Rules, Paper, Status

Rules, Paper, Status

Migrants and Precarious Bureaucracy

in Contemporary Italy

Anna Tuckett

Stanford University Press
Stanford, California

Stanford University Press
Stanford, California

Printed in the United States of America on acid-free, archival-quality paper

Library of Congress Cataloging-in-Publication Data

Names: Tuckett, Anna, author.
Title: Rules, paper, status : migrants and precarious bureaucracy in contemporary Italy / Anna Tuckett.
Description: Stanford, California : Stanford University Press, 2018. | Includes bibliographical references and index.
Identifiers: LCCN 2018003994 (print) | LCCN 2018005224 (ebook) | ISBN 9781503606500 | ISBN 9781503605404 (cloth : alk. paper) | ISBN 9781503606494 (pbk. : alk. paper)
Subjects: LCSH: Immigrants—Italy—Social conditions. | Emigration and immigration law—Italy. | Italy—Emigration and immigration—Government policy. | Bureaucracy—Italy.
Classification: LCC JV8132 (ebook) | LCC JV8132 .T84 2018 (print) | DDC 325.45—dc23
LC record available at https://lccn.loc.gov/2018003994

Cover design: George Kirkpatrick

To Ibrahim and the next generation

Contents

Acknowledgments

Without the generosity, openness, and support of many people in both Italy and London, this project would not have been possible. I regret that I cannot name them all. I am deeply indebted to staff members and regular clients at the advice center who shared their stories with me and tolerated my endless questions. Outside of the center I am very grateful to Manuela Alfieri, Chiara Candini, Angela Giancristofaro, and Claudio Negri for welcoming me into their lives and sharing them with me. Thank you also to Ledia Andoni and Valmir Dibra.

The project on which this book is based was funded by a U.K. Economic and Social Research Council Studentship, and by further research studentships from the Newby Trust and the London School of Economics. I am very grateful for this generous assistance. Sections of revised material in this book appeared in articles published in *Focaal* and *Critique of Anthropology*.

At the London School of Economics (LSE) I am indebted to many people. I am extraordinarily grateful to my supervisors, Deborah James and Mathijs Pelkmans. I thank Deborah not only for her meticulous attention to my chapters (and patience with my writing), but for always pushing me in the direction I want to go and helping me get there. Mathijs supported this project since its beginning, and I am grateful for his challenging advice, which both guided and inspired me throughout. I also thank the conveners and participants in the LSE writing seminars 2011–13. Thanks to my current colleagues on the Ethnography of Advice team for their useful comments during our book writing workshop.

The feedback of many friends and colleagues both at LSE and beyond was invaluable at various stages of this book's development. I am grateful to Tony

Good and Ralph Grillo for their detailed and insightful comments. Thank you to Rita Astuti, Laura Bear, Max Bolt, Ryan Davey, Matthew Engelke, Ana Gutierrez Garza, Insa Koch, Giulia Liberatore, Bruno Riccio, and Alpa Shah. I also wish to thank Adam Kuper for his encouraging and useful comments. The book's peer reviewers provided highly valuable, detailed, and thoughtful feedback.

Warm thanks to Stanford University Press. I am very grateful to Michelle Lipinski for her enthusiasm and support and to others at the press for their help in finalizing the manuscript.

My family has been tremendously supportive. I am deeply indebted to my parents, Lesley, David, and Paola, for their constant support and encouragement over the years. Matt Wilde was an enormous influence on this book. His enthusiasm, interest, patience, and care kept me going during my hardest and most frustrating moments. I am deeply grateful not only for his tireless proofreading, but also for his support in helping me to develop and articulate my ideas. Thank you also to our son Gwyn for his patience with my one-armed breastfeeding while I put the finishing touches on the manuscript in the first weeks of his life.

Last, I thank my second family in Italy: Anna, Mohamed, and Ibrahim. Anna profoundly influenced this book and is an inspiration to me.

Glossary

amnesty/ sanatoria/ emersione. Amnesty is a law that regularizes employed "il-legal" migrants on Italian territory. The 2002 amnesty allowed undocumented migrants in all occupations to regularize their status. A further amnesty in 2009 was introduced but this time was designed to legalize only domestic work-ers. In common parlance, both amnesties were referred to as the *sanatoria* or *emersione.*

Bossi-Fini law. The current immigration law in Italy. It was introduced in 2002.

carta d'identita. Identity card. All those legally living in Italy (Italians and non-Italians) are required to have an identity card. Italian citizens may use it as a travel document, but non-Italian citizens may not.

carta di soggiorno. Card to stay, also known as *permesso di soggiorno di lungo periodo* (long-term permit to stay). The long-term permit is valid indefinitely unless a migrant is convicted of a criminal offense.

comune. Municipality.

contratto di soggiorno. A work contract that migrants from non-European Union (EU) countries must hold and present when renewing their permits.

decreto flussi. An accord between the Italian state and "sending" countries. It allows for the legal entry of workers who are desired by employers in Italy.

kit. This is the name of the application form for immigration permit–related applications.

permesso di soggiorno. Permit to stay. The permit that non-EU migrants must hold to live legally in Italy. It usually lasts for two years.

prefettura. The prefecture, which plays a role in the process of family reunification and citizenship applications

questura. The police headquarters in which the immigration office is situated. Permit applications are processed here.

Rules, Paper, Status

Introduction

Extract from fieldnotes, December 2009

I arrive at the *questura*[1] (the immigration office) at 7:45 a.m., much later than everyone else. The entrance's steel gates are open, revealing a concrete slope leading up to the long and flat immigration office building situated at the police headquarters. Metal barriers snake around the slope, forcing people into an orderly but bulging line as they wait for a police officer to hand out numbers. The numbers are for appointments to collect permits, submit applications, and various other processes and procedures. From the size of the queue, it is evident that people started to arrive some time ago. It is freezing, although there is some warmth created by the large number of people crammed inside the barriers. There are all sorts of people waiting: old, young, and groups of families with small children and strollers. Most people are tightly clasping plastic folders filled with paperwork.

At 8:00 a.m. a policeman emerges. His manner is aggressive as he waves the raffle-style tickets in the air and asks people to calm down and stop pushing; he has plenty of numbers to distribute, he states. Confusion is paramount, as people are unsure what the ticket numbers refer to. At one point the policeman says the tickets he is distributing are only for the afternoon. I repeat this to Ahmed, an Algerian man who is standing next to me in the queue, but he seems to think otherwise.

After the numbers have been distributed, some people leave to get coffee, but most wait for the immigration office to open. We stand around in the small courtyard directly in front of the building observing the well-dressed police officers purposefully entering and exiting the adjacent buildings that house other police departments. At around 8:30 a.m. the immigration office opens

Figure 1. Photograph of a *questura*. Photograph by author.

and people begin to shuffle in. It is a long corridor-like room with strip lighting and very limited seating, and it soon fills up. After a while, Ahmed and I go outside, joining others who can no longer bear the cramped and oppressive atmosphere inside.

At about 8:35 we rush back in as they start to call the first appointment times and corresponding names. Ahmed explains to me that the people who are being called are those with appointments to provide their fingerprints for permit renewal. The appointments are scheduled every minute, which explains the huge backlog. Although it is still only 8:35, the police officers call the names of those with appointments up to 8:45. I realize that those with the earliest appointments are in the best position, since the next roll of names (those with appointments for 8:49 and later) are not called until after 10:00.

By 11:00 a.m. there is an increasing sense of chaos because those with the early appointments (and also those with the later appointments, as everybody arrives early) have now been waiting since 8:30. People are becoming tired, and the sound of small children's crying rises above the loud din of the crowd. Just after 11:00 a different policeman starts calling out the names. His manner is aggressive and intimidating, his large physique lending extra menace. Under

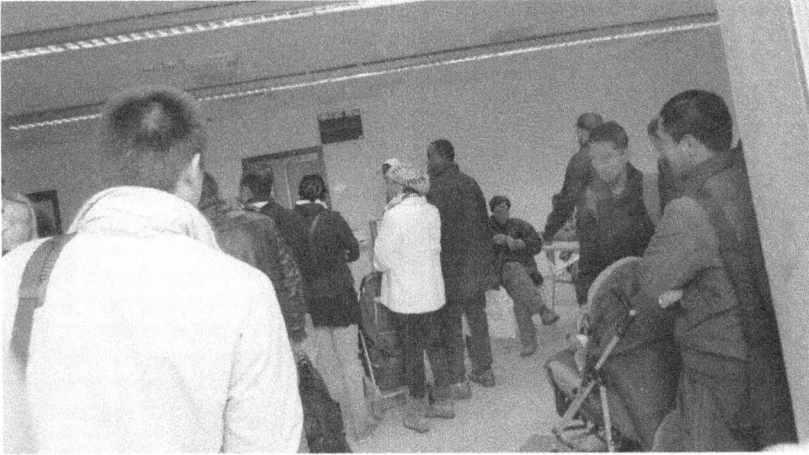

Figure 2. People waiting inside a *questura*. Photograph by author.

his breath Ahmed mumbles, "This one is tough [*duro*]." Taking a different approach from the first officer, he calls people by their names. This slows down the roll call as people struggle to hear through the noise and mispronunciation. The tension, frustration, and confusion mount, and people begin to complain to the policeman. He quickly becomes angry and tells people to calm down and move away from the door. Responding to the crowd's lamentations, he says that there is one appointment scheduled for every minute and they simply cannot work any faster.

The use of space exacerbates the intimidating atmosphere. More metal barriers divide the long room, and at tense moments people are rudely told to stay behind the barrier. At one point, a policewoman harshly shouts: "You are like crocodiles! Don't you see the barrier? Get outside!" At other times, toward the end of the morning when the crowds have diminished, people flout the rules: they stick their heads around the door to see what is going on or lean against the front wall on the forbidden side of the barrier.

In the pauses, between the episodes of number calling, the mood relaxes slightly and fleeting camaraderie develops among the waiting. Conversations turn to past experiences of long waits, horror stories of being issued expired permits, and accounts of how early people woke up in order to receive a number. During the exchange of these stories people raise their eyebrows and shake their heads; their anxiety is accompanied by annoyance about the chaos and delays.

At 11:30 a.m. the appointments from 9:26 a.m. are announced. At this point most people have been waiting on their feet for three hours inside the *questura* and since 5:00 a.m. in the queue outside. As the morning nears lunchtime, the tension starts to lift. There are fewer people waiting, and those who have been there all morning slump against the walls, exhausted. When I leave at 1:15 p.m., the last few people have been called and the room is empty.

Immigration, and how to control it, is perceived to be one of the biggest concerns currently facing the world. Since the early 1970s, when a long phase of foreign labor recruitment ended, immigration to Europe has largely become a story of allegedly unwanted migration (Finotelli and Sciortino 2013). Migration flows have become increasingly bureaucratized and regulated in efforts to restrict and control the number and "type" of migrants allowed entry. Increased regulation has led to the emergence of what Xiang and Lindquist (2014) label migration infrastructures, which exist within and across nation-state borders. The migration infrastructure includes interlinked technologies, institutions, and actors that facilitate, regulate, and condition the migration process. Migration, in other words, is "intensively mediated" (Xiang and Lindquist 2014: 124). Drawing on in-depth ethnographic research conducted in Italy, one of Europe's biggest receiving countries, this book homes in on one aspect of the migration infrastructure, what I call the documentation regime: the nexus of documents, paperwork, and legal and bureaucratic processes that migrants must engage with in their efforts to become and stay "legal," to bring family members into the country, and to attain citizenship.

While there has been much focus on the regulatory mechanisms that must be negotiated when migrants cross borders (Andersson 2014; Collyer 2012; Feldman 2012; Xiang and Lindquist 2014), the initial act of migration is only the start of what becomes a long and enduring relationship with migration bureaucracy. In large part this is because, across different destination settings, secure—or any kind of—legal status is increasingly difficult to attain; migrants must continuously and enduringly navigate the "host" country's "webs of administration" (Reeves 2013: 511) in order to become or remain documented. Arriving in the host country and obtaining one's initial permit, therefore, is only the first of many interactions with immigration bureaucracies. Even in cases where migrants manage to attain permanent citizenship, encounters with the documentation regime continue through their efforts to support family and friends.

Through ethnographic research conducted with migrants, immigration advisers and advocates, brokers, officials, and others within the immigration nexus in Italy, I examine everyday encounters with the immigration bureaucracy and the diverse processes of inclusion and exclusion it engenders. Although encounters with the immigration bureaucracy are characterized by frequently changing laws, discretionary implementation, and unlawful practice, the bureaucracy's precarious nature also allows a certain degree of flexibility. In the Italian context, successful navigation of the immigration bureaucracy involves taking advantage of loopholes, cultivating contacts, and knowing when and how to bend the rules. Moving away from debates about whether immigration policies "work" or not, this book shows that these informal strategies of navigation are productive in other ways. On the one hand, they produce affective and meaningful outcomes for migrants and those who work on their behalf. These include measurable results such as legal status, material profit, friendships, solidarity, and professionalism, as well as the more abstract values of cultural citizenship, political subjectivity, and self-worth. On the other hand, these individualized strategies are limited in their ability to challenge the broader structural, economic, and legal frameworks in which migrants and their labor are made and remade as marginal. Although such strategies offer individual migrants certain opportunities, they also reproduce the structural inequalities they are attempting to overcome.

This book explores the dynamic tensions created by the divergent affects and meanings produced through encounters with the Italian immigration bureaucracy. It offers insights into the disjunctures produced by bureaucracies in general, and by immigration regimes in particular. By learning to navigate the immigration bureaucracy, migrants become cultural insiders, yet exclusionary laws can transform this social and cultural learning into the very thing that endangers their right to live in the country.

A note on the term "illegal"

Throughout the book I sometimes use quotation marks around the terms "legal" and "illegal" when referring to migrants with or without permits in order to emphasize the arbitrariness of these seemingly strict categories. These statuses are the product of legal and political processes and are not accurate descriptive terms for people (Andersson 2014: 17; Coutin 2000; De Genova 2002). The status "illegal" does not exist outside of the state but is formed by and exists in relation to it (De Genova 2002: 422). I use these terms for two reasons, in spite of both their offensiveness and their inaccuracy. First, they are emic terms used by my interlocutors (alongside the term *clandestino* [clandestine]). And, second, in employing these terms together with ethnographic data, I hope to show how they are constructed, shifting, and contingent. Migrants' everyday encounters with immigration law highlight the temporariness and fluidity of the categories "legal" and "illegal," as well as "official" and "unofficial." Law creates "illegality" by its definitions; illegal practices are in fact necessary in order to fulfill legal requirements. By closely examining the ways that policies play out in everyday life, I show how these categories are not only constructed but also mutually productive.

Needed but not wanted: migrants in Italy

In comparison with some of its other European neighbors, Italy was a relative latecomer as a destination for migrants, but in the past decade it has become one of the main receiving countries in Europe (see figure 3). The migrants discussed throughout this book are those whom Italians consider to be *immigrati* (immigrants) or *extracomunitari* (non-EU citizens). *Extracomunitario* is an ideologically loaded term. It refers to a non-EU citizen, but the term is primarily used to refer to migrants from the global South and post-Soviet countries, notwithstanding their home country's EU member status. For example, Romanians and Poles, who are EU citizens, are labeled *extracomunitari*, while Australians and Americans, who *are* technically *extracomunitari*, are not labeled in such a manner. Accordingly, the term refers to migrants who are deemed to originate from less-developed nations, and its use is related to the notion that migrants are low-level workers, criminals, or objects of charity.

As the widespread use of *extracomunitario* indicates, migrants have not been universally welcomed onto the nation's shores, but low birth rates and a very large aging population make their presence crucial. As "useful invaders" (Ambrosini 1999) migrants fill positions that Italians—with ever increasing levels of education—refuse to. These largely include manual labor jobs in construction, manufacturing, agriculture, the service industry, and domestic work. As Emilio Reyneri observes, "Immigrants tend to be concentrated in jobs where conditions are hard, requiring physical strength, willingness to do shift-work, and where occupational hazards are high (Reyneri 2004a: 78). The demand for unskilled manual labor in the Italian economic context, alongside young natives' unwillingness to do such work, explains how high local unemployment coexists together with high rates of immigrant employment (Ambrosini 2001: 54; Reyneri 2004a). Kitty Calavita (2005a: 73) notes, "They are part of the same phenomenon of a late capitalism that is made up of pre-Fordist and post-Fordist work, with little in between." That is, the domestic work and agricultural sectors that are overwhelmingly dominated by migrants are based on

Country	Number (million)	Percent of population
Germany	8.7	10.0
United Kingdom	5.6	8.6
Italy	5.0	8.3
Spain	4.4	9.5
France	4.4	6.6

Figure 3. Largest numbers of nonnationals living in EU member states on January 1, 2016. Data from Eurostat.

pre-Fordist employment relations, yet exist in a context of a post-Fordist globalized economy where the principle of flexibility—or precarity—rules. Labor in the small and medium-sized enterprises typical of Italian capitalism, meanwhile, are hybrid spaces of pre- and post-Fordist labor relations and employment structures. The effect of this combination, argues Calavita, "helps explain the paradox of high local unemployment and high immigrant employment: too few good jobs and too many bad ones" (74). While young Italians, who are able to rely on their parents, can wait for better opportunities to arise, migrants fill the badly paid, precarious, and low-status jobs.

Scholars have argued that the stigmatization of, and discrimination toward, migrants must be understood in the context of Italy's peculiar relationship with nationhood and nationalism. It was only in the second half of the nineteenth century that an Italian nation-state was constructed from historically diverse regions (Grillo and Pratt 2002: 11). Regionalism is a significant feature in understanding identity and nationalism in Italy, and Italians often identify more strongly with their region than with the nation as a whole (Pratt 2002; Stanley 2008: 46). Conversation in Italy frequently revolves around the variations in food, language, and culture in different regions. "To be Sicilian, Piedmontese or Neapolitan is not only a matter of geographical origin but also carries strong cultural identities" (Maritano 2002: 62).

In addition to regional differences, the country's north-south split is also highly significant. A considerable body of literature has analyzed the "southern question" as a key component of the Italian reaction to outside immigration (Giordano 2008; King and Mai 2002; Mai 2003; Maritano 2002; Pratt 2002). The title of Jane Schneider's 1998 book *Italy's "Southern Question": Orientalism in One Country* reflects the legacy of exclusion and prejudice that lies at the heart of questions of Italian nationhood. The south has historically been stigmatized by the north as lazy, backward, and "African" (Pratt 2002: 30): it is commonly referred to as the *mezzogiorno*—land of the midday sun—and those who are from the south are derogatorily referred to as *terroni* (country bump-kins). Nicola Mai and others have argued that the stigmatization of southerners has been "translated on" to modern-day non-EU migrants (Giordano 2008: 590; King and Mai 2002; Mai 2003; Maritano 2002; Pratt 2002).

As these analysts have suggested, this is part of a discourse that aims to pres-ent contemporary Italy as compatible with a new-EU, post-Maastricht identity: "The representation of the arrival and presence of foreign immigrants worked to construct a positive image of Italian people in terms of efficiency, tolerance and civility through the devaluation and criminalization of the image and identity of the newcomers" (Mai 2003: 83). In this context, these scholars have argued that migrants have come to represent the ultimate "other."

With its focus on the entry and control of flows of migrants, rather than on the potential for meaningful integration (Cachafeiro 2002), the media have played a key role in perpetuating and normalizing anti-immigrant sentiment (Mai 2002). The right-wing separatist party the Lega Nord (Northern League), which has taken advantage of people's fear of immigration in order to promote its political platform (Geddes 2008; King and Andall 1999: 154; Zaslove 2004), is a key player in refining and perpetuating the normalization of an exclusionary and discriminatory discourse. In his work on migrants' political participation, Davide Però (2002: 96) has explored how the Left is also to blame for the normalization of such anti-immigrant discourse. In his study of the Forum—a project based in Bologna that aims to enable migrants to voice, organize, and channel their politics—Però argues that, as well as the Right, the mainstream Left in Italy has "contributed to the construction of immigrants as political minors." He notes that there exists a sharp discrepancy between the Left's inclusionary multicultural rhetoric and its exclusionary everyday practice, which—rooted in paternalism and essentialism—ultimately constructs migrants as second-class, ethnically marked subjects. Giovanna Zincone (2006a: 13) likewise discusses the limitations of movements supporting migrants' rights. She notes that although campaigns to improve the basic rights and legal status of migrants do exist, the "commitment to political and citizenship rights for long term residents is less tenacious." Similarly, other scholars have noted that because advocacy on behalf of migrants is focused on emergency situations, often dominated by Catholic associations, the assistance migrants receive tends to be aimed at helping to achieve short- rather than long-term ends (Cole and

Saitta 2011: 528; King and Andall 1999: 152). Such advocacy on behalf of migrants is thus paternalistic in nature and does not challenge the unequal inclusion that they encounter.

Encouraged by inflammatory media and a normalized discourse about discrimination, politicians limit their discussions about immigration to the perceived need to control borders and emergency solutions, rather than focusing on the potential for meaningful social inclusion. When advocacy does take place, it is not concerned with rights but instead focuses on offering basic care, which only works to perpetuate means of differentiation. These social and political attitudes are reflected and contradicted in immigration law and policy.

Ambiguities in law

The tension between popular anti-immigrant sentiment and the economic need for migrant labor is reflected in Italian immigration law. Curiously, harsh anti-immigrant-driven policies exist alongside regular amnesties through which "illegal" migrants can regularize their status. In addition, there are regular *decreti flussi*, policies that allow for the legal entry of foreign workers. Reflecting Italy's relatively late status as a host country, its first comprehensive immigration law was passed in 1986. This law was introduced following expression of concern from trade unions and opposition parties about the exploitation of a growing number of "illegal" immigrants, and from the EU, which wanted to protect its borders (Calavita 2005a; Zincone 2006b). Other acts were later introduced, including, most significantly, the Turco-Napolitano law, which was brought in under a center-left government in 1998. This law aimed to prevent and combat illegal entry, regulate new flows of foreign workers, promote the integration of immigrants holding valid residence permits, and grant basic rights to "illegal" immigrants.

In 2002 the Bossi-Fini law was introduced under Prime Minister Silvio Berlusconi's center-right government. Drafted by Gianfranco Fini, a right-wing politician, and Lega Nord's ex-leader Umberto Bossi, the law has been criticized as discriminatory and driven by anti-immigrant sentiment. It has two main purposes: first, to make legal status more dependent upon employment; and second, to combat illegal entry (Zincone and Caponio 2006: 4, 5). Reflecting the government's restrictive approach to immigration, under the new law the length of the job-seeking work permit was reduced from twelve to six months and the duration of other permits was also shortened. Under this law a migrant's legal status is contingent upon presenting a regular work contract. Consequently, regardless of how many years one has lived in the country, losing one's job or being employed unofficially in the "black market" can result in the loss of legal status. In 2009 the so-called Security Packet (*Pachetto di Sicurezza*) reinforced this apparently tough stance on immigration. The bill dramatically increased the cost of permit renewal and made the status of illegality a crime.

Despite the restrictive nature of Bossi-Fini, which works to make migrants' legal status both temporary and contingent, since its introduction there have been two large-scale regularizations and a number of programs for the entry of foreign workers (*decreti flussi*).[2] The first regularization in 2002 allowed 630,000 migrants to regularize their status (Ambrosini 2015: 3). Initially the amnesty was designed only to regularize domestic workers, but following pressure from the Christian Democratic Party (which formed part of the governing coalition at the time) and employers' organizations, the opportunity to regularize was opened up to all undocumented migrants. A second amnesty followed in 2009, which regularized approximately 270,000 workers, although this time it *was* restricted to those with domestic work contracts. Given Italian families' need for this kind of labor, domestic worker regularizations are not politically controversial. In the intervening years between these regularizations, a series of *decreti flussi* have also allowed for the legal entry of workers from abroad, both permanent and seasonal, who already have a work contract with an employer based in Italy. The Bossi-Fini law, therefore, is characterized by exclusionary and harsh policies alongside the provision of relatively frequent regularizations and quota policies that allow for legal entry. In the words of one migrant respondent: "It is easy to get in [to Italy], but hard to legally stay."

Amnesties are, therefore, the "principal tool" (Ambrosini 2008: 567) of Italian immigration policy. In part this is because political regulation on migration has been reactive rather than proactive in responding to the pressing demands for migrant labor from individual families and the broader economy. The institution of *decreti flussi* that allow authorized entry to a certain number of both permanent and seasonal migrant workers every few years is an effort to resolve the delayed outcomes of migration policy. Actual market trends, however, tend to exceed the "cautious forecast made at the time of determining the quotas" (568), meaning that governments have been forced to realign immigration policy with economic trends *after* the event through the use of further regularizations. As a result, prime ministers from both sides of the political divide have admitted that the *decreti flussi* have not served to bring in new migrants from abroad, but in the majority of cases have enabled migrants already on Italian territory to regularize their status. Effectively, therefore, these *decreti flussi* work as another form of regularization. The significant role that amnesties play in

Italian immigration policy highlights two of its central characteristics. First, the majority of migrants in Italy complete a stint of "illegality" in the country before obtaining legal status (568). And second, owing to the contingency of legal status on work, individuals can very easily fall into "illegality." Overall, Italian immigration policy treats migration as an emergency and short-term problem, rather than actively developing longer-term policies that aim to achieve integration and stability (Cole and Saitta 2011: 528).

The seeming contradiction between anti-immigration public discourse and frequent regularization policies has been explained in a number of ways. Zincone (2011: 259) has discussed the influence of the so-called advocacy coalition, which includes Catholic organizations, industries desiring foreign labor, left-wing nongovernmental organizations (NGOs), trade unions, and Italian families who employ migrant domestic workers. As noted above, because of the recognized need for such a labor force, and the kind of migrant associated with domestic work—female and "unthreatening"—Italian families do not object to such migration and in fact actively demand it. Zincone notes that the pressure from such advocacy groups has led to immigration policy being on a "zigzagging path" (278), in which immigration law is harsh and exclusionary yet also allows for large-scale and fairly frequent legalization programs. Accordingly, the voting public's hostility to immigration, the pressure exerted by the advocacy coalition, and Italy's "objective need for foreign manpower" (278), in particular caregivers, create contradictory immigration policies that are simultaneously harsh and lenient.

The fact that immigration policy follows a "zigzagging path" is not unique to Italy. Scholars focusing on states' immigration laws have examined the "gap" between the objectives and outcomes of migration policy (Collyer 2012; Favell and Hansen 2002; Freeman 1995; Hollifield, Martin, and Orrenius 2014; Joppke 1998; Sassen 1996). They point to the different groups who, driven by divergent interests, pressure states to exercise leniency in their immigration policies. Similar to the advocacy coalition, other influences on immigration policy include businesses and employers, humanitarian groups, unions, community organizations, and a host of interest groups from both within and beyond the nation-state (Collyer 2012: 507; Sassen 1996: 98). Further, leniency or restrictiveness toward immigration is not determined by one's political views (de Haas and Natter 2015). On both sides of the political spectrum there is internal disagreement about immigration policies. In left- and right-wing political parties, Giuseppe Sciortino (2000: 225) argues, migration divides those close to the party's economic tradition and those close to its sociocultural tradition.

However, in opposition to these diverse groups that advocate leniency in immigration policy, across Europe there is also an established bedrock of hostility to migrants. The electoral success of politicians and parties espousing anti-immigrant sentiments in Europe and North America demonstrates a relative spike in such attitudes over the past two decades. Accordingly, it is unsurprising that national governments have pursued immigration policies that appear restrictive.

Last, and particularly pertinent to EU member states, migration policy is not only designed and implemented by individual nation-states. The Schengen Agreement, for example, allows for freedom of movement for EU citizens and documented migrants within the Schengen Area; and the Dublin I and II Regulations share biodata to ensure that asylum seekers claim asylum at their first point of entry. Thus there is considerable convergence between EU member states' immigration policies (Eule 2014: 6; Geddes and Scholten 2016). The supranational decision-making power of the European Courts of Justice and Human Rights adds a further dimension to individual nation-states' design and implementation of policies (Boswell and Geddes 2010). Writing about Italy, Andrew Geddes (2008: 350) observes that the "gap" between rhetoric and reality that characterizes immigration policy should not, therefore, be presented as a puzzle or a paradox but, rather, as "suggestive of political and institutional limitations on state capacity to regulate international migration." Rather than dismiss the paradoxical nature of immigration policy, however, I suggest it is productive to engage with and attempt to unravel it. For it is the paradoxical nature of immigration policies and how they take place on the ground that reveals how everyday experiences of immigration law connect to broader political-economic frameworks.

Overall, therefore, as a "destination" country Italy's immigration policies are exclusionary and discriminatory, making it difficult for migrants and their children to build secure lives with hope for a better future. This is particularly notable among the second generation who, excluded from Italian citizenship by the *jus sanguinis* nationality policy, can find themselves "illegal" or in legally precarious situations on turning eighteen years old (see Chapter 5). Yet, alongside these harsh realities, which relegate migrants and their children to second-class citizenship, migrants' encounters with Italian immigration law and bureaucracy are also characterized by a flexibility and maneuverability that is unusual in other contexts, such as the United States or the United Kingdom (Bloch, Sigona, and Zetter 2011; Dreby 2015; Sigona 2012). As a result, this book's accounts of migrants' encounters with immigration law are different from those found in other settings, where possibilities for migrants to strategically navigate the law seem increasingly impossible and the lives of both documented and undocumented migrants are haunted by harsh regimes of enforcement and deportation (De Genova and Peutz 2010; Dreby 2015).

This is not to suggest that Italian immigration law is not also punitive. Long-term residents and those born in Italy can easily fall into "illegality" and the contemporary reality of multiculturalism is not acknowledged in law or society, resulting in experiences of everyday racism and discrimination for those not considered "Italian" (Cole and Saitta 2011). Yet the immigration law's inherently contradictory nature—oscillating between exclusionary policies and large-scale legalizations—also gives migrants room to maneuver. As the case studies that follow show, migrants are able, as well as expected, to exploit loopholes and make the law work to their advantage. Encounters with the immigration bureaucracy cause anxiety and uncertainty, but through processes of strategic navigation they also produce possibilities for self-fashioning and social mobility. It is precisely this strategic maneuvering, however, that in other moments may preclude the chance to obtain more secure legal status or citizenship.

Zigzagging path: immigration law's contradictions

The ambiguities in Italian immigration law are characteristic of immigration policies studied elsewhere and relate to a fundamental tension between what governments say and what they do. "Illegal" immigration, argue some scholars, should not only be viewed as the result of competing pressures and dysfunctional immigration policies, but must be contextualized in relation to the demand for cheap and disposable labor (Coutin 2000; De Genova 2002; Heyman 1995; Kearney 1991; Portes 1978). Perpetual fear of arrest and deportation guarantees undocumented migrants' acceptance of poor and unfair working conditions, while their status of "nonexistence" ensures they are unable to make claims on the state (Coutin 2000: 27).

Immigration laws, therefore, do not exclude migrants, but rather include them under certain conditions. Following earlier work (Portes 1978; Kearney 1991), Nicholas De Genova (2002: 429) has argued that immigration laws act tactically to create undocumented migrants who are socially included "under imposed conditions of enforced and protracted vulnerability." With this in mind, the categories of "legal" and "illegal" must be deconstructed, showing how official procedures of legalizations play a role in the production of "illegality." Premising a theory of "deportability," De Genova argues that migrants' endurance of years of "illegality" serves as a "disciplinary apprenticeship in the subordination of [their] labor, after which it becomes no longer necessary to prolong the undocumented condition" (2002: 429). That is, after a prolonged experience of "illegality," even after having obtained documents, migrants sustain a sense of "deportability" and thus continue to accept poor working conditions.

Immigration law does not only create illegality through the legal inclusion of some and the exclusion of others; illegality is also created through processes of legalization. In the Italian case, where legal status is contingent upon employment, illegality is inevitable: without proof of employment, migrants lose their legal status. The law both "institutionalizes irregularity" (Calavita 2005a: 43) and perpetuates migrants' occupations in low-paid and insecure jobs. Immigration law and migrants' labor are thus inseparable and, owing to their precarious and temporary legal status, migrants remain perpetually "other." This status, Calavita argues, is a "critical ingredient of their flexibility" (64), ensuring that they remain in low-level, poorly paid, and insecure jobs—the so called "non-EU" jobs (those that native European citizens refuse to do).

While migrants' labor may be desirable for the economic benefits it provides, appearing tough on immigration, particularly "illegal" immigration, has nonetheless proven to be politically profitable (Hollifield, Martin, and Orrenius 2014). The result is immigration laws riddled with contradictions (see Calavita 1989: 43 for a U.S. example). In the Italian context, the capitalization on, and fueling of, anti-immigrant sentiment by right-wing politicians has pushed parties at both ends of the political spectrum to favor tough immigration policies. But, as Calavita (2004: 375) notes, those politicians who demonize immigration flows must also cope with the economic and demographic realities in Italy that make migrant labor essential. This conflict leads to simultaneously restrictive and lenient immigration policies which, in their execution, are fueled by contradictions and inconsistencies, and are highly contingent on the implementation of low-level officials (Calavita 2004: 376; Heyman 1995; Triandafyllidou 2003). How then do these contradictions play out on the ground?

When examining migration systems, accounts tend to focus on borders and their regulatory mechanisms. Gregory Feldman (2012), for example, shows that neoliberals and neonationalists can find agreement over migration matters through the EU's increasingly dominant policy of circular migration. Circular migration allows for some labor migration but ensures that migrants are unable to hold secure or long-term legal status in the "destination" country. Josiah Heyman's study of immigration officials on the U.S.-Mexico border, meanwhile, explores how contradictions in immigration policy are made coherent through Immigration and Naturalization Service (INS) officers' worldviews. The result is the production of the contradictory "voluntary departure complex," which ultimately results in satisfying the INS's desire for visible arrests while permitting "labor migration in numbers well beyond those permitted by law" (Heyman 1995: 261, 267). Finally, Ruben Andersson's (2014) focus on the "illegality industry" and its "business of bordering Europe" reveals how the industry produces exactly what it is designed to "combat"—more "illegality."

Although illuminating in some ways, an exclusive focus on the border and its regulatory infrastructures obscures the way in which "legality" and "illegality" are produced well within nation-states' boundaries, as well as the role that migrants themselves play in the production and implementation of immigration law. Given the labyrinthine nature of the immigration bureaucracy, migrants must necessarily be active agents in its navigation. My focus on migrants' interaction with law *inside* the border through mundane paperwork procedures uncovers the diverse strategies that can be employed to bend the law to one's advantage. These strategies also highlight how migrants' and states' economic interests converge, as well as how migrants play key, if silent, roles in the working out of contradictory policies on the ground.

The domestic work contract

Domestic work contracts feature prominently throughout this book and tell us much about the changing structure of Italian society, the role that migrants play within it, and how immigration law can be creatively manipulated. In the Italian context, where little if any state-provided welfare is available, it continues to be families, or more specifically women, who are responsible for the care of the young, elderly, and sick. To fill the care gap produced by increasing female participation in the workforce, alongside an aging population and insufficient public services, households turn to migrant domestic workers. Pensions, public allowances, and economic aid from their children mean that even the elderly in low economic positions are able to be cared for in their homes by live-in caregivers (Ambrosini 2015: 4). Migrants who take on this arduous and poorly paid work are overwhelmingly female and often also undocumented. Given this widespread demand for migrant domestic workers it is not surprising, therefore, that immigration policies are soft on those in that category while remaining restrictive overall.

It is not only genuine domestic workers and their employers, however, who are able to benefit from this leniency in the immigration policy. The domestic work contract enables large numbers of migrants who are not genuine domestic workers to regularize and maintain their legal status, benefiting a range of employers and the economy more generally. The private and relatively unregulated nature of the domestic work contract in Italy means that any migrant, with the appropriate resources and knowledge, is able to regularize his or her status, provided somebody is willing to act as an "employer." As many case studies throughout this book illustrate, in the 2009 domestic worker amnesty it was commonplace for migrants who were not domestic workers to present "inauthentic" domestic work contracts in order to regularize their status. Such contracts are also used by migrants who do not have jobs or do not want jobs but are obligated to present a work contract in order to renew their permits. Domestic work contracts, therefore, are a tool through which individuals can regularize their status or renew their permits, notwithstanding their actual occupation status.

Domestic work contracts, in sum, play a crucial role in the Italian political economy. On the one hand, in a context of changing household structure, aging populations, and insufficient state provision of welfare, migrant domestic workers—or what Maurizio Ambrosini (2015) calls "invisible welfare"—help to manage and pacify the relationship between the state, the household, and the labor market (Sciortino 2004: 126). And on the other, the domestic work contract enables migrants who are likely to be employed in manual, unskilled, and low-tech labor to regularize their status and/or gain entry into the country, while concealing this from a voting public who would disapprove.

Law and uncertainty

A growing body of work has explored how encounters with immigration law produce deep uncertainty in the lives of migrants—in particular those without legal status (Cabot 2014; Coutin 2000; De Genova and Peutz 2010; Mahler 1995; Menjívar 2006; Sigona 2012; Willen 2007). For migrants who are undocumented, fear of arrest and deportation profoundly affects subjective experiences of embodiment, time, space, sociality, and sense of self because mundane decisions such as what form of transport to use, how to dress, and where to walk are made according to the risk of being stopped by the police (Coutin 2000: chap. 2; Gonzales and Chavez 2012; Mahler 1995: chap. 5; Willen 2007: 10). It is not only a lack of legal status, however, that produces uncertainty. Restrictive immigration and asylum regimes and the worldwide proliferation of permit systems based on migrants' temporary stay (Calavita 2005a; De Genova 2002) often cause even those with legal status to live in "legal limbo," unsure of their future. The profound uncertainty that immigration law creates in migrants' lives is not, therefore, exclusively produced by the empirical fact of an individual's "illegal" status. It is also constructed through the "inherent uncertainty over where the boundary between 'legal' and 'illegal' presence actually lies." Research on "webs of administrative regulation" such as that on which this book is based, highlight two central reasons for this uncertainty (Reeves 2013: 511).

First, the actual processes of completing legal applications related to immigration often require engaging in "illegal" or "extralegal" practices (Coutin 2000; Mahler 1995). In her work, Susan Bibler Coutin (2000: 104) describes how Salvadorans "bargain in the shadows of the law." They purchase fake papers and engage with unofficial immigration "experts" in order to be granted "legal" status: "Official law is thus inextricably entangled with the illegalities that it creates" (70). In my fieldsite, a center that provides advice to migrants in navigating the immigration bureaucracy, such activities include: producing paperwork containing false information; paying individuals to act as employers, wives, or husbands; and rule-bending by officials; in addition, there are numerous immigration "experts" who charge high rates for their bureaucratic services. As Josiah Heyman and Alan Smart (1999: 11) argue, although "the line between 'legal' and 'illegal' is held to be clear and definitive inside a given state," in practice legality and illegality are "simultaneously black and white, and shades of gray." The case studies in this book describe how migrants' strategies, which involved illegal or extralegal practices, took place within the parameters set by the state bureaucracy.

Second, as the literature on law and migration has elucidated, illegal migrants do not live the underground lives they are assumed, in popular perception, to live. Rather, like most legal citizens, they are in some senses integrated into the everyday social fabric through work, family, public spaces, and friends. It is common for people to live in mixed-status families, where different members hold different citizenship or (non)legal statuses. In particular moments, lack of legal status may come to the fore, but in much of everyday life, legal status is inconsequential (Coutin 2000: chap. 2).

The fluidity of statuses and their temporary nature is particularly pertinent to the Italian setting. Owing to the contingency of permits on work and salary, under Italian immigration law, legal status can easily be lost. At the same time, however, the relatively frequent legalization programs make it fairly easy for those who have lost legal status to reregularize, providing they possess the appropriate resources. Holding legal or illegal status, therefore, was often experienced by my interlocutors as transient and temporary, and it was common for them to have experienced both statuses, as well as others in between. In fact, during renewal periods, which usually last at least six months and sometimes longer, migrants inhabit a limbo status in which they are legally resident in Italy but unable to access all the rights and services to which legal migrants are entitled (see Chapter 2). Further, because of the particularities of immigration and citizenship laws, it is not uncommon for long-term migrants—even those born in the country—to fall into illegality (see Chapter 5). Legality and citizenship status are not, therefore, necessarily indicators of integration or belonging in Italian society. But this is not to suggest that these statuses are insignificant. The very real effects of lacking legal status restrict a whole range of everyday activities: employment opportunities, access to health care and social welfare, everyday transactions requiring the signing of a contract (such as buying a SIM card for a mobile phone or connecting one's home to the internet), and, perhaps most seriously, one's freedom of movement (see also Dreby 2015). Yet because of the "institutionalization of irregularity" (Calavita 2005a: 43) inherent in the Italian system, becoming illegal was always possible and had usually been experienced by migrants at some point in the past.

Experiences of uncertainty, therefore, result not from being undocumented per se, but rather from migration regimes that make legal status highly precarious and contingent (Calavita 2005a; De Genova 2002). The contemporary proliferation of migration policies across the world allows for short-term migration—such as circular migration—but ensures that attaining long-term legal status is much harder (Feldman 2012: chap. 6; Lindquist, Xiang, and Yeoh 2012: 10; Vertovec 2007). Permit systems that authorize only temporary residency create more bureaucratic regulation and administration, as migrants must continuously apply and reapply for their status. Equal attention, therefore, must be given to the uncertainties produced by both the processes of legalization and the processes of illegalization.

Alternative affectivities

Focusing on legalization processes—rather than specifically lack of legal status—highlights the other affective outcomes produced through encounters with the immigration bureaucracy, besides uncertainty and anxiety. Migrants in Italy are certainly constrained and marginalized by the socioeconomic and political context in which they are situated; at the same time, the legal and bureaucratic domains they navigate are frequently disordered, conflicting, and contradictory. For these reasons, my analysis moves beyond the deterministic modes of subjectification and governmentality found in Foucauldian-influenced anthropological accounts (Auyero 2012; Ferguson 1990; Ong 1999; Ong 2003) to show how the affects produced through encounters with legal and bureaucratic processes are varied and ambiguous.

As is also the case in the navigation of welfare (Auyero 2012; Sarat 1990), development (Ferguson 1990; Lewis and Mosse 2006), and planning and regulatory bureaucracies (Hull 2012a), for those caught up in these "webs of administrative regulation" (Reeves 2013: 511) anxiety and uncertainty are not the only things produced. Legal and bureaucratic engagements can produce opportunities for self-fashioning, social mobility, and forms of cultural citizenship. Tracing migrants' encounters with paperwork and documents offers key insights into these alternative affectivities, as the divergent meanings that bureaucratic and documentary processes can hold, as well as the purposes they can serve, are revealed. False but authentic domestic work contracts can enable migrants without jobs or working in the informal market to regularize their status or to renew their permits. Those who agree to act as domestic work "employers" can be motivated by business opportunities, altruism, or kinship obligations. Meanwhile, domestic work "employees"—secure with work permits that are valid for two years—can pursue employment opportunities either in Italy or abroad or choose not to work at all. As well as leading to tangible outcomes, documentary practices have affective qualities, producing new forms of subjectification. Learning how to complete permit renewal applications and other basic paperwork, for example, provides an opportunity for savvy migrants to acquire both material gain and social status by becoming informal immigration advisers (Chapter 4). Strategically navigating the immigration bureaucracy through the presentation of authentic but false documents is a means through which migrants become Italian cultural insiders (Chapter 3). Closely tracing paperwork and documents, therefore, highlights that although uncertainty and anxiety haunt migrants' experience of the immigration regime, bureaucratic encounters can also produce alternative affects and outcomes.

The multiple meanings that immigration law and documentary practices can hold simultaneously is also explored by Heath Cabot (2014, 2012) in her work on asylum seekers in Greece. She shows that, similar to the domestic work contract, the "pink card"—the identity document that asylum seekers are issued with by the Greek state—is granted new meanings. Despite its official purpose, for Bangladeshi migrants the pink card was understood to be a residence permit as it enabled them to work and live legally in Greece, if only temporarily. But, as suggested to Cabot by a lawyer research respondent, the police and bureaucrats' interpretation and employment of the document was different from its official aim. For them, the pink card was a means to enact an informal census of undocumented migrants in Greece (Cabot 2012: 21). Bureaucratic and documentary practices can, therefore, have multiple and contradictory effects that often diverge from their officially stated purpose. They are evidence of how laws actually work and of the varying purposes they can serve to different actors within the immigration nexus.

Encounters with bureaucracies, in particular those that regulate immigration regimes, seem to be universally characterized by long waiting times, changing policies, misinformation, and lost documents, which produce profound uncertainty, frustration, and anxiety for their users (Auyero 2012; Cabot 2014; Hoag 2010; Sarat 1990; Triandafyllidou 2003; Tuckett 2015). Yet, as research conducted on the documentation processes shows, the indeterminate nature of documentary regimes (Kelly 2006) also creates room for maneuver (see Sarat 1990 on navigating welfare bureaucracies in the United States). In the Italian context, false but authentic domestic work contracts, along with other strategies, which are documented throughout this book, enable migrants to obtain legal status, renew permits, and bring over family members.

The effects of indeterminate documentary practices, however, must be continually contextualized within the broader political-economic context in which migrants are situated, so as not to exaggerate or romanticize the power that migrants—documented or not—might have in relation to the state in which they are bordered. The marginalized position to which migrants are restricted in Italy is crucial to understanding the meaning and significance of the effects of their immigration encounters. Further, while useful in achieving basic ends such as permit renewal, migrants' strategies of navigation did not ultimately help them to develop more secure lives for themselves in Italy.

Fieldwork

This book is based on research conducted from 2009 to 2016 in a city in the northern Italian region of Emilia Romagna.[3] Following migrants' bureaucratic encounters as they sought to become and stay "legal," I conducted nineteen months of intensive fieldwork between 2009 and 2011 followed by annual visits. Emilia Romagna is characterized by a proliferation of small and medium-sized industries; it provides a fruitful terrain for migrants seeking work opportunities. They do so predominantly in the manufacturing, agricultural, construction, and domestic care sectors. Mirroring the diversity of migrants' nationalities in the country as a whole, the city's migrant population is heterogeneous, and migrants account for approximately 10 percent of the population. Overlapping partly but not completely with the list for Italy as a whole, the "top ten" nationalities in the region are Moroccan (14.6 percent), Romanian (13.1 percent), Albanian (12.6 percent), Ukrainian (5.1 percent), Tunisian (4.9 percent), Chinese (4.6 percent), Moldovan (4.6 percent), Indian (3.2 percent), Pakistani (3.2 percent), and Polish (2.6 percent) (Caritas 2010).

I began my research by tracing migrants' trajectories as they contacted landlords, employers, and the *questura* in different parts of the city in their application processes. By observing the system of documentation at its various stages and in its various sites, my fieldwork focused on how documentary practices played out in the city itself. Two months into my fieldwork, thanks to Mohamed—a Tunisian migrant I met while conducting participant observation at the *questura*—I discovered an advice center for migrants run by a trade union, which is where much of my fieldwork came to be based.[4]

In the first stage of my research I visited the *questura* early in the mornings, mirroring the routines of migrants who, in the midst of completing applications, arrived there beginning around 5:00 a.m. to obtain a ticket that allowed them to see an official when it opened at 8:00 a.m. I waited with them in the queue, observing the goings-on and occasionally conducting informal interviews. One morning, squashed between the metal barriers set up to order the queue, I met Mohamed. After a brief chat in which I told him about my research, he advised me to visit the center: "You see everything there," he told me.

Following his advice, the next day I went to the center to ask permission to conduct participant observation there. After speaking to a volunteer named Naveed, I was told to e-mail the center's director. Receiving no response, I e-mailed Naveed, who told me to return to the center that week. On arriving I was placed behind the reception counter and briefly introduced to the other volunteers and staff members. Several minutes later another volunteer, Mehdi, told me that I ought to make myself useful. He thrust a list of requirements for permit renewal into my hands and ordered me to explain the application process to a client. "Come on, come on!" he barked at me while I looked at him hesitantly, unable to understand half of the technical terms on the list. Obediently, I began to go through the list with the client, looking to Mehdi for confirmation and explanations of the terms. This was how my fieldwork began and continued. As a volunteer at the center, I learned the ins and outs of Italian immigration law and how they were experienced by migrants every day.

Methodology

I frequented the center most days, spending many hours at the reception counter. There I checked the status of permit renewals on the computer, handed out information regarding requirements for particular applications, and answered clients' queries. I also consulted with staff members on behalf of clients and observed the interactions between clients and staff members, both at the reception counter and at the desks in the back office. At times my research at the center required me to visit other sites: I accompanied clients to the *questura*, delivered citizenship applications to the *prefettura* (prefecture—where some immigration paperwork is completed), and participated in protests and strike days.

The center was also where I met other research respondents involved in the immigration nexus, such as migrants, advice center workers, lawyers, brokers, and officials. These meetings served as a first point of contact, enabling me to use the extended case study method (Mitchell 2006). Once I had developed relationships with particular individuals, I accompanied them across the city as they completed tasks related to their or their clients' applications. We visited the *questura*, the *prefettura*, post offices, the offices of the *comune* (municipality), and other sites. I also developed more social relationships with clients and staff members I met through the center: I saw them for drinks or dinner, I went to their homes, and, on the weekend, we regularly went shopping together or met in the squares to socialize.

Long-term fieldwork at the center offered several key advantages. It enabled me to develop close relationships with staff members and some clients, and to collect and compare hundreds of case studies. The catalogue of case studies I created enabled me to analyze the nature and frequency of particular encounters with the immigration bureaucracy. In addition, given the highly complicated and technical nature of the Italian immigration bureaucracy, long-term fieldwork allowed me to develop an understanding of the law and its everyday workings. I also met several of my close respondents outside of the center. At one point I lived with foreign students (from Albania and Israel), and I accompanied them and their friends on their document trails. My conversations and interviews with respondents were usually conducted in Italian. On occasion I spoke English with those who came from the Philippines, Pakistan, India, or anglophone countries in Africa. At times, I also acted as a translator between clients and staff members at the center.

Owing to my position behind the counter, many of the center's clients thought that I worked there. I explained my background and research project to some of them, although often my conversations with clients were very brief, so I could not always elaborate on my situation. Clients frequently asked about my origins, often assuming that I was eastern European or Italian. When I said I was British, they were surprised. "What would an English girl be doing here?" they asked, reflecting the commonly held view that the United Kingdom was a superior destination to Italy. On some occasions eastern European migrants reacted in a hostile manner toward me after I told them I was unable to speak or understand Russian, presuming that I was an arrogant compatriot. Staff members and volunteers were also puzzled about my origins. They detected that I was not Italian and, since it was usual for migrants to volunteer at the center, assumed that I must be eastern European. On learning that I was from London, staff members and clients responded in awe: "from London? London, London?" Their attitude toward me also shifted. From being slightly suspicious and disdainful, staff members became intrigued and respectful. On learning about my background, migrants who visited the center also responded excitedly, frequently relating to me their hopes (past or future) to move to the U.K. or stories of family or friends who lived there. My status as a privileged European did not create the perception that I would provide them with material benefits. But they did think that I, like other staff members, might be able to do them favors.

My greatest ethical concern during my fieldwork was the fact that I became an adviser myself, and thus potentially responsible for the outcomes of applications, which may have had serious repercussions on individuals' lives. At first I tried to stand at a distance, observing the interactions between staff members and clients, listening to common inquiries and concerns, and talking informally to visitors as they waited for their appointments. In the busy and sometimes understaffed center, however, such a position was untenable. "You have to work! Brigadini [the head of the center] will kick you out if you just stand there," Mehdi, the volunteer, barked at me in my first week at the center. Early on, my role was confined to the computer, taking appointments, and checking permit renewal status. As the months passed, however, I became more knowledgeable and I was asked to give information as well as take appointments. When I began to feel more confident at the center I moved around the space more freely, sitting at different staff members' desks as they advised individual clients. In particular, I developed a close relationship with Alberto, a senior staff member and spent many hours with him at his desk observing more in-depth interactions. I largely resisted filling in *kits* (application forms for permit renewal). Technically, completing permit renewal forms was exclusively the role of paid staff members, but when the staff were running behind schedule some volunteers also took on this responsibility. In order to avoid being asked to complete forms, and thus run the risk of making mistakes that could have an impact on migrants' applications, I purposely did not learn how to fill them in (although occasionally staff members did ask me to do so under their guidance). In January 2011 I was asked to assist in the completion of *decreto flussi* applications. Although I was concerned about the ethical implications of completing application forms and potentially making an error, the online application was very simple, and the procedure led to valuable insights. I continuously emphasized my role as a student-researcher and nonexpert to staff members and clients but, despite my unwillingness, through my role at the center I did become an actor in the immigration nexus that I was analyzing. This required reflexivity, but also provided me with insights that would not have been otherwise available.

Where are they from?

Anthropological ethnographies on migration, whether based in "host" or "sending" countries, tend to focus on migrants from the same nationality or regional area. Undoubtedly nationality and cultural background are significant factors in how people engage and interact with systems of immigration bureaucracy, as are factors such as the length of time spent in the country, language abilities, education, class, gender, and occupation. Given my interest in legal and bureaucratic encounters, however, selecting a nationality group, and assuming some homogeneity of experience due to nationality or background, would have been arbitrary, obscuring as much as it revealed. Given my specific interest in the immigration bureaucracy itself, my interlocutors turned out to be those who were in some way engaged with it. Besides migrant applicants and their families, they included activists, brokers, officials, advisers, lawyers, and post office workers.

I do not make distinctions between types of migrants according to their legal status. Owing to the specificities of Italian immigration law, people held different kinds of permits, depending on their circumstances—work permits, student permits, family permits, political asylum permits, and others. Although the application procedures for asylum seekers were different, applying for and renewing most other kinds of permits usually resulted in similar processes, interactions, and experiences.[5]

Chapter outline

Chapter 1 introduces the book's central fieldsite: a trade union–affiliated migrant advice center that provides support and assistance to migrants in their completion of application forms, as well as navigation of the immigration bureaucracy more generally. Trade unions have a central function in the Italian welfare state, and the center's role in completing migrants' application forms is closely connected to this. Although affiliated with the trade union, in the eyes of its visitors, and in practice, the center's role is often blurred with that of the *questura* (immigration office) and the state in general. Because the center acts as a mediator between migrants and the *questura,* the assistance that clients received could determine application outcomes. Not all staff members were equally knowledgeable about or interested in migration matters, however, and the quality of assistance they provided was highly variable.

Through detailed case studies, Chapter 2 illustrates how everyday experiences with the Italian immigration bureaucracy are characterized by uncertainty, arbitrariness, and frustration. This close examination of migrants' bureaucratic encounters, however, reveals that the bureaucracy's arbitrary and uncertain nature also makes it flexible and relatively easy to manipulate. Using effective strategies of navigation, migrants are able to manipulate the law's loopholes and succeed in getting their applications accepted. Tracing migrants' strategies, this chapter argues that "formal" and "informal" spheres are interdependent and symbiotic: migrants, brokers, advisers, and officials all must engage in informal and extralegal practices in order to successfully navigate the immigration bureaucracy.

Chapter 3 argues that rule-bending reveals the broader attitudes toward the state and bureaucracy in Italy that, through their bureaucratic encounters, migrants also come to hold. Bureaucratic engagements are thus forms of citizenmaking. Socially acceptable rule-breaking, however, is accompanied by strict compliance with proceduralism in relation to paperwork. Successfully navigating the immigration bureaucracy requires expertise in the management of documents: paper trails must seem authentic even if false. Yet given the documented nature of migrants' lives, rule-bending in one application can potentially create problems in others, meaning that even skillful rule-bending can be risky for migrants, causing them to lose legal status or foreclosing the attainment of citizenship. There thus exists a mismatch between a migrant's social knowledge—which is required to navigate the bureaucracy—and exclusionary citizenship laws that make this knowledge dangerous.

Chapter 4 focuses on the role of community brokers—informal immigration advisers with migrant backgrounds—and describes how they style themselves as bureaucratic experts. Doing so enables these brokers to develop new subjectivities and fashion themselves in affective terms. Becoming advisers gives them the appearance of professionalism, helps them gain standing in their community, satisfies their charitable impulses, and places them center stage in the fight for social justice. Taking on the role of a community broker offers possibilities for gaining social status that are not otherwise available to most migrants in Italy.

Reflecting on the second generation's experiences with the immigration bureaucracy, Chapter 5 considers the contradictory and divergent effects of immigration law encounters. If dealings with the immigration bureaucracy produce opportunities for first-generation migrants and their advisers, for the second generation they create upset and disjuncture. This generation is more vulnerable to immigration policies since its members may suddenly find themselves labeled "undocumented immigrants" after turning eighteen, owing to Italy's *jus sanguinis* nationality policy, which confers citizenship according to ancestry rather than birthplace. Although they are at ease in and largely integrated into Italian society, they are still subject to the country's restrictive immigration and citizenship laws. The disjuncture highlights the profound injustices and inequalities that such laws create for all migrants.

The final ethnographic chapter explores migrants' feelings of disappointment about their migration trajectory in Italy and their desire to leave the country. The disappointment of those who aspire to migrate but ultimately never leave their homelands has been extensively discussed in the migration studies literature. Chapter 6 places the focus on those who *have* migrated but who still feel they have failed owing to their lack of onward mobility from Italy. Focusing on those migrants' feelings of disappointment and personal failure, it describes the differentiated inclusion of migrants in the global marketplace. Their desire to leave Italy, whether imagined or acted upon, shows how the mobility enabled by neoliberal globalization reproduces hierarchies within the EU. By viewing Italy as a stepping stone on a longer trajectory, migrants—both those who leave and those who remain—conceptualize the country as an inferior destination.

Drawing the preceding chapters together, the conclusion argues that the "border spectacle" (De Genova 2002) produces a lopsided view of migration by obscuring how immigration policies relate to broader political and economic processes of contemporary migration and globalization. Migrants' navigation of the documentation regime seems to provide them with only meager benefits, while employers, lawyers, policy makers, and other stakeholders within the immigration nexus reap the rewards. The final section of the conclusion reflects on policies that could improve the migration landscape in light of the problems I have identified.

1   The Center

My central fieldsite was a trade union–affiliated migrant advice center that helps migrants complete application forms, as well as navigate the documentation regime more generally. Although affiliated with the trade union, in the eyes of its visitors and in practice the center's role is often blurred with that of the *questura* (immigration office) and the state in general. In what follows I outline the history and daily functioning of the center and illustrate the ambiguous role it holds.

Good advice is essential for migrants navigating the immigration bureaucracy, and the center played an important role in helping migrants to effectively navigate the documentation regime. Providing advice, however, is a difficult task that requires experience, knowledge, and finesse. There were vast discrepancies in the quality of advice offered by different staff members at the center. After introducing the center's staff members, who provide an important backdrop to the subsequent chapters, I briefly describe the immigration regime's shifting terrain, which profoundly shaped the workings of the center.

History and daily operations

At the time of my fieldwork the advice center was the most frequented migrant advice organization in the city. Its long opening hours, free services, and regular meetings with the *questura* made it in high demand among its mainly migrant client base. Its established role in the city's immigration nexus was due to Paolo Brigadini, an activist passionate about social inequality, discrimination, and migrants' rights, who set up the center in the early 1990s. When it first opened, the only paid staff member was Brigadini himself, and its single room, a cupboard-like office, was staffed by volunteers. It grew rapidly, and by

2009, when my fieldwork began, the center employed seven staff members and several volunteers.

The center was situated around the corner from the central trade union offices that housed the trade union federation groups serving different categories of workers. For example, there is a federation that represents workers in the commerce, services, and tourism sector; separate federations represent workers in construction and woodwork and other employment sectors. The center's space was divided into two halves: the inner office, where the majority of administrative duties were carried out, and the outer waiting room and reception counter (*sportello*). The waiting room was usually extremely busy. Families, friends, and individuals sat in plastic chairs either chatting or sitting in silence. Mothers breast-fed babies, children ran around playing, and people made and received phone calls. Notices of upcoming protests relating to the trade union decorated the walls, alongside posters showing migrant children accompanied by slogans reading, "We are all the same" (*Noi siamo tutti gli stessi*).

Staff members at the center, and from other departments in the trade union, often remarked that the migrant advice center was the trade union's busiest office. Before the center opened in the morning, and after the lunch break, queues of people waited for its doors to open. The reception counter was the center's hub and was typically busy and hectic. People gathered around it trying to make appointments to complete their applications or to check the status of their permit renewals online. Queries ranged from those concerning the requirements for a particular application to those involving complex and often unsolvable situations. How the latter were dealt with depended on who was working at the counter and how many other people were waiting. Some staff members dismissed such queries, telling clients that they needed to go elsewhere or that what they were asking was not possible. Others consulted more experienced staff members, who were usually in the inner office, and the issue was either dealt with immediately or deferred. It was common for clients to return multiple times before their problem was resolved, and without persistence their cases could easily become forgotten.

In addition to help with documentation, many clients asked for help with housing, social services, the police, bills, fines, and employment. Again, the attention and service that people were given depended on which staff member they saw and when, but they were usually referred to different offices specializing in the particular issue. Working at the reception counter was stressful, and staff bore the brunt of migrants' frustrations with the immigration bureaucracy and long waits. Both clients and staff members frequently raised their voices. Clients were sometimes accusatory, believing that they were not receiving fair treatment, and staff members were sometimes openly aggressive or irritated by clients' failure to understand or perceived rude manner. In contrast, the atmosphere of the inner office was more relaxed. Here there were six desks where staff members completed application forms on computers, usually by appointment. Staff members and clients chatted as their applications for permit renewal, family reunification, and citizenship were completed. Those working at the reception counter would come in and out to photocopy or ask advice from other staff members.

The center's growth reflected both the increasing number of migrants in Italy and the increased bureaucratization of immigration processes. Given the necessity of employment for permit issue and renewal, it was logical for the trade union to become involved in the immigration bureaucracy for two reasons. First, migrant workers dominate the trade union's strongest sectors—industry, construction, services, and domestic work. Therefore, by offering permit application completion and advice, the trade union was providing an essential service to its current members, as well as potentially cultivating new ones. Second, as part of the original "advocacy coalition," trade unions have historically played a role in the formation of immigration policy in Italy (Zincone 2011). The center's services were free, but clients who were not already members of the trade union were gently encouraged to join. Membership cost 1 percent of a member's monthly salary. Similar migration advice centers existed across the trade unions in Italy, but because of Brigadini's activism, the center where I conducted fieldwork was considerably larger, better staffed, and open more days a week than its counterparts across the country.[1]

The center's role as a trade union affiliate was ambiguous, as reflected in migrants' attitude toward it. Many clients did not know about its trade union connections and presumed that it was affiliated with the *questura* or *comune*. The services the center offered were also available in other sites across the city, but usually at a cost (see Chapter 4). Because this center's services were free, many were suspicious of the quality of the services available, presuming that quality and value could only be bought and not freely given. In response to complaints about delayed applications, staff members emphasized to clients that the center was "*il sindicato*" (the trade union), not the *questura* or the state. The organization of the Italian welfare state, however, which is closely intertwined with trade unions and other nonstate bodies, makes clients' confusion understandable. The key function played by the center in completing application forms related to its position as a *patronato. Patronati* are intermediary institutions attached to trade unions in which workers can receive free advice, assistance, protection, and representation. They play a central role in the history of the Italian welfare state, and trade unions have been key players in both their implementation and operation since the Second World War (Agnoletto 2012: 22). Besides immigration-related issues, assistance provided by *patronati* includes help with pensions, welfare benefits, sick leave, and unemployment. Their role is to protect and advocate for welfare users and ensure that the social security system is functioning correctly. Although they are not part of the state infrastructure, the state pays the *patronato* for each assistance file opened. Thus trade unions are protagonists in the Italian welfare state (Agnoletto 2012: 13, 22), playing the roles of provider, advocate, and protector. Because *patronati* hold a unique position as gatekeepers to public assistance, as well as guarantors that they function correctly, Stefano Agnoletto has described them as a "peculiar institution wherein the distinction between public and private is poorly defined, its trade union identity overlapping its public utility function" (18). The center's role as a *patronato* exemplified this peculiarity.

The center received state funds for each permit renewal, long-term permit, and family reunification request it completed. It was paid by the state to complete paperwork but, as a *patronato*, was not an arm or representative of the state in name or practice. Rather, the center acted as a mediator between the state—in this case usually represented by the *questura*—and migrants. This mediation was crucial for migrants in their encounters with Italian immigration law. As the following chapters illustrate, the *questura* frequently acted in "unlawful" ways, including denying applications on unfair grounds, making errors on official documents, requesting unnecessary documentation, and delaying applications. In the Italian legal system, it is common for recently passed laws to directly contradict existing ones. The laws that the *questura* chooses to implement are at the discretion of individual *questura* directors, meaning that in practice immigration law differs in different Italian cities. Ministerial *circolari* (circulars), which are designed to clarify acts of law, create further discrepancies as there is no obligation on the part of the *questure* to follow the directives of the *circolari*. Because the *questure* officials had such decision-making discretion, migrants were highly dependent on the protection of institutions such as the center, which held weekly meetings with the *questura* director or vice director, during which its representatives challenged the reasons for delayed or rejected applications. In Chapter 2 I explore examples of these issues in more depth.

This setup put the center in an ambiguous role. Reflecting this, clients frequently directed their complaints and dissatisfaction about their ongoing applications, and the law in general, toward the center. Their confusion was due to the indistinct boundary between the work of the state and that of trade unions, as well as the fact that the *questura* had no procedures for allowing migrants to contest decisions.

The *questura* was responsible for processing applications and making decisions, but it did not officially disseminate information about applications to individuals or to the broader public. On entering the heavy metal gates, visitors saw a cabin where a police officer sat. Taped onto the cabin's glass window was letter-size sheet of white paper that read, in capital letters, "NO INFORMAZIONI" (see figure 4). When people tried to ask this officer for help, he mutely pointed to the sign.[2] Sometimes, though, visitors to the center repeated information that the officer occupying the cabin had given them, suggesting that some officers were friendlier than others. This information, however, was frequently incorrect, and center staff members were then left with the task of trying to convince skeptical clients that the police officer was misinformed.

Inside the *questura* there were also no opportunities to ask about submitted applications or general procedures. Interaction between officials and applicants was confined to three kinds of meetings: appointments to give fingerprints, which occurred at the beginning of the renewal phase; appointments to collect issued permits; and permit renewal appointments for family members of Italian citizens, whose applications were submitted directly at the *questura* rather than via the postal system.[3] These interactions took place at either the beginning or the end of the application phase, excluding any opportunity for individuals to inquire about ongoing applications. When individuals did attempt to request information, for example, by attracting a passing official's attention while at the *questura*, they were either ignored or told to send an e-mail. E-mails sent to the *questura*, however, consistently bounced back to the sender's e-mail account.

The impenetrability of the *questura* meant that the kinds of interactions clients desired to have there instead took place at the center. This was partly because some thought that the center was affiliated with the *questura*. It was also due to the existence of the reception counter and the center's relative ease of access. In relation to his study of French benefit offices, Vincent Dubois (2010: 4) notes that, in administrations, reception counters usually bear the brunt of users' frustrations. This was certainly true at the migration advice center, whose reception counter absorbed the anger and complaints caused not only by its own errors and delays, but also by the *questura*.

On hearing that a permit renewal was still delayed or that an application

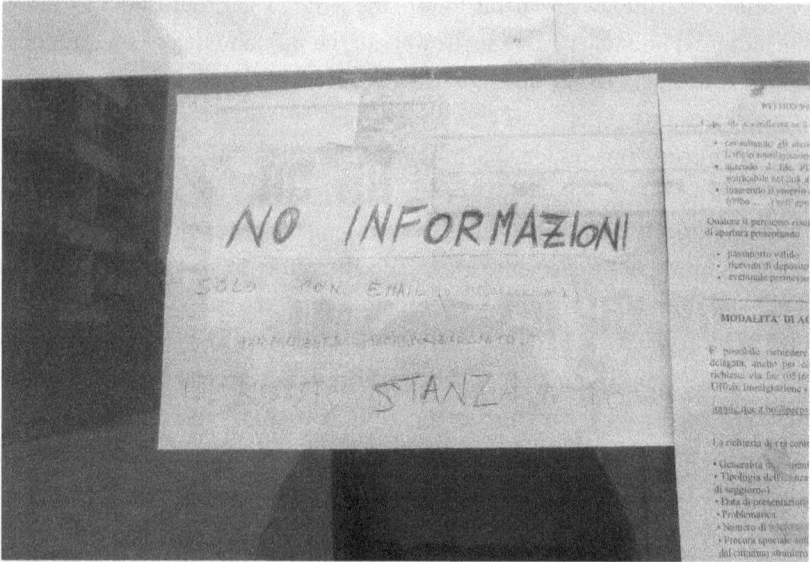

Figure 4. Photograph of sign at the questura. Photograph by author.

had been rejected, people frequently responded with raised voices, tears, and panic. Staff members' reaction to such behavior varied according to the individual and the atmosphere of the center at a given moment. Some responded sympathetically but told the client they were unable to help; others became angry, telling clients, "We are not the *questura*"; and others were proactive, asking the client for paperwork, which they photocopied before asking Alberto or Ginetta to make inquiries at the *questura* at the next meeting. This last option was not always available to even the most sympathetic staff members. The load of inquiries that Alberto and Ginetta took with them to the weekly *questura* meetings was always heavy, and not everybody's case could be given sufficient attention. When applications were delayed, it was usually futile to make further inquiries. The standard wait for a permit to be issued was several months, and only those applications that were considered to be abnormally delayed would be inquired about at the weekly meetings. Therefore, because space (physical or temporal) for contestation and complaint was limited at the *questura*, many encounters between bureaucrats and nonbureaucrats took place at the center, despite the fact that it was not a state bureaucratic office (Dubois 2009, 2010).[4]

New leadership

After the departure of Brigadini in the summer of 2010, the character of the center changed in both its working patterns and its ethos. The official story was that Brigadini had retired. He was replaced by Maria, a forty-year-old woman who had previously worked in the central trade union administration. Prioritizing the political struggle for migrants' rights, Brigadini had had little interest in using the center to raise money for the union. The center ensured funding for the trade union in its role as a *patronato,* but it had a low record for membership recruitment, since under Brigadini clients were not strongly encouraged to enlist. Writing in the 1990s, Zincone (1998: 72–73) noted that migrants' "free-riding" of trade unions' services was encouraged by unions on both sides of the political spectrum as they were investing in the unions' future: the aim was that migrants would join the union once they found more stable work. But by 2010 such free-riding was no longer considered acceptable by the trade union administration.

Unlike Brigadini, Maria had no previous connections with migration associations, *questura* officials, or others who may have been useful to a person in her role. Staff members largely interpreted her entry into the center as motivated by the trade union administration's desire to bring the center into line and to increase its membership. People told me that the trade union was suffering because of the economic crisis, as members who had become unemployed or were no longer able to afford the dues were canceling their memberships. This was a problem across the trade union, and those I knew from other sectors told me they were under increasing pressure to recruit new members.

Fueling these rumors, Maria introduced various initiatives designed to increase membership. These included encouraging clients to enlist, restricting access to the center's lawyers to members only, introducing a type of unemployment membership for those who did not work but wanted to attend the center's "free" Italian language courses, and organizing training about the history and principles of trade unionism for staff members and volunteers. Staff members and volunteers implemented these initiatives unevenly, with most considering the new rules nonsensical. For example, the idea of an unemployment membership to a trade union was considered a contradiction in terms, as were the new rules about who could consult with the center lawyers. Most of those who needed to consult with the lawyers were waiting to hear about the outcome of applications that would give them legal status. One could hardly expect "illegal" migrants to sign up as members of a trade union. Last, many staff members viewed it as futile to enlist people who were likely to cancel their subscription soon after joining.

Maria's new rules showed how the trade union's need to reproduce itself financially was clashing with the everyday running of the center and the realities of the documentation regime more widely. Many clients were unaware that the center was part of a trade union at all, and did not necessarily understand the concept of *sindicalismo* (unionism). In addition, many of those who frequented the center were not technically eligible to become trade union members, being either undocumented migrants or unemployed holders of family permits. Further contradicting Maria's uncompromising emphasis on *sindacalismo* were the realities of the documentation regime. As Chapter 2 explores, many migrants hold fake domestic work contracts in order to renew permits while working *in nero* (off the books) in other sectors. For these individuals, joining the union would have been futile because their actual employers were not listed on their contracts.

In contrast, under Brigadini the running of the center had been fairly relaxed. He employed a hands-off approach and was seldom present. When he was at the center he was usually in his office. Under Brigadini staff members worked hard and consistently, but were free to act as they saw fit. If the center was not too busy, staff could drink coffee at the bar, smoke cigarettes outside (and sometimes inside), and hold personal phone conversations. As reflected by my own experience, volunteers were not formally interviewed or trained, but were required simply to be eager and ready to work.

On her arrival as the new head, Maria quickly implemented changes. She was far more selective about potential volunteers and formalized their role through the issuing of contracts. Another example of her more rigorous approach was how she ran Thursday mornings, when the center was closed to the public for staff training sessions and meetings. Before Maria's arrival, few meetings or training sessions actually took place. Instead staff members used the time to catch up on work or run personal errands. Maria, however, made sure that meetings and training sessions occurred. Representatives from the trade union made presentations to center staff about their work. At other times, Maria asked Alberto (a senior staff member) to hold training sessions for staff and volunteers on immigration matters in order to ensure consistency in disseminated information. This was challenging because the rules themselves regularly shifted and were implemented differently by *questura* officials.

Overall, with the arrival of Maria the center changed in both the way it was organized and its ethos. While Brigadini was motivated by a strong sense of social justice for migrants, Maria, sent from the central administration, seemed more concerned with increasing membership numbers and making the center run like a trade union. She was less interested (or was perhaps unable to be interested, given her lack of knowledge and contacts in the immigration world) in politics regarding migrants' rights. Her approach had an impact both on the running of the center and on the treatment of clients. Where Brigadini had espoused the humanitarian attitude that all were entitled to the services the center offered, Maria argued that it was unfair to union members to make services available indiscriminately. In reality, because the center's status as a *patronato* meant that its services were open to all, and because many migrants needed the services, it was impossible for these discriminatory rules to be effectively applied.

In the next section I introduce some of the central figures who worked or volunteered at the center. These individuals are featured throughout the book.

Staff and volunteers

Paid staff

Staff members varied greatly in their knowledge and interest in migration matters and had followed rather different trajectories. Some had originally worked in other sectors of the trade union, and others had started as volunteers and subsequently became advice center employees. Some held strong ideas about migrants' rights, but others cared less, if at all. Several staff members were migrants themselves, although most were native Italians. Almost all staff members had fallen into work in this sector rather than aspiring to it. Alberto, from southern Italy, had previously worked in the fiscal office of the trade union after graduating with a philosophy degree from the local university. He had no previous professional experience in the field of migration but had been transferred to the center when more senior staff were required. Despite his lack of experience in the field, Alberto had a natural flair for the job. Chiara (one of the center volunteers) described to me how in his first few months he voraciously lapped up information, incessantly asking questions and browsing the internet for information. Reflecting this thirst for knowledge, his comprehension of legal migration matters quickly developed, and he was usually better informed than officials or lawyers. His good humored manner, ability to make people laugh, and willingness to spend time with clients put them at ease and made even the mundane task of filling out forms a sociable event.

Another staff member, Ginetta, who was close to retiring, had been hired by the center following years of volunteering there. Her entry into the world of migration was motivated by goodwill and a desire to learn new skills. Her decade-long presence in the office had propelled her into a senior position and she shared with Alberto the responsibility of visiting the *questura* for weekly meetings to follow up on delayed and complicated cases. While Alberto enjoyed what he called "finding the right road for each case," Ginetta found the process stressful and was erratic in how she dealt with cases. She did not share Alberto's flair and finesse for quickly understanding different laws, how they overlapped or contradicted each other, and how they could be manipulated. In contrast to Alberto's easy-going style, Ginetta had a strict and formal manner. At moments when tensions were running high she would become frustrated with migrants' lack of understanding or assertiveness. Yet despite her shortness of temper, she never refrained from employing the formal mode of address with clients. This respectful mode is always used in public offices in Italy, but was rarely heard in the center. Moreover, although she did not have the same expertise as Alberto, many clients were deeply grateful to Ginetta for issues she had resolved for them, particularly in her role in charge of citizenship applications. On Tuesday mornings I often accompanied her to the *prefettura* (where citizenship applications are processed), helping her carry the stacks of applications that she needed to deliver. She was always in a good mood on these Tuesday mornings, commenting on the respect and good manners of the officials at the *prefettura* in contrast to the police officers (*poliziotti*) at the *questura*. Staff members and clients viewed officials at the *prefettura* more positively than those at the *questura*, in part because *prefettura* officials were considered to be more sympathetic to migrants. Ginetta, despite her severe demeanor, was a kind, generous, and warm-hearted individual, though she suffered from the heavy workload and stress of her job.

After Ginetta, the longest-standing staff member was Biniam. Originally from Eritrea, Biniam had arrived in Italy almost ten years earlier. His sister, Chiara (an original volunteer at the center), encouraged him to volunteer in order to keep busy while he sought full-time employment and sorted out his documents. After years of volunteering and being paid only his expenses, Biniam was finally hired on a temporary contract but with a salary considerably lower than other staff members'. Five years on, Biniam still held this temporary contract. He attributed his lowly position to racial discrimination and the fact that he lacked the connections within the central trade union offices considered essential in order to be granted a permanent position. Like Alberto, Biniam was highly knowledgeable about legal issues pertaining to migration, particularly those concerning asylum. Like many Eritrean migrants, Biniam had applied for asylum himself, an application he later withdrew after being granted citizenship thanks to his Italian grandfather.

Working between the advice center and the trade union's engineering sector were Al Alami and Al Badisi, both originally from Morocco. Their trajectories were common to the very few migrants employed at the trade union who, after working in factories and acting as trade union delegates, eventually become employed full-time by the union. The employment of such individuals is essential to the trade union, since increasingly those who work in the dominant sectors it represents are also migrants. Those such as Al Alami and Al Badisi, who were long-time union members themselves, were perceived to be able to bridge the gap and recruit more members, as well as provide the necessary assistance to current members. As Arabic speakers, both were regularly called away from their desks to act as interpreters at the counter.

Volunteers

Volunteers were central to the running of the reception counter. Most were drawn from the ranks of socially conscious Italian students who wanted work experience or were migrants themselves. Those who were migrants tended to be motivated by a desire to help others, or in some cases by the possibility of financial gain. On several occasions it was discovered that volunteers had been charging clients for services that were intended to be free at the center. As Chapter 4 discusses, volunteering at the center offered migrants possibilities for financial gain and professional standing that were not easily available in Italy.

Chiara, Biniam's sister, was one of Brigadini's first volunteers and still volunteered at the center several times a week. Originally Eritrean, Chiara arrived in Italy when she was thirteen years old, preceding her brother's migration by almost two decades. Like Biniam, thanks to their paternal grandfather's Italian ancestry, Chiara was an Italian citizen. She occupied an in-between position in Italian society. She strongly identified as an "immigrant" but saw herself as, and was considered to be, different from other migrants. Her fluent Italian language skills, manner of gesticulation, style of dress, and name identified her as Italian. Yet her dark skin and braided hair excluded her from being considered Italian, and thus she found herself betwixt and between. Chiara brought a fun and energetic atmosphere to the center during her afternoons there. Bossy, strong-willed, and very knowledgeable about migration issues, Chiara would interrupt if she heard a less experienced volunteer or staff member giving incorrect information and, unlike most staff members, would "go the extra mile" for clients. If their needs were beyond that of the center's remit, rather than just referring them to a different office she would make phone calls and do her utmost to help. The last remaining volunteer from Brigadini's original group, Chiara was keen to foster a sense of migrant communal identity and support, and she treated clients with compassion, warmth, and respect. In the twenty years she had spent in the city, Chiara had cultivated a network of friends and contacts in the *questura*, the *comune*, social services, trade unions, and political parties. She activated these networks to help individuals in need at the center, and those whom she encountered elsewhere.

Unquestionably also motivated by a desire to help others was Mehdi, a Moroccan volunteer. Mehdi held radical left-wing views and was dedicated to struggles against inequality and racism. He was frequently called on to help other Moroccans, but unlike other staff members and volunteers who were migrants themselves, he felt equally responsible for the plight of those from other communities. His working style on the counter was manic, and he would flit from case to case, sometimes leaving people confused and uncertain how to proceed. When he felt someone was being rude he became angry, tearing up the piece of paper or list of requirements that he was writing on. In spite of his mood swings, he was dedicated to helping those he felt were in need and upheld strong principles of social justice. He did not hold regular employment and survived by doing irregular translation work. In addition to Mehdi and Chiara, a number of other volunteers also staffed the center. They will be introduced in the following chapters.

The center also employed two lawyers who were paid a minimal fee by the trade union to consult with clients. The lawyers offered clients a free consultation and reduced rates if the case needed to be continued. In theory, only trade union members were entitled to this service, but in practice staff members and volunteers referred clients whether they held membership or not.

"The practical stuff": the indeterminacy of advice

The great variety of working practices among staff members meant clients' experiences at the center and, in some cases, the outcome of their applications, were contingent upon which staff member they were seen by. Staff members' official role was to complete forms and advise clients about the documents they needed to submit for particular applications. Staff members in back office completed forms, while those at the reception counter distributed lists that outlined the requirements of applications and checked the status of permit renewal. Many clients, however, presented problems that could not be solved by filling out forms or distributing lists of requirements. Often clients required practical advice that was not written down in laws.

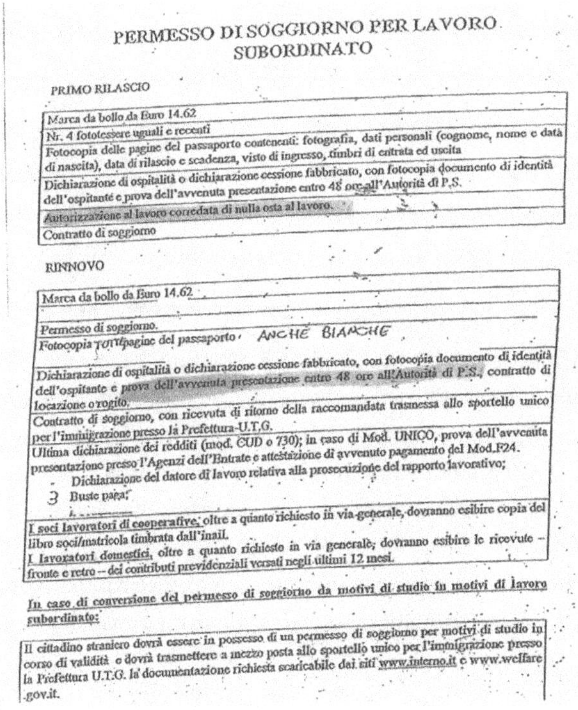

Figure 5. Photograph of list of paperwork needed to renew a work permit. Photograph by author.

As a law student, my Albanian friend Jovan was well versed in official immigration law. Visiting the center because he needed information about how his parents could obtain the long-term permit, he told me the following: "There is always a gap between what is written and what is actually put into practice. This place [the migration advice center] is good with the practical stuff." It was this practical stuff that constituted much of the center's work. Reliably advising on the practical stuff, however, was difficult, and not all staff members were sufficiently knowledgeable to do so. As Alberto informed us during one Thursday morning training session:

There is the law, but then there is the *questura*. How they [*questura* officials] choose to implement the law changes, and it changes from *questura* to *questura*, from official to official, and from day to day. If a case is complicated or does not have a straightforward answer, make sure you come and talk to me. In some cases what might seem impossible *is* possible. But at the same time we have to be careful not to tell people that something is possible that is not.

At the bar later that evening Alberto told me that he was irritated by the way in which one staff member, Giorgio, had handled a case. Giorgio had told a Cuban client, Carla, that she was required to redo a family reunification application for her daughter because she had failed to attend the necessary appointment a year ago. "Her daughter is a minor—she can't be expelled. In situations like this, there *is* a way around," Alberto told me. Alberto was annoyed with Giorgio because, instead of attempting to help Carla or simply referring her to Alberto, he had dismissed her. He had demonstrated both his lack of desire to help and a poor understanding of the law.

Familiar with Alberto because he had advised her on a separate occasion, Carla sought him out after her unsuccessful consultation with Giorgio. She had applied for her daughter to join her in Italy through the family reunification process. When completing the original application, Carla had applied through the *questura* of Naples, where she held residence but did not live (in Italy residence and domicile can be different).[5] She lived and worked in the city where I conducted fieldwork, but according to the requirements of family reunification her accommodation was not sufficiently capacious to accommodate both her and her daughter. In consideration of these circumstances, on the application form Carla had declared her Naples address (the house of her former employer) to be where her daughter would live. When the daughter finally arrived, however, Carla could not afford to pay for the train to Naples. Consequently, she missed the obligatory meetings at the *prefettura* and *questura* of Naples where her daughter's permit would have been issued, meaning that officially the daughter was not present on Italian territory. As a result, the girl did not hold a permit and was technically illegal. Alberto gently berated Carla. She should have put the address of a friend's house on the application form, he told her. A friend who lived in a big enough apartment could have done Carla a favor and, for the purposes of the application, given "hospitality" to the daughter. In reality this would not be the residence of the girl, and when she arrived a different address could be declared. Now the situation was more complicated because Carla's daughter had been living in Italy for over a year without her presence being declared at the *questura*.

Although complicated, and contrary to Giorgio's advice, there was a way around this problem. As a solution Alberto wrote a cover letter to the local *questura* asking them to overlook this mistake and completed the application form manually rather than on the computer. Application forms were usually filled out electronically via the *patronato*'s online portal. This was essential in order for the center to receive funds from the state for each application completed. In some cases, however, the applications were completed by hand (and consequently the center did not receive funding). This occurred if staff members were behind schedule and a volunteer completed the form (in theory only *patronato* staff should complete the electronic forms) or if the staff member did not want a particular application form to be registered with the *patronato*. When I asked Alberto why he had not used the electronic version for Carla, he told me that the *questura* would be more likely "to turn a blind eye" if the application form had been filled out by hand because, unlike an electronic version, it would not be officially recorded or archived. By writing a cover letter and completing the application form by hand, Alberto was hoping that the *questura* would overlook Carla's error and process the application. Under Italian immigration law minors cannot be expelled; therefore it was likely that the *questura* would, in this case, rule in Carla's favor.

Cases such as these were presented at the center daily and usually referred to Alberto or Ginetta, in view of the fact that it was they who attended *questura* meetings. Not all such cases, however, reached their desks, and it was down to luck or migrants' own initiative and persistence whether their cases were pursued. Clients at the center thus received advice of variable quality. The nature of the law itself made giving good advice difficult, the attitude and knowledge of particular staff members differed, and the center's heavy workload meant that not all visitors could obtain equal attention.

A note on the term "client"

So far I have referred to those who frequented the center as "clients."[6] Given the fact that the center was a trade union, and that its services offered were free of charge, I recognize that clients is not a wholly appropriate term. But finding a more appropriate term is difficult given the ambiguous role of the center and the nature of its visitors. Those who were trade union members would be better described as members, while those who visited the center for help completing their forms should perhaps be labeled recipients or applicants. Also, the term "client" suggests the exchange of money, which was a contentious issue at the center.

According to the Oxford English Dictionary, a client is "a person or organization using the services of a lawyer or other professional person or company" and "a person being dealt with by social or medical services." Although not accurate in every case, these definitions do encompass the various roles of those who frequented the center. Thus for want of an alternative I will continue to call those who frequented the center "clients."[7]

Conclusion

The center's ambiguous role and the importance of individual staff members' knowledge, expertise, and personality were deeply intertwined with the wider ambiguities within the documentation regime. The shifting nature of immigration law in top-down policymaking and on-the-ground discretionary implementation meant that providing good advice required expertise and could not be disseminated in a generic fashion. Chapter 2 explores the shifting terrain of the immigration bureaucracy, showing how particular kinds of attitudes are necessary in order to navigate it, or even to obtain advice on how to do so.

2

Working the Gap

Migrants' Navigation of the Immigration Bureaucracy

Extract from fieldnotes, January 2010

My Albanian flatmate, Eva, has invited me to accompany her to the post office today in order to complete the first stage of her permit renewal process. Eva is a twenty-five-year-old university student studying economics. Although she has lived in Italy for only four years, she speaks Italian with no hint of a foreign accent. Eva's student permit, which must be renewed every two years, is about to expire.

The first step is to photocopy all of the documents, certificates, and other paperwork that must be submitted for the renewal, so Eva and I head to a nearby copy shop on one of the city's main shopping streets. We wait for about half an hour in the small shop as the woman behind the counter makes copies of Eva's entire passport (including the blank pages), her bank statements, a declaration of hospitality from our flatmate who has the rental contract in his name, her expiring permit, and a university exam transcript. With the paperwork still warm from the copier, we head to a post office to collect a *kit* (application form for permit renewal) and to submit the application.

At the post office Eva takes a numbered ticket to join the queues for two different services. The first is to submit the paperwork for medical insurance, which students are required to hold in order to renew their permits. There is barely a line for this and Eva quickly submits the relevant paperwork and makes the 100 euro payment. The line to submit the *kit* is considerably longer (Eva has number 36, and 21 is currently being assisted.) While we wait, Eva completes the *kit*, a relatively straightforward task if one is literate in Italian bureaucratic language. Eva completes the form in silence, checking, double checking, and triple checking it. When she finishes, there is still a long line of people ahead

Figure 6. Photograph of photo booth outside a *questura*. Applicants must provide photographs when submitting their applications. Photograph by author.

of us. After waiting for over an hour, Eva complains about how ridiculous and inefficient this system is and semi-seriously jokes that she should get married in order to change her nationality. Becoming increasingly frustrated, she goes to the counter and politely asks how much longer the wait will be. The person behind the desk tells her that each person's application takes about twenty minutes to submit and there are ten people ahead of her. Sighing with exasperation Eva suggests that we get a coffee at the bar next door to kill some time.

As we drink our coffees, she tells me that she fears the permit will not be ready in time for her to take the flight to Paris that she booked several months ago in order to visit her boyfriend. She is worried because, during renewal periods, migrants are only allowed to travel to their home countries. Her situation, however, is not without hope. She tells me she will try to board the flight even without the correct documentation. In the past she has simply presented her identity card with her finger covering the line that denotes her nationality. The problem, Eva says, is that Ryanair, the airline with whom she has booked her flight, tends to check the nationality on identity cards. Although Italian nationals are permitted to travel with their nonelectronic paper identity cards, foreign nationals are not. If she is caught, she will simply book another flight with a different airline. In any case, she explains, it is only the outbound flight she would have to rebook, as Italy is much stricter about checking identity cards than other countries.[1] I ask her if she feels nervous about doing this. "No," she replies nonchalantly, "I have done it loads of times." I strongly suspect, however, that a migrant with weaker Italian language skills, a stronger foreign accent, and darker skin would not be able to fool the system so easily.

We return to the post office and, as we wait, I observe the interactions between those ahead of us as they submit their applications. Unlike Eva, most of these applicants do not speak fluent Italian and arrive with their *kits* precompleted, likely because they received assistance with filling them in. The Asian couple directly ahead of us have considerable difficulty understanding the woman behind the counter, who is explaining to them, in a rather aggressive and frustrated manner, that they must purchase a *marca da bollo* (specific kind of stamp) with which the application will be sent to the *questura*. This stamp, however, is unavailable from the post office and can only be purchased at *tabaccherie*. Eventually the couple leave the desk, but it is unclear if they have understood what they must do. Finally it is Eva's turn, and we approach the desk where a blond, middle-aged woman assists us. The post office worker is noticeably more cordial to Eva and me than she was to the previous couple. As she checks over Eva's form, she chats to us with an air of camaraderie, as if she too is befuddled by the complex bureaucratic system. After almost three hours at the post office, the form is finally completed, sealed, and ready to be sent to the *questura*.

Encounters with the immigration bureaucracy are critically important to individuals' lives. Application outcomes determine whether one's child can come to Italy, if one can leave the country to see a dying relative, or whether one can go home for a visit and then return to Italy. Most migrants face permit renewal every two years. For those lucky enough to have secure legal status, encounters with the regime continue through family and friends. Thus, dealing with the documentation regime is a defining feature of what it means to be a migrant in Italy and was experienced by my interlocutors as all-pervasive and intrusive. The bureaucracy's arbitrary and uncertain nature, however, also make it relatively flexible and, through engagement with it, migrants develop strategies to manipulate its loopholes and facilitate the acceptance of their applications.

The necessity to engage in the informal sphere in order for the formal one to function has been well established by anthropologists. Strictly following the official rules often leads to individuals losing out, the system itself ceasing to function, or the production of structural violence (Gupta 2012). Showing how migrants, brokers, advisers, and officials all must engage in informal practices in their navigation of the Italian immigration bureaucracy, this chapter argues that formal and informal spheres are interdependent and symbiotic. The banal and everyday practices of completing forms and other bureaucratic activities reveal the strategies migrants employ to take advantage of the law's uncertainty. As well as creating anxiety, therefore, the ambiguous character of the documentation regime also creates possibilities for its users. Though useful, however, these strategies hold only limited advantages.

Bureaucratic encounters

Long waiting times marked migrants' experiences of the Italian documentation regime and were often the primary reason for anxiety. These waits included queuing at the *questura* to provide fingerprints for permit renewal or collection, waiting months for a renewed permit to be issued or to hear about a family reunification request, and waiting years to hear about citizenship applications. Other sources of anxiety included renewing expired permits, permit renewal paperwork being suspended without notification to the applicant, and the *questura*'s denial of having received submitted applications.

Migrants often attributed the long waiting times to mistakes they must have made in the completion of applications. During my fieldwork, applicants could wait six months or longer for a two-year permit. "Is there something wrong with my application?," clients anxiously asked when checking the status of their permit renewal at the advice center. "It doesn't say anything here. Only that it is *in trattazione*" (they are still working on it), was a common response from advice staff members as they looked at the police webpage on the computer monitor. "You just have to wait." Yet such replies offered little comfort. The *questura* often failed to inform applicants when the reason for delay was that documents were missing, causing applications to be "blocked" for months. In other cases the *questura* did inform applicants about problems with their applications. Letters would be sent to applicants' addresses detailing additional documents that needed to be presented or stating that the application had been rejected. These letters consisted of generic statements in technical and legalistic language that did not specify the reason for the rejection (see also Good 2007: 104). Much of the center's work involved translating these letters to applicants and, sometimes, contesting the *questura*'s decisions.

The months of waiting for permit renewal were long and frustrating, not least because during the renewal phase migrants inhabited a limbo state in which they were neither illegal nor entitled to the rights and freedoms of a valid permit holder. Those renewing their permits lamented their inability to make large purchases, take driving lessons, or sit for university exams, since such activities required the presentation of a valid permit. Worse still, they were limited in their freedom of movement, access to health care, and to employment opportunities. These migrants felt disenfranchised and humiliated, as everyday events such as buying a television or signing a phone contract became impossible. In addition to causing inconvenience, the renewal period was also highly stressful. Applicants who had lost a job or had not earned a high enough salary the previous year risked rejection of their application. Even when applicants held all the correct requirements, their distrust of the *questura* and its seemingly ever-changing rules made many unsure of their status until the priceless new permit was delivered.

Waiting
Pushing a laden baby carriage and a full leather shoulder bag with documents poking out, Sandra struggled into the center on a quiet afternoon with her tiny newborn, Daniel. She had visited the center several times and, having previously acted as her interpreter, I remembered her well. She had been to her fingerprint appointment at the *questura* eight months earlier and for several weeks had made frequent visits to the center to check the status of her permit, always being told to wait "a little longer" as the *questura* was processing permits of those who had provided their fingerprints before her. "Next time we'll take a copy of your *ricevuta* (receipt for renewal) they said (see figure 7). In cases where the waiting time was proving abnormally long, *ricevute* were photocopied and Alberto or Ginetta took them to inquire about at the *questura*. On this particular day, when Sandra was told that she would have to wait a little longer before inquiries about her application would be made, she broke down. "I have moved to a different city [about thirty-eight kilometers away]. I can't keep coming back and forth with the baby. Before

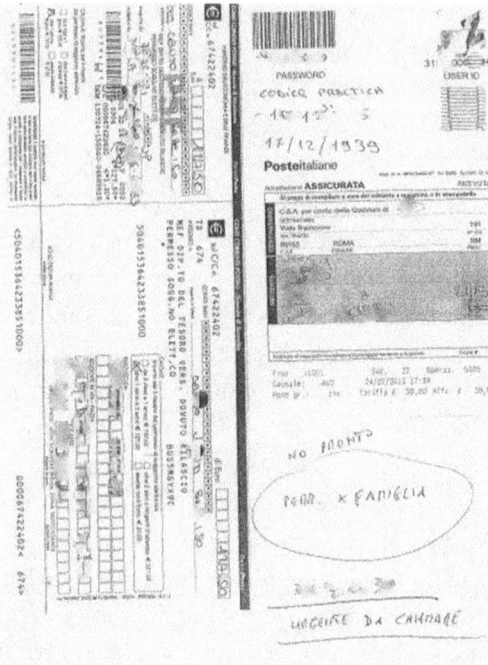

Figure 7. Photograph of a *ricevuta* (receipt given to applicants when they submit their applications). Photograph by author.

my sister was here to help me, but now she has gone back to Ghana."

Seeing how distressed she was, the staff member at the counter photocopied Sandra's *ricevuta* for Ginetta to take to the following Friday's *questura* meeting. Having promised Sandra I would phone her as soon as there was news about her permit, the next week I asked about the *questura*'s response. "Suspended for grave motives," Ginetta read out. "What motives?" I asked her. "I don't know. Truly, I am getting more and more fed up with the *dottoressa*'s [vice director of the *questura*'s] responses!" It was Friday afternoon, Ginetta's afternoon to "receive the public," and the queue of people waiting to see her was growing and becoming increasingly impatient, so she implored me to follow up on the issue with Alberto instead. Seeing me approach, Alberto excused himself from the group of clients sitting around his desk and led me to the side entrance of the center where he could smoke. I explained Sandra's situation to him and the response Ginetta had been given by the vice director. Alberto rolled his eyes with frustration at Ginetta's meek acceptance of the vice director's response and promised me that he would take the *ricevuta* with him to the following week's meeting at the *questura*. I reported back to Sandra, making up an excuse as to why there was still no information about her permit.

The following Friday, Alberto returned with news that Sandra's permit was actually ready. The previous week's misinformation, therefore, had resulted from an error by either Ginetta or the vice director. I phoned Sandra to tell her the good news. Her relief, was short-lived, however, as two days later Sandra returned to the center distraught again. Earlier that morning she had been to the *questura* to collect the permit but had discovered that it would expire in three months (instead of two years).

On collection of issued permits it was common for applicants to discover that their newly issued *permessi di soggiorno* (permits to stay) were either expired or close to expiring. This meant that the costly process of renewal had to be repeated and the semi-legal limbo status that accompanied it resumed. In cases such as these, migrants would turn up at the center fuming. Once the permit had been issued and accepted, however, there was nothing the center could do. "You shouldn't have signed for it," staff members told clients. Their bewildered facial expressions communicated that they had not realized it was optional. Besides, after months and months of waiting for the desired permit, one was hardly likely to reject it. Similar events took place when migrants applied for the long-term permit but were then issued the regular permit with no explanation. Those in such situations were required to reapply and repay the application fees. Once the permit had been accepted and signed for, it was too late.

As I later discovered, the reason for Sandra's desperation lay in her intention to travel with her baby to Ghana, where she planned to leave him with relatives to be cared for while she returned to Italy alone. "It's not possible otherwise," she told me, "I can't work and look after him here." With her permit expiring in three months, however, she would be forced to return to Italy before it expired or risk not being able to return at all. After mulling over Sandra's situation, Alberto told her that she should submit the application for her permit renewal now. Holding the receipt for renewal plus the expired permit, she should be able to return to Italy without problems. Since permits can only be renewed up to two months before expiring, there was a risk that Sandra's application for renewal could be rejected, but the receipt for renewal would nonetheless allow Sandra to return to Italy even if her new permit had already expired. I did not see Sandra again and can only assume that this plan was successfully executed.

Misinformation

In addition to the long waiting times and other effects of a seemingly chaotic bureaucracy, migrants suffered from the perception that the law was constantly changing. Joy, a Nigerian woman, arrived at the center early on a typically chaotic Monday morning. She had come in the previous week to ask for a list of the documents needed to apply for a long-term permit as the mother of an Italian citizen. Applications for permits as the family member of an Italian citizen entailed a specific set of bureaucratic requirements, with applicants obliged to submit paperwork in person at the *questura* rather than via the postal system. Accordingly, Joy had arrived at the *questura* at 5:00 a.m. to obtain an appointment number in order to be seen when it opened at 8:30 a.m. Since officials routinely turned migrants away because of missing paperwork, applicants often had to make repeated visits. On this day, Joy's Monday morning trip was wasted, as the policeman she eventually saw informed her that she was missing documents, and she was sent away with a scrap of paper on which the policeman had handwritten:

—*Certificato di idoneità alloggiativa* (certificate attesting to the size of accommodation and how many people it can accommodate)
—*Contratto di locazione registrato* (registered rental contract)
—*Atto di nascita del figlio* (son's birth certificate)

In fact, according to the usual *questura* practice, Italian immigration law, and the advice center's list, these three documents were *not* required for relatives of Italian citizens. Presuming that the *questura* had not understood that she was the mother of an Italian citizen, a staff member at the center told Joy that she should return to the *questura*, this time with the birth certificate of her son, and explain again that it was on these particular grounds that she was applying for the long-term permit.

Two days later, Joy returned, deeply frustrated and anxious about the situation. She was also concerned that her work contract might be suspended—her permit was due to expire the following week and McDonald's, where she worked, had a strict policy that workers must have a valid permit, or a receipt for permit renewal, at all times (in spite of the fact that the law allows a sixty-day grace period to renew permits after their expiration). On this occasion Alberto came out from the back office and saw Joy in tears. He ushered her to his desk and phoned the *questura* to find out if these documents were really required. The policeman who answered said that in "some particular cases" these documents were indeed required, but did not explain why this was so in

Joy's case. Trying to find a solution that would allow Joy to procure the receipt for renewal as soon as possible—fortunately, Joy did have these documents at home—Alberto completed the usual postal application: the one that applies to migrants who have *no* family connection to an Italian citizen. In doing so, he circumvented further face-to-face contact with the police officer, enabling Joy to obtain a receipt for renewal as soon as she had sent the application from the post office.

These kinds of occurrences led migrants at the center to lament that "the law changes from day to day." In reality, there is little change in immigration law, but the great inconsistencies and myriad *interpretations* of the law by different actors means that individuals experienced it as fickle and shifting. As the next case study illustrates, *questure* frequently interpreted and implemented the law differently. Requirements for long-term permits or family reunification, for example, differed according to locale.

"Changing law"
Diverse implementation of law according to locality led Chiara to joke that migrants should hold residency in cities across Italy and choose which *questura* to use depending on its reputation for strictness regarding particular applications. In fact, when Chiara's partner's mother came to Italy from Morocco, on Chiara's advice he ensured that his mother took residency with his sister in a nearby town (seventy-two kilometers from where he lived), where permit issue was considerably faster.

One reason for the high level of discretion by officials in different *questure* is the nature of Italy's legal system: new laws are imposed that supersede earlier laws, without the revocation of the previous ones. The result is inevitable: confusion prevails and many acts of legislation are simply ignored (Pini 1995: 11). In the implementation of immigration policy, the existence of different and sometimes contradictory laws leads to individual *questura* directors personally deciding which law to follow. Alberto and Chiara explained to me that the implementation of laws by *questure* hinged on the political stance of the *questura* director and the particular pressures to which that director might be subjected. According to Alberto and Chiara, the current director of the local *questura* was "*alla destra*" (right-wing) (see also Triandafyllidou 2003: 276) and was strict in his implementation of policy.

The long-term permit—otherwise known as the *carta*—was a source of much contention and stress during my fieldwork at the center. The long-term permit does not expire and, as Ginetta once said, "is every immigrant's dream."

This statement may be an exaggeration, but holding the long-term permit did mean an end to the continual cycle of permit renewal since one's legal status was no longer contingent upon employment status or annual salary—a comforting and reassuring prospect. The *questura* in my fieldsite was, however, strict regarding the issuing of the long-term permit and frequently changed the application requirements.

During my fieldwork there was much controversy over whether the long-term permit needed to be updated. In 2006 all new permits issued were electronic, the size of credit cards with chips containing the holder's anagraphic data and fingerprint records. On the front of these new electronic permits there was an "expiration date" that was five years from the date of issue; although the permit itself did not expire, after five years the document's anagraphic data needed updating. Crucially, there was no need for the migrant to file a new application or for employment and salary status to be reassessed. In spite of these rules, this type of long-term permit came to be known as the "five year *carta*," while those with the old paper versions would proudly say, "I have the *carta indeterminato*" (permanent permit).[2]

In 2011, when the first batch of the new electronic long-term permits needed to be updated, there was great uncertainty about the exact procedure. The holders of the "five-year electronic *carta*" were very worried that their document might expire, and some staff members and volunteers were wary about reassuring clients, unsure of the *questura*'s future behavior. To complicate matters, in 2010 the format of the electronic long-term permits was changed. On the front they no longer displayed an expiration date but instead read "*illimitato*" (unlimited). Yet on the reverse side, hidden in the barcode, there was the expiration date (indicating when the anagraphic data were to be updated). Consequently, although all the different formats of the long-term permit bestowed the same rights, those who had the "five-year" version felt shortchanged and wanted to complete the application for the new *illimitato* permit. Staff members and volunteers tried to convince clients that the update was a waste of money (nearly 100 euros per application) since both provided the same rights. The anagraphic data on both needed to be updated every five years, but both were *indeterminato*. In general, however, clients were obstinate in their desire for the "*illimitato* one." "It is better to be safe than sorry," they said—100 euros seemed a small price to pay for security.

Migrants thus drew on their own understandings of the legal processes that blurred "official" and "unofficial" versions of law (see also Coutin 2000). The blurring was evident not only in migrants' understanding of the situation but also in *questura* practice and the center's advice. Although staff members informed clients with conviction that the law—*la legge*—says that the "five-year *carta*" did not need to be renewed but merely updated, cases did exist of applicants being newly required by the *questura* to present evidence of salary or employment. Reflecting this uncertainty, for a period of time when completing applications for updates, staff members began to include evidence of applicants' salary and employment (if available)—"just to be on the safe side," they said. Thus both migrants and advisers were drawing on official and unofficial versions of law. As a result, migrants were required to make decisions and take action according to conflicting and contradictory information. In the case of the long-term permit, migrants tended to place their trust in the materiality of the written word *illimitato*. The material document was more than simply a signifier of particular laws and policies. It came to affect legal and social relations itself (Cabot 2014: 69; Hull 2012a).

Another contentious issue regarding the long-term permit was whether spouses of *carta* holders were required to demonstrate they had lived in Italy for at least five years in order to obtain their own. Five years of residency in Italy is a requirement for the long-term permit. But a separate piece of legislation, *Articolo 30*, states that spouses of *carta* holders, by virtue of their marital status, are automatically entitled to hold such a document, notwithstanding the length of time they have spent in the country.[3]

In spite of this piece of legislation, the *questura* in the city where I conducted fieldwork enacted a discretionary policy requiring spouses to have lived in Italy for a minimum of five years to be eligible for the *carta*. Reacting to this, clients came into the center complaining that their friends' spouses living in nearby places had been successfully issued long-term permits after only a year of residency.

Fatos, who was well dressed, spoke fluent Italian, and had lived in Italy for a long time, frequently visited the center to seek advice from Alberto. His wife had arrived in Italy from Kosovo several years earlier, and in the past year they had had their first child. When migrants' children are born on Italian territory they do not obtain Italian citizenship, but rather are born nationals of their parents' country of citizenship. Therefore, as foreign citizens, they must be included in the permit of one or both of their parents. Following his son's birth, Fatos completed the paperwork so that his baby could be added to his wife's long-term permit. This was a simple update rather than a renewal. Months later, however, when they went to collect the newly issued document, Fatos discovered that a permit lasting only two years had been issued to his wife. He stormed furiously into the center and asked Alberto what could be done.

After making inquiries at the *questura*, Alberto discovered that Fatos's wife's long-term permit had been revoked because the *questura* deemed that it had been erroneously issued. At the time of her original application, the local *questura* allowed spouses of long-term permit-holders to apply for the *carta* regardless of how long they had been resident in the country (as the law dictates). Because the *questura*'s interpretation of the law had since changed, the official who handled her new application considered that the permit had been unlawfully issued the first time because at the time of the original application she had been in Italy for only two years. When I left my fieldsite, months after the revocation, the issue was still unresolved.

This divergence between the law and how it was interpreted and practiced by different *questure* and their officials was a central feature of the instability and insecurity of the documentation regime. On Thursday mornings at the staff and volunteer training sessions Alberto would emphasize the importance of appreciating the gap between what the law *says* and what the *questura does*. He told us to exercise caution in disseminating information since there was often not a straightforward answer to people's queries. Clients should be informed of their options yet not be told things that might not be possible to achieve. Complex cases, Alberto told us, should be referred to him.

As I discuss later, this instruction was problematic, as almost all cases were complex and Alberto had a heavy workload. The situation of spouses' rights to the long-term permit was a case in point. What applicants were told depended on staff members' assessment of each individual's capacity to understand. If individuals were persistent and seemed astute, and if the counter was not overrun by clients, they would be told that they could *try* applying for the long-term permit. At the same time, they were told to prepare for the application to be rejected and that overturning any decision would require the services of a lawyer and be a lengthy and expensive process. Staff members thus tended to inform clients that five years of residency was a strict requisite in applications for the *carta*, despite the fact that this was a misinterpretation of the "official" law by the local *questura*.

In her work with Salvadorans in the United States, Coutin (2000: 11) has described how migrants devise their own understandings of "what legal status consists of and how to get it." She notes that although these understandings may be "factually incorrect," they "provide an account of law as seen from the realm of 'illegality' in which the undocumented are located." Building on this point, the case studies here highlight not only migrants' understandings of legal processes, but also the way in which these understandings were interlinked with other understandings and practices of legal processes that may not be factually correct.

What emerged was a matrix of circulating (mis)information and practices that were passed between and among migrants themselves, as well as between officials, advisers, and others involved in the immigration nexus. In some moments the law appeared stiff and impenetrable, in others flexible and fluid, and sometimes both simultaneously. It was not, however, only the circulation of misinformation that gave the impression of the law as malleable. Not only were specific laws interpreted and practiced differently according to locality, but in some instances the details of particular acts of legislation were undecided.

Undecided laws

In September 2009 the Italian government opened an amnesty for migrant domestic workers without permits. This amnesty gave undocumented domestic workers who had been working in Italy before April 2009 the opportunity to be regularized in relationship to their employer. In reality, however, the law gave the opportunity to be legalized to anybody who was able to find, and usually pay, an "employer." In the months after the amnesty, young Moroccan, Pakistani, and Tunisian men (groups who were unlikely to be hired for domestic work) frequently came into the advice center.[4] Having secured fake employers, they were now checking the status of their applications. If the application was successful, after the issuing of the first permit, applicants could then change their reported job. As the following case study shows, amnesty applications revealed the lack of centralized information about laws, the way in which rules for applications were made and changed during the process, and the extent to which locality determined the law's practice.

Khan, a thirty-year old from Bangladesh, made his living selling plastic trinkets and roses on the street in the city's main shopping areas. He had lived in Italy for ten years, previously holding a valid permit and working in a factory. However, after losing his job and being unable to renew his permit he fell into "illegality." Since the expiration of his permit, Khan had been stopped and fingerprinted by the police twice, both times being issued with an expulsion order (*foglio di via*) requiring him to leave the country within forty-eight hours. Those issued with expulsion orders are expected to leave the country independently. Like most others in this position, Khan nonetheless remained in Italy, and when the amnesty for domestic workers was publicized he jumped at the chance for legalization. As he told me, life without a permit in Italy was not impossible, but it was hard. He described it as akin to living in a "big prison" because he was trapped within the country's borders. Because Khan was not a domestic worker, in order to submit an application for the amnesty, he paid an acquaintance to act as his domestic work "employer."

At the time of the amnesty application period the Ministero del Interno (Interior Ministry) had not specified whether those who had previously received an expulsion order were eligible to apply. Accordingly, migration advice centers across the city encouraged people to apply and "see what would happen," as one staff member described it to me. However, as their applications became increasingly delayed, rumors circulated that those who had been previously stopped and fingerprinted by the police, like Khan, would be refused a permit. Six months after the submission of their applications, Khan and several others came into the center holding copies of the newspaper *La Repubblica*. The paper contained an article questioning whether holding a previous expulsion would lead to negative outcomes for amnesty applicants. It said the responses would depend on the individual *questura*.

> inflexibility in some provinces and elasticity in others . . . Rigidity in Trieste, Rimini, Perugia. Clemency in Milan, Venice, Bologna, and other provinces. Consequently, uncertainty everywhere. [*inflessibile in alcune province, a maglie larghe altrove . . . Durezza a Trieste, Rimini, Perugia. Clemenza a Milano, Venezia, Bologna e in altre province. Incertezza ovunque, di conseguenza..*] (Rumiz 2010, my translation).

"So what about here, then?" Khan asked me. Unsure how to respond, I took the newspaper into the back office to show to Alberto. He quickly read the article and replied that, in the case of this city, those who had received only one expulsion should not experience any problems. As I re-entered the waiting area Ginetta ran after me. She grabbed my arm and pressed her hand to my ear, whispering: "Be careful what you tell them. None of us are sure how this is going to turn out!"

The newspaper article pointed out that local areas interpreted the amnesty's rules (or lack of) in different ways, resulting in serious consequences for applicants. The issue related to the contradiction between the fact that being "illegal" in Italy is a criminal offense, yet the amnesty was exclusively for "illegal" migrants who had been living in Italy for at least five months.[5] This policy, which layers illegality on top of illegality, resulted in a large number of illegal migrants remaining on Italian territory with expulsion orders in hand. Since, in this case, the punishment and reward were the same—leaving the country—there was no advantage to be gained by following the deportation order unless forced to. At the local *questura*, applications by those who held several expulsion orders were put on hold until the Ministero del Interno confirmed whether or not holding an expulsion would disallow an amnesty applicant. But other *questure* behaved differently. In March 2010 a Senegalese citizen was summoned to the *questura* of Trieste for an appointment about his amnesty application. On arrival, the man was arrested and put on a plane to Senegal. His crime was that he had been previously expelled for his illegal status but had never left the country.[6] Unlike the Senegalese man, Khan's amnesty application was eventually accepted despite his two expulsions, proving, as the newspaper article reported, that the law was being inconsistently applied.

Thus it is clear that migrants' encounters with contradictory and inconsistent information were due not only to the ignorance, incompetence, or favoritism of officials or staff at advice centers, but also to the lack of specificity in the law. The resulting confusion, among both migrants and advice center staff, made advice centers very difficult to run and manage.

The uncertain terrain of immigration bureaucracy

As the above cases have shown, experiences with the Italian immigration bureaucracy were characterized by long waiting times, misinformation, and ambiguous laws. Encounters with the documentation regime were not isolated moments of uncertainty, but rather formed ongoing *conditions* of crisis in migrants' lives. The intensity of these conditions varied according to individual circumstances. Whether issues relating to the immigration bureaucracy were dominant anxieties or only minor niggling worries, encounters with the regime cast an enduring shadow over migrants' lives. Yet, while the uncertain nature of the documentation regime caused daily anxiety and frustration, it also created opportunities to manipulate it, engendering a social navigation based on resilience, persistence, and creative manipulation of rules.[7]

Despite their continual complaints about the bureaucracy's unfairness and incompetence, migrants learned not to dwell on its lack of rationale, logic, or consistency. Instead they learned to accept, if disdainfully, the immigration law's uncertainty and to take advantage of its contradictions. While the uncertainty produced by immigration regimes, therefore, undoubtedly creates deep anxiety and stress in the lives of migrants (Bloch, Sigona, and Zetter 2011; Cabot 2014; Calavita 2005b; De Genova 2002; Dreby 2015; Gonzales and Chavez 2012; Willen 2007), in the Italian setting the documentation regime's ambiguous nature also enabled its manipulation. Migrants' tactics to ensure that their paperwork was accepted involved working around and managing the misinformation, ambiguities, delays, and contradictions that characterized the bureaucracy.

Writing about the actions of agents in uncertain and opaque terrains, Henrik Vigh (2006, 2009) notes the usefulness of the concept of social navigation, which is not a metaphor for agency "but rather designates the interface between agency and social forces" (2006: 14) and highlights "the *interactivity* of practice" (2009: 420, my emphasis). Migrants employed social navigation in their interactions with the uncertainties of Italian immigration law. In navigating the bureaucracy they positioned themselves as actors interacting *with* immigration law, rather than exclusively acted on *by* immigration law (see also Collyer 2012).

As the following case studies illustrate, therefore, by accepting the fact of the system's unpredictability and chaos, migrants used strategies of navigation to turn the system's uncertainty to their advantage. Yet, while the "law cannot be characterized as exclusively hegemonic" (Coutin 2000: 12), migrants' strategies of navigation were not acts of resistance or subversion. Their navigation of the documentation regime worked to the advantage of, and was sometimes encouraged by, immigration policy makers and officials. As will be discussed further in Chapter 3, the bending of laws and manipulation of loopholes were considered to be the dominant mode of practice in the Italian setting. Actors who did not want to engage in such practices risked social disapproval, as well as rejected applications.

Working the gap: migrants' navigation of paperwork

Migrants' strategies of navigation were necessitated by the ways in which their paperwork did not always reflect real-life circumstances. Although the *questura* was strict about the presentation of the correct documentation for permit issue, these documents often presented a very different "life" from the real one. The center played a key role in helping migrants take advantage of the law's flexibility. Sometimes staff members helped migrants shape their stories and fill in the forms so that they would be accepted, while in other cases migrants presented an already embellished story that staff members tried to unravel and reconstruct. Staff also made phone calls to officials and wrote cover letters to accompany applications when an applicant's situation could not be sufficiently conveyed via the standard application form; and sometimes staff were able to challenge "unlawful" decision-making by the *questura* (see also James and Killick 2012: 13). The center thus acted as a broker between the migrant and the *questura,* giving applicants the opportunity to find their way around an otherwise impenetrable bureaucratic maze.

The most successful and popular advocate for migrants at the center was Alberto. Much of staff members' work was mundane form-filling, but Alberto transformed the role, acting as mediator, broker, legal adviser, counselor, and contact with the *questura.* He thrived in his role at the center and was adored by clients. Long-term clients remembered Alberto's invaluable assistance and sought him out when another bureaucratic issue arose. Many felt they had a personal relationship with him after he had helped them secure a permit for a spouse, child, or parent. In addition, his warm and witty demeanor lightened the mood at the center and made clients feel respected—a rare experience for migrants in their encounters with bureaucratic offices.

During our regular after-work *aperitivo,* Alberto plied me with stories of his successes in helping particular individuals "get around" the system. Between rushed puffs on cigarettes, he recounted episodes from his ongoing cases. He had managed to convince a trade union colleague to "employ" a young Chinese woman, Valentina, in the upcoming *decreto flussi;*[8] Sho Wa had been issued the long-term permit even though her salary was too low; and he had managed to get Tatyana's baby a temporary permit so that the family could visit their grand-mother who was dying in Moldova. In difficult cases where all possible avenues were considered and then creatively manipulated, Alberto became excited. He frequently stayed late at the center searching through material to find possible ways to solve problems that the center's lawyers had said were insoluble.

Alberto's reputation was not only related to his "*possibilista*" nature (as Chiara called it), but also because he was constantly checking the facts and searching for new ministerial circulars (*circolari*) or legislation that could be used to the advantage of one of his clients. He was usually better informed than the lawyers or police officers themselves. This was made strikingly clear when, on occasion, officials at the *questura* would send clients in difficult situations to find "Alberto at the center." In other words, *questura* officials referred migrants to the center in order to obtain advice on how to exploit a loophole or ma-nipulate an application form. Alberto's ability to help migrants navigate im-migration law reflected his mastery of the "multiplicity of law" (Coutin 2000: 79). Well versed in immigration legislation and circulars, he was often able to provide individuals in difficult situations with several options as to how the law could be made to work best for them.

His advice to a Chinese couple with two young children is one example. On a busy Wednesday afternoon, two separate sets of Chinese clients were waiting to be seen by Alberto—a mother and her Italian-born eleven-year-old son and a young couple. The mother and son had arrived at the center earlier for an appointment to complete applications for their permit renewals. Given the son's fluent Italian, Alberto had asked them to stay behind so the boy could act as an interpreter while he consulted the young couple who spoke no Italian. Through the boy, Alberto learned that the couple were there to inquire about how the wife could become legalized. The husband worked in a Chinese-run factory and held a valid work permit, but the wife was technically illegal. Attempting to ascertain the wife's situation and document history, Alberto first asked whether the couple had any children, to which they answered that they had two, both born in Italy. "Damn!" Alberto exclaimed in response. Both children being born in Italy meant that the couple had already lost two chances for the wife to obtain a permit. Under Italian immigration law a pregnant woman can claim a temporary permit for *cure mediche* (medical reasons), which is valid until the baby reaches six months of age. On the expiration of this temporary permit, providing the husband has legal status, employment, certified income, and suitable housing, the woman can apply for a family permit through a process called family cohesion (*coesione familiare*). Further inquiries revealed that during one of her pregnancies the wife had in fact held a temporary medical permit, but the couple had been unaware of the family cohesion option and, when it expired, the permit had not been converted. Since the children were older than six months at the time of the meeting with Alberto, converting the permit was no longer an option.

Exhibiting his familiarity with the law's multiple layers, Alberto explained that the couple had four options. One, the wife could become pregnant again, which would give them another opportunity to transform a temporary medical permit into a permanent one. This option would be slightly problematic as, according to the official requirements, the husband's salary was too low to support a wife and three children. Unsurprisingly, given the age of the interpreter, the retelling of this option caused an embarrassed giggle from him and the couple. Second, the couple could complete the usual family reunification procedure. This, however, would involve the wife returning to China once a valid visa had been issued because, in the usual procedure for family reunification, the family members to be reunited reside in the country of origin. Third, they could submit an application for the wife to be employed in the upcoming *decreto flussi*. This option would also involve a return to China for a visa, and was not guaranteed. Fourth, with legal representation, the couple could make a case that the wife's presence on Italian territory was necessary for the well-being of her children. In a recent case, a father had won the right to a permit on such grounds. The success of this case created some optimism for those in similar situations, but only a limited amount, as in the Italian legal system previous court rulings do not bind judges' decisions as they do in jurisdictions founded on common law (Audisio and Colombo 1995: 74; Silvestri 2009: 139). This last option was preferable to the others because it offered the least disturbance to the couple's lives, but it would be expensive (paying for legal costs) and did not guarantee success. In addition, this fourth option was risky. Through the process, the wife's illegal status would become known to the authorities. If the case were to be rejected she would receive a deportation order.

As well as demonstrating the invasive impact that immigration law has on people's private lives and personal decisions, this case draws attention to Alberto's ability to provide the couple with several options for solving their problem. His suggestions included using the law "legitimately" (family reunification); manipulating the law's loopholes (having a third child or applying in the *decreto flussi*); and contributing to the reshaping/challenging of law (arguing that the children's welfare depended on the mother's presence in Italy). As a successful broker and adviser, Alberto was aware of "the multiplicity of law" (Coutin 2000: 79), both official and unofficial.

However, not all clients had the good fortune to be seen by Alberto. Clients' access to him depended on timing, contacts, and whether they managed to establish a relationship with him. Alberto did not intentionally privilege certain individuals over others, but the hectic environment of the center meant that a certain process of selection occurred. The center received a large number of clients every day, and each client's situation was unique and needed individual attention. It was a question of luck and/or favoritism as to whether a client received his attention.

Thus, the center acted as a broker and advocate on behalf of migrants, but, like much else in the documentation regime, its service was inconsistent. Migrants' strategies of navigating the regime were often enabled by center staff members. Eliciting help from an effective and dedicated staff member was, sometimes, part of the strategy itself.

Decreti flussi and amnesties

Manipulation of the law's loopholes was particularly evident when migrants obtained their first permit. As the case of Khan showed, many nondomestic workers took advantage of the 2009 domestic worker amnesty to be legalized. The previous amnesty had taken place in 2002 and was used in a similar way as the 2009 amnesty.

Another way in which migrants were able to gain legal status in Italy was through a *decreto flussi*. Distinct from an amnesty, and in part serving in the absence of amnesties, the *decreto flussi* is a policy that allows employers in Italy to bring over foreign nationals who live abroad. These opportunities are offered every two to four years, and one was offered during my fieldwork period. *Decreti flussi* are accords that the Italian state has with "sending" countries in which a designated number of citizens can gain permits through work contracts with employers based in Italy (see figure 8). For example, the 2011 *decreto flussi* allowed for the legal entry of one thousand citizens from Pakistan and four thousand citizens from Tunisia. Both Tunisia and Pakistan, among many other countries, hold accords with the Italian state, but other countries, such as Eritrea and China, do not. Given this, the 2011 *decreto flussi* also allowed for the entry of thirty thousand citizens from nation-states that do not have such accords. Those in this category are, in theory, restricted to employment in the domestic work sector. While the *decreto flussi* is officially intended to enable legal entry to those not yet in Italy, in practice it has a different purpose. The following extract from *La Repubblica* describes how the law often functioned:

> In reality, as all immigrants know well, for years the *decreto flussi* has been the only chance for migrants to escape illegality and access a permit (owing to a lack of amnesties). The procedure however is not simple or without risks. First a migrant submits the application. If the application is successful, the migrant returns to his/her home country. Subsequently he or she then leaves the home country with a valid visa and finally re-enters Italy. Thus, he or she exits in a clandestine manner and re-enters in a regular one. (Polchi 2008, my translation)

As the extract says, the *decreto flussi* was typically used by "illegal" migrants who were *already* on Italian territory. As one staff member commented, "Who would hire somebody they did not know from abroad?" Rather, in both the *decreto flussi* and amnesty, "employers" were often friends, family, or acquaintances who charged high rates to "employ" a migrant. If the application was successful, the migrant returned home and then re-entered Italy (this time legally) with a visa. Media coverage of the *decreto flussi* often referred to it as a *beffa* (hoax), acknowledging the law's informal function as a second amnesty for migrants on Italian territory without permits. Given the contingency of permits on work and salary, it was easy for migrants in Italy to fall into illegality, meaning that opportunities to be reregularized were in high demand.

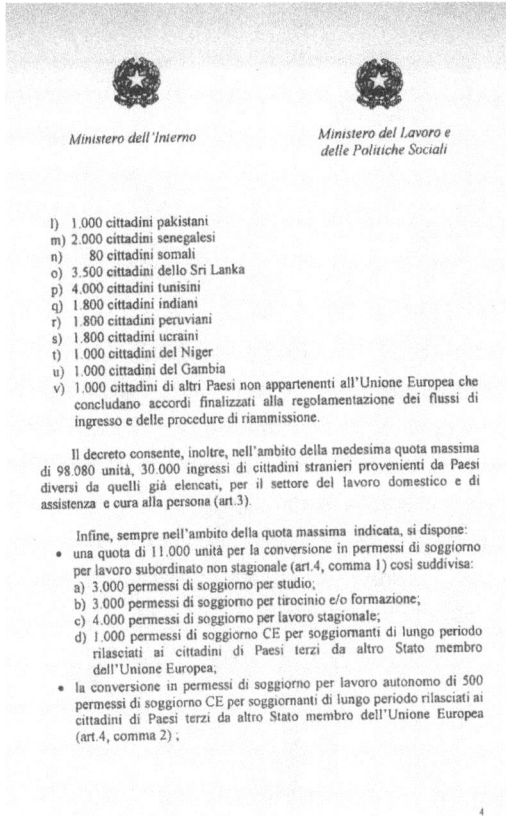

Figure 8. Second page from the Ministero del'Interno document that outlines the quotas for the 2011 *decreto flussi*.

Rumors of *decreti flussi* and amnesties opening were rife throughout my fieldwork period. In January 2011 a *decreto flussi* did finally open, but its practical use was somewhat different than in previous years. One Saturday morning, Marlena, a young woman from the Dominican Republic, was sitting at Alberto's desk. The two were discussing possible ways in which Marlena's sister might be able to enter Italy. Marlena had Italian citizenship, so once on Italian territory her sister would be entitled to a permit on the grounds of family reunification. The problem, however, was whether her sister would be permitted to enter at all. Aware that siblings of Italian citizens have the right to permits once on Italian territory, Italian embassies are reluctant to issue tourist visas to those in that category. One solution, Alberto suggested, was for Marlena's sister to apply for a Spanish tourist visa and then, taking advantage of the Schengen Agreement, travel from Spain to Italy. Looking pensive and tapping the unlit cigarette in his hand, Alberto added that Marlena should consider the possibility that the long rumored *decreto flussi* might open in the near future. He explained that if this happened Marlena could submit an application to "employ" her sister as a domestic worker. If the application was successful, Marlena's sister would be issued with a visa and once in Italy could apply for a family permit as the sister of an Italian citizen. Marlena looked unsure and said she would think about it. Her skepticism was justified. The *decreto flussi* works in a semi-arbitrary manner in which those submitting online applications sooner than others stand a greater chance of acceptance. Furthermore, if the previous *decreto flussi* in 2007 was any indication, responses to applications could take up to three years.

As this example suggests, migrants used the 2011 *decreto flussi* differently than in previous years. Rather than being used as a kind of general amnesty, in 2011 it was a means of reunifying families. By December 2010 the rumors that a *decreto flussi* would open were spreading like wildfire. Comments made by the Ministero del Interno hinted at its likelihood, and at the center's reception counter we began to tell people that a *decreto flussi* was likely, although we did not know when, or what the conditions would be.

On December 31, 2010, the decree was passed, inviting applications beginning on January 31, 2011. In the new year the center was particularly busy. The counter was inundated with people who dropped in looking for information about the procedure. Staff members and volunteers explained the procedure countless times. In mid-January the application form was made available, and the center offered the service of filling in the application forms in advance of their online submission.

During this period, staff members and volunteers worked without stopping for hours on end, day after day, completing application forms and disseminating information. When I remarked on the busy and hectic environment, however, the more experienced staff members and volunteers told me that this was "nothing" compared to previous years. One particular volunteer recounted that, "in 2007 they were queuing all the way down the street before opening. Some arrived at 5 a.m. in order to be the first!" Staff members believed the recent 2009 amnesty was responsible for smaller crowds in 2011. As they explained, "Many of those without permits who could be legalized [that is, had kinship or financial capital] have already applied in that amnesty." The previous 2007 *decreto flussi* had been massively oversubscribed, but because the 2011 procedure was taking place fewer than two years after the 2009 amnesty, there were far fewer applicants.[9]

In sum, the 2011 *decreto flussi* was used primarily as a means of family reunification for relatives who were otherwise not permitted to migrate to Italy. While I was completing application forms for clients in the center, the conversation would inevitably turn to which relative they were bringing over. People told me how they hoped to help a sibling, nephew, niece, or cousin. In the hundred or so applications that I completed, I did not come across a single genuine employer/employee relationship. Both the *decreto flussi* and amnesty offered opportunities for migrants to become legalized or relegalized, or to bring over a relative. But the official terms and conditions were perceived as flexible by both staff and migrants. The fact that the 2009 amnesty was intended exclusively for domestic workers was not conceived as restrictive. If one paid the right fees and completed the correct paperwork, it was immaterial whether the domestic work contract actually existed. Similarly, it was not an issue that the *decreto flussi* was designed for people living outside Italy; an applicant could simply exit the country and then return.

As the article from *La Repubblica* suggests, the existence of these tactics was no secret. Although form-filling was manipulated, people's practical circumstances were not reshaped (cf. James and Killick 2012: 441). Migrants felt no need to hide the details of their situation, and state officials—provided the paperwork was in order—were not interested in their circumstances. In the aftermath of the 2009 domestic work amnesty, Mirkena, who had previously volunteered at the center, was employed on a temporary basis at the *prefettura*, which handles some immigration paperwork. Amnesty applicants (both "employers" and "employees") were required to present themselves at the *prefettura* to check that their declaration of income, housing situation, and documents were all in order before passing the paperwork on to the *questura*, which would eventually issue the permit.

Shadowing Mirkena one morning at the *prefettura* while she made her way through the day's appointments, I saw that the applicants were not afraid they might be found out or turned away if their "work" relationship were discovered to be false. Domestic work "employers" and "employees" included spouses, siblings, and, contrary to the stereotype of eastern Europeans doing domestic labor, an older eastern European woman "employing" a twenty-year old Tunisian man as her "cleaner." What counted was that the paperwork was in order; applicants were only turned away if they had brought the wrong declaration of income, housing document, or residence certificate.

Contacts count

The loopholes offered by domestic work contracts were also utilized by those renewing their permits. For the renewal of a work permit, the *contratto di soggiorno* (a work contract for non-EU migrants) is an essential piece of paperwork. Yet it is common for people to hold a *contratto di soggiorno* with one employer while in reality being employed informally by a different employer.

Yasmina, a twenty-three-year-old Moroccan woman, although technically unemployed, was not seeking work. She lived with her relatively affluent family and had no need or desire to enter the workforce. However, being twenty-three years old and unmarried, she was not permitted to renew her permit for family motives.[10] Accordingly, if she did not renew for "work motives" she would risk losing her legal status. Yasmina had come into the office with her brother, Karim, to ask about the practicalities of his hiring her as the family's domestic worker. Given that domestic work contracts are informal and subject to few controls, migrants were easily able to acquire and hold inauthentic domestic work contracts in order to renew permits. The lack of controls and the ease of finding a fake employer who, either through kinship or in return for payment, will sign a *contratto di soggiorno*, gave migrants considerable flexibility. Consequently, the domestic work contract was a useful resource for migrants: those who did not want or could not find work with a legal contract were nonetheless able to renew their permits.

As the case of Yasmina demonstrates, migrants' diverse navigation of the documentation regime's loopholes was, of course, contingent on access to money and social networks. For those who did not have contacts or family networks to help them, components of applications such as work contracts and hospitality declarations could be purchased. For example, it was common for recent migrants to live in temporary accommodation for which they had no contract or proof of residence. This proved a problem when submitting an application, but it also provided others with an opportunity for a small informal trade.

Taking advantage of this potential market, Chiara told me that Aidan, the owner of an Eritrean bar, sold hospitality declarations for 10 euros each. Those who paid for the declarations did not actually live in Aidan's house, although the certificate attested that they did. Having the certificate enabled the purported guests to submit applications with the requisite documents in place. Similarly, I heard rumors of other bar owners who sold migrants *contratti di soggiorno*. The migrants would appear to work for the bar, while in reality they were either unemployed or employed informally elsewhere. As Chapter 4 will

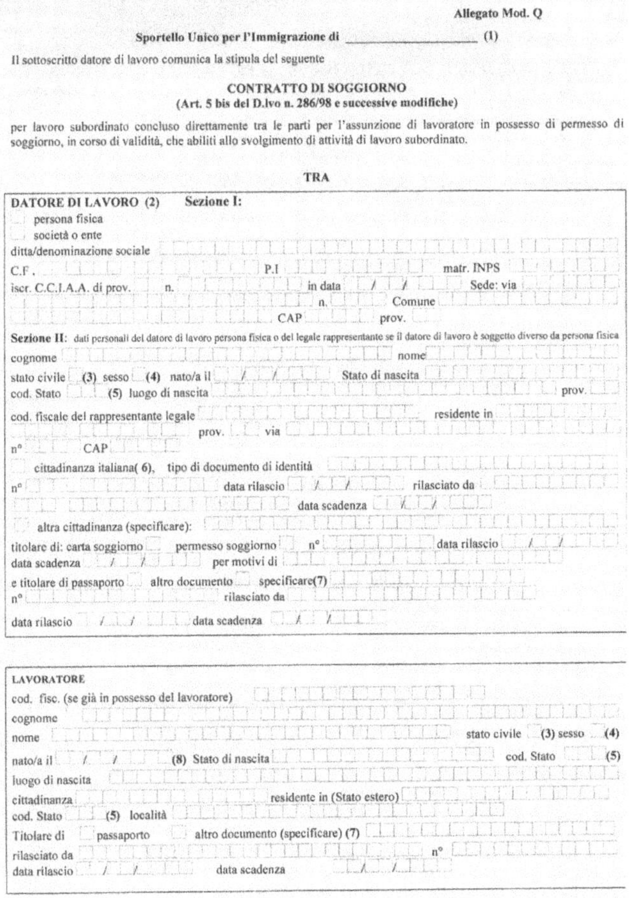

Allegato Mod. Q

Sportello Unico per l'Immigrazione di _____ (1)

Il sottoscritto datore di lavoro comunica la stipula del seguente

CONTRATTO DI SOGGIORNO
(Art. 5 bis del D.lvo n. 286/98 e successive modifiche)

per lavoro subordinato concluso direttamente tra le parti per l'assunzione di lavoratore in possesso di permesso di soggiorno, in corso di validità, che abiliti allo svolgimento di attività di lavoro subordinato.

TRA

DATORE DI LAVORO (2)   Sezione I:
persona fisica
società o ente
ditta/denominazione sociale
C.F.   P.I   matr. INPS
iscr. C.C.I.A.A. di prov.   n.   in data / /   Sede: via
n.   Comune
CAP   prov.

Sezione II: dati personali del datore di lavoro persona fisica o del legale rappresentante se il datore di lavoro è soggetto diverso da persona fisica
cognome   nome
stato civile (3) sesso (4) nato/a il / /   Stato di nascita
cod. Stato   (5) luogo di nascita   prov.
cod. fiscale del rappresentante legale   residente in
prov.   via
n°   CAP
cittadinanza italiana(6), tipo di documento di identità
n°   data rilascio / /   rilasciato da
data scadenza / /
altra cittadinanza (specificare):
titolare di: carta soggiorno   permesso soggiorno n°   data rilascio / /
data scadenza / /   per motivi di
e titolare di passaporto   altro documento   specificare(7)
n°   rilasciato da
data rilascio / /   data scadenza / /

LAVORATORE
cod. fisc. (se già in possesso del lavoratore)
cognome
nome   stato civile (3) sesso (4)
nato/a il / /   (8) Stato di nascita   cod. Stato (5)
luogo di nascita
cittadinanza   residente in (Stato estero)
cod. Stato (5) località
Titolare di   passaporto   altro documento (specificare) (7)
rilasciato da   n°
data rilascio / /   data scadenza / /

Figure 9. A *contratto di soggiorno* (a work contract for non-EU nationals)

illustrate, there existed a host of organizations and individuals that, for a price, offered to provide applicants with the requisites for applications or the necessary contacts to obtain those requisites.

Perhaps even more valuable than money were contacts. Samir approached the counter one morning to ask for advice on renewing his permit, which had already expired. He was fashionably dressed in a designer puffer jacket, jeans, and high-top sneakers: his sense of style and fluent Italian demonstrated that he had grown up in Italy. He took his permit out of his wallet, showing me that it had expired several months ago. It was an unemployment permit, a type of permit issued only once that lasts for just six months.

Regardless of how long a person has been living and working legally in the country, if at the time of renewal they do not have a job, they lose the possibility for renewal, effectively becoming *clandestino* (undocumented). Furthermore, permits can be renewed only within two months of their expiration date, and Samir's had expired five months previously. The reason he had not renewed his permit, he said, was because he had been unable to find a job. Despite being technically illegal and holding an expired permit that was apparently unrenewable, Samir appeared remarkably calm. Looking doubtful, my colleague at the counter advised him to make an appointment with the advice center's lawyer to see if there was any possibility of "saving" his permit. The next day, Samir popped into the center to tell me that he had resolved his problem. He had a friend who worked at the *questura* who would help him renew his permit. The permit would be for unemployment and would last two years, despite the fact that the law dictates that unemployment permits are nonrenewable without a work contract and have a maximum duration of six months. Samir was told to fill out the usual application form and deposit it at the *questura*.[11]

These cases show that access to particular resources was indispensable in order to take advantage of the flexibility in the system and effectively exploit its loopholes. To buy a *contratto di soggiorno* one needed money; Yasmina relied on her family network to help her; and, without contacts at the *questura*, Samir would have fallen into illegality. Money and contacts were thus essential resources for exploiting the system's flexibility and openness to manipulation.

Conclusion

Despite the heterogeneity of migrants in Italy, experiences of managing the uncertain and time-consuming immigration bureaucracy are shared by all. The opacity and ambiguity that characterize encounters with the regime create daily anxiety, frustration, and anger, yet the bureaucracy's uncertainty also holds advantages. While the *questura* was strict with regard to paperwork and migrants' demonstration of correct requisites, the real circumstances of applicants' lives were not scrutinized. This "gap" between paper and practice enabled migrants to take advantage of the law's loopholes in order to become and stay legal and be reunited with family members. These strategies, however, also had clear limitations. Because they were often unofficial or technically illegal, if the strategies failed, migrants had no recourse. For example, although nondomestic workers conveniently made the domestic worker amnesty serve them, engaging in authentic but false domestic work contracts not only incurred considerable financial cost but also made these applicants vulnerable to being scammed with no possibility for compensation. And these strategies often provided only short-term solutions. Samir, for example, was able to find a temporary solution to his legal status, but this security would only last for two years, despite the fact that he had grown up in Italy.

These paradoxes and contradictions go to the heart of Italian immigration law. On one hand, the law offers migrants more flexibility than would perhaps be available in other settings; on the other, it is premised on an exclusionary vision that institutionalizes migrants' marginality and precarity.

Chapter 3 further explores migrants' agency and resourcefulness in manipulating and navigating immigration law. These strategies have limits, however, and remind us of the serious constraints that migrants faced. Further, because migrants' tactical navigation enabled them to "get by," the institutionalization of illegality, precarity, and exclusion within the immigration law remained unchallenged.

3 The Rules of Rule-Bending

Extract from fieldnotes, January 2010

Eva, my Albanian flatmate, has just returned from visiting her boyfriend in Paris. Her plan to travel with only her identity card worked. The officials did not notice the word "Albanian" printed on her document as she confidently approached the boarding gate and passed through without a valid permit. It is two weeks since she sent off her permit renewal application at the post office. Yesterday I accompanied her to the *questura*, where she had an appointment to provide her fingerprints. Eva is uncharacteristically quiet at the *questura* and while waiting tells me how anxious she becomes in these moments. I comment to her that she was not nervous, however, to travel to Paris with an invalid document, and she replies, "No but the worst that could happen is I have to get another flight. When I'm here [at the *questura*], my situation as just a poor foreigner is made real to me. If I don't finish all my exams this year, I could lose my permit."

The *questura* is quiet today, and Eva is called relatively quickly from the central waiting area into a second room where we join a small line of people also there to be fingerprinted. This second room is lined with several glass counters, most occupied by police officers processing migrants' applications. Pointing to a police officer behind one of the counters, she tells me that she hopes she is not seen by him. "He is a complete *stronzo*" (bastard), she says. "He always finds some problem or other with your paperwork and makes you come back." Fortunately, we manage to avoid this officer and are soon leaving. Eva's paperwork will now be sent to the central offices in Rome where, providing there are no problems with her application, the new permit will be printed before being sent back to the local *questura* to be issued. The official she sees tells her that

Figure 10. Photograph of the entrance to a *questura*. Photograph by author.

the new permit will be ready in two to three months. I know from my work at the center, however, that most applicants wait six months to a year for their permits to be issued.

Today Eva has realized that she has lost her identity card and has been to the *carabinieri* (section of the police department) to report it. At home she tells me and our other flatmate that the *carabiniero* she saw asked her for her phone number, which she gave him. "Maybe I can ask him to help me speed up the permit renewal," she says cheekily. I can't tell if Eva is joking or not, but I find out soon enough that she is serious. Her permit is ready for collection by the end of the following week.

This chapter explores the way in which migrants' strategies of navigation fit into broader rule-bending practices that are prevalent in Italy. In recent years, anthropologists have observed that bureaucracy and documents are central to forms of statecraft and the reproduction of the state (Gordillo 2006; Gupta and Sharma 2006; Hull 2012b; Scott 1998). In particular, it is through bureaucratic practices that the "state comes to be imagined, encountered and re-imagined by the population" (Gupta and Sharma 2006: 12).

In what follows I examine the dominant discursive construction of the Italian state and bureaucracy as inefficient and corrupt, and the accompanying expectation that its rules should be bent. It is through their encounters with the Italian bureaucracy that migrants come to participate in the production and reproduction of this collectively shared imagined state and become "cultural citizens" (Ong 1996). In the Italian bureaucratic context, however, prevalent rule-breaking is accompanied by strict compliance with proceduralism in relation to paperwork. Paper trails must be authentic even if false (Hull 2008), and successfully navigating the immigration bureaucracy requires expertise in the management of documents. Given the documented nature of migrants' lives, however, rule-bending in one application could create problems in others; even skillful rule-bending can be highly risky for migrants. Paradoxically, therefore, developing cultural citizenship can also result in migrants' risking the attainment of actual juridical citizenship or other forms of secure legal status.

"Every law has a loophole": rule-bending and cultural citizenship

Successfully navigating the immigration bureaucracy in Italy involves manipulating loopholes, making the best of the law's flexibility, and seamlessly managing the gap between paper and practice. Staff members and long-term migrants referred to accessing contacts, paying for paperwork in the informal economy, or learning to accept and make the most of the changing and flexible laws, as "*il sistema paese*" (the system of the country). The term referred to the way in which Italian bureaucratic and legal systems are both manipulated and open to manipulation. "In Italy things work like this!" (*In Italia le cose funzionano cosi!*) my respondents would tell me exasperatedly when I repeatedly asked how a Bangladeshi street-seller was able to be legalized in the 2009 domestic worker amnesty, or how undocumented migrants already on Italian territory were able to make use of the *decreto flussi* contrary to its official purpose. The process of completing bureaucratic applications was far from straightforward, and learning to maneuver to one's best advantage was a sign of an integrated and long-term migrant.

The notion that crafty navigation of laws is somehow a quintessentially Italian modus operandi corresponds to stereotypical representations of the country that have long been rehearsed in scholarly work, as well as in film and fiction (Foot 2003: 5–6; Sabetti 2000). Historians trace contemporary attitudes toward, and experiences of, Italian bureaucracy to the early stages of nation-state formation, when unification was, says Paul Ginsborg (1990: 145), "consciously sacrificed to an all-powerful central bureaucracy." The will to produce a single nation from the highly diverse regional areas meant that the state soon "earned a reputation for being unnecessarily oppressive and interfering" (145). In addition, the administration was originally based upon the Germanic, highly legalistic principle of Rechtsstaat (the state based on the rule of law), under which "every activity carried out on behalf of the state had to be set within the framework of administrative law" (145). The creation of an all-powerful central bureaucracy, in order to promote unity, was accompanied by the "promulgation of laws, statues, circulars and internal directives" (145) which, although designed to safeguard citizens against the centralized bureaucracy's use of arbitrary power, resulted in "the minute regulation of administration activities" (145).

The current abundance of laws, statutes, circulars, and internal directives have, therefore, existed since the inception of Italian bureaucracy (Ginsborg 1990). Although this highly legalistic system was intended to protect disparate citizens against a centralized bureaucracy, in reality it led to confusion and inefficiency (145–146). Scholars have argued that the vast number of laws—many of which are obsolete—as well as the technical language in which they are written, have been "particularly important for the history of Italy and the difficult relationship between citizens, state bureaucrats and law-makers" (Foot 2003: 75–76), which has led the Italian state to lack legitimacy in the eyes of its citizens. As John Foot writes, "The Italian state has found legitimation extremely difficult to obtain since unification . . . The basic 'rules of the game' have never been accepted by most Italians . . . They have, instead, been partly replaced by other, unwritten 'rules' that have institutionalized patronage, clientelism, inefficiency and informal modes of behavior and exchange" (55). In contemporary Italy, the effects of these historical processes are evident in the predominance of an overly legalistic culture, in which the population must grapple with an abundance of laws written in an obtuse and incomprehensible language (Foot 2003: 77, 99; Ginsborg 1990: chap. 5; Pini 1995: 11; Sabetti 2000). Contrary to popular belief, therefore, "a chief problem in contemporary Italian public affairs is not the absence of law but rather the rule *by* law, or too many laws" (Sabetti 2000: 245).

Whether or not contemporary attitudes toward law and bureaucracy can be traced back to the *Risorgimento* (the nineteenth-century movement for Italian independence and unification), the understanding that the bureaucracy is inefficient and possibly corrupt is a dominant narrative in Italian society, as it is in many other parts of the world (Gupta 1995; Herzfeld 1992; Nuijten 2003). Following Gupta (1995: 374), in this chapter I explore the way in which discourses of inefficiency, corruption, and rule-bending are a key arena through which the state comes to be imagined. Through their interactions with the Italian immigration bureaucracy, migrants partake in this prevailing discourse about the Italian state and bureaucracy and develop the rule-bending practices that are deemed appropriate for navigating its institutions; in doing so, I argue, they become "cultural citizens" (Ong 1996).

In her formulation of cultural citizenship, Ong (1996: 738) distances her analysis from the legal-political aspects of citizenship and instead focuses on the "cultural practices and beliefs produced out of negotiating the often am- bivalent and contested relations with the state and its hegemonic forms that establish the criteria of belonging within a national population and territory." She provides an insightful account of how Asian migrants in the United States are disciplined through a range of state and nonstate mechanisms and placed at different points on a black-white spectrum. Poorer migrants are blackened and richer ones whitened, indicating "the degree of their closeness to or distance from ideal white standards" (751).

My account of cultural citizenship, however, reinstates the legal-political aspects —intentionally neglected by Ong— to highlight the dynamic interplay between forms of cultural belonging and actual juridical citizenship. I argue it is precisely through their encounters with state processes and institutions that migrants develop culturally specific modes of behavior. Through every- day encounters with officials, advisers, documents, paperwork, landlords, em- ployers, and others involved in the documentation regime, migrants develop understandings of the Italian state and how best to navigate it. While these understandings and experiences induce particular kinds of behavior, migrants are not being disciplined into specific subjects. Rather, moving beyond Ong's Foucauldian perspective, which provides a somewhat deterministic portrayal of migrant's subjectification, I argue that in the Italian context the process of migrants' subject-making is more informal, accidental, and a product of their own encounters with bureaucratic institutions, in which they learn the best way to make the system work for them. As I explore at the end of this chapter, however, actual citizenship status is crucial to fully understanding this process of subject-making. Although culturally learned rule-bending was necessary for migrants to successfully navigate the immigration bureaucracy, it was their so- cially embedded modes of behavior that could lead to their applications for citizenship and other forms of secure legal status being denied.

Il sistema paese

Practices of *il sistema paese*, therefore, are connected to both the reality of a labyrinthine bureaucracy and a culturally informed imagination of the Italian state. *Sapa'fa'* (a particular mode of cleverness) (Pardo 1995: 48), the art of *arrangiarsi* (to sort out/manage) (Mignone 1998: 412), the "real system" (Galt 1974), and *furbizia* (a cultural code that celebrates astuteness particularly when legal norms are flouted) (Schneider 1998: 85) are all terms that scholars of Italy have used to describe the crafty and skillful manipulation of rules and laws that are commonplace in the Italian setting. The point is also reflected in the saying "*fatta la legge, trova l'inganno*" (every law has its loophole) (Shore 1989: 70).

The understanding that rules should be bent and loopholes manipulated was commonly held among migrants in their navigation of the immigration bureaucracy. Conversations at the center and at other sites in the documentation regime frequently revolved around the necessity to follow the rules of *il sistema paese* when completing applications. Examples of engaging in *il sistema paese* in relation to the immigration bureaucracy included: buying and selling hospitality declarations, producing false but authentic *contratti di soggiorno* (specific work contracts for migrants), or hiring one's brother as a live-in cleaner in order for him to renew his permit.

Discussing the long waiting times for permit renewal, clients at the center often complained that, even if they had submitted all the correct requirements, the *questura* had nonetheless found a problem with their application or had delayed it for no apparent reason. Referring to her belief that the *questura* worked inefficiently if one did not have the appropriate contacts, one client stated:

> You can't just follow the rules [official rules] here. First of all, they change every day, and in any case it's not enough to complete your application correctly or present all the documents. If you don't want to wait a year for your permit to be issued, you have to know somebody.

Others remarked: "You have to be *furbo* [clever/ cunning] to get by here." *Furbizia*, which Dorothy Zinn (2001: xxii) calls an Italian cultural code, literally translates as "individual 'cunning' and 'cleverness' for the pursuit of one's own interests" (Cole 1997: 32). It refers to those who are wise, clever, and crafty (Galt 1974: 195) and who successfully recognize and negotiate the blurred boundaries between "legal" and "illegal." My interlocutors believed that strictly following the official rules was not only unhelpful but also potentially risked damage to applications because "everybody else was *furbo*." This belief echoes Anthony Galt's (1974) Sicilian research participants' views on what he refers to as the "real system" and the "official" system. The latter refers to written laws, circulars, and statutes, and the former refers to a mode of behavior that will be effectual. In spite of the illegal or extralegal nature of the "real system," for Galt's respondents it is the "official system" that is viewed as ethically problematic and corrupt, and that compels his interlocutors to engage in the "real system."

The prevalence of rule-bending is not only pertinent to immigration-related processes. My respondents spoke in a similar manner about access to social housing, declaration of income and taxation, and university exams. In all spheres, they saw bending the rules as necessary not only to get by but also to not lose out. A striking example of this social attitude is given in Emanuela Guano's (2010: 475) article on tax evasion in northern Italy. As she describes in relation to Berlusconi's 2003 fiscal amnesty, which enabled tax evaders to pay a fine in order to avoid much graver legal consequences, following the official rules could lead to paying twice. In fact, at the time of the fiscal amnesty, accountants advised their clients that to *not* partake in the amnesty would alert the attention of the officials and possibly lead to an audit. Guano notes that, "since the common belief is that an audit inevitably brings about fines even in the face of the most transparent fiscal conduct, many professional and business owners decided not to take the risk" and paid the fine *on top* of the taxes they had already paid. Such an experience would hardly encourage these business owners to continue paying regular tax.

Further justification for not following the official rules is the commonly held belief that politicians produce laws in their own interests and not those of ordinary citizens (Foot 2003; Ginsborg 2003; Guano 2010; Pardo 1995; Zinn 2001). My interlocutors echoed this belief, frequently describing how they felt that Italian politicians, lawmakers, *questura* officials, and the public were against them and purposively made the immigration bureaucracy difficult to manage. Referring to the 500 euro fee required to submit an application in the 2009 domestic worker amnesty, many made comments such as, "They [politicians] introduced the amnesty to make money [*incassare*]. They are in *crisi* [economic crisis], aren't they?" The understanding of laws being passed in the interest of those who make them provides a justification and motivation for individuals to bend them (Guano 2010; Zinn 2001). On the other hand, those who follow the official rules can feel forced to do so in order to avoid losing out.

Rule-bending, therefore, is not based exclusively on individuals' assessment of how to best profit, but also on complex reasoning based on their understanding of slow, unfair, and possibly corrupt administrations whose rules do not seem designed to aid the users. Such rationales make it difficult for people to reject tactics of evasion, not only in the belief that "everybody is doing it," but also because past experiences have taught them that by not being *furbo* one misses out.

The hegemony of this attitude toward the Italian state and its bureaucracy, and how it should be navigated, became especially apparent when individuals did not follow the typical rule-bending behavior. The expectation that individuals *should* bend the rules in order to successfully navigate the documentation regime was underscored by the unusual cases of Stefano and Ivan, who rejected the immigration bureaucracy's "pragmatic rules" (Bailey 2002). These two young men did not want to engage in what they saw as underhanded practices in order to obtain documents. This unusual attitude elicited almost universal disapproval at the center.

Not following the rules

Reflecting his bias in favor of bright and engaged university students in unusual circumstances, Alberto was enthusiastic about Stefano's case. Stefano was a Chinese citizen who had recently graduated from university. He was visiting the center because he needed advice on how to renew his permit. Students who have graduated are able to convert their student permits to work permits, but they must secure a signed work contract before the student permit expires. Stefano's permit was to expire in the following days, and he still had not found a job. Alberto had advised Stefano that he should find somebody who would be prepared to "employ" him as a domestic worker. As described earlier, domestic work contracts were frequently used by applicants who were unable or did not wish to find employment. Through family or friendship networks, Stefano needed to find an "employer" who, in friendship or in return for financial reward, would sign a work contract. This would enable Stefano to convert his student permit to a work permit and continue with his job search without fear of becoming undocumented. Stefano responded, however, that he did not wish to renew his permit in this manner. He politely explained to Alberto that he had studied very hard for his degree and was confident that he would soon find a job. On hearing Stefano's story other staff members in the center thought him foolish, but Alberto admired Stefano's unusual attitude: Stefano was aware of how the system worked but rejected it.

Two days later Stefano returned to the center to inform Alberto that he had been successful in his job search, but he needed Alberto's assistance. He was caught in a "Catch-22" situation. The new work contract was not due to begin until after the expiration date of his permit, but without a receipt for permit renewal he would not be able to sign his work contract. Stefano needed Alberto to persuade the *questura* to accept his conversion application before his work contract began. The following Friday, along with other cases about which he was inquiring at the *questura*, Alberto presented Stefano's situation to the vice director. At the bar later, Alberto described to me the vice director's response. She had exasperatedly asked Alberto, "Doesn't he [Stefano] have any friends or family who could have done him a favor?" Alberto noted the irony of the situation in which the official was encouraging Stefano to manipulate the system and exclaimed, "It is the honest ones who get screwed in this system of delinquency!" (*In questo sistema di delinquenza sono gli onesti che sono fregati!*) The unwritten and unofficial rules of *il sistema paese* were perceived as those that *should* be followed, even by officials.

Alberto felt that the vice director's reaction was evidence of a system that perpetuated corruption by encouraging Stefano to procure a fake domestic work contract. The vice director was attempting to bend the rules rather than break them, however. She acknowledged the difficult situation Stefano was in, but felt obligated to process his paperwork in the "correct" manner. By following the pragmatic rules (Bailey 2002), which involved accepting a domestic work contract even though she may have known it was false, the vice director would have been able to mediate the tension between the demands of the formal rules and the practicalities of Stefano's situation. The fact that the domestic work contract would be false was insignificant.

As Galt (1974: 195) notes with regard to his respondents in Sicily, "Everyone recognizes its [the official system's] fundamental incompleteness and unfairness. Few see operating within it as a mode people *should* adopt." This case, therefore, presented an unusual and paradoxical situation because Stefano desired to follow the "official rules" rather than the pragmatic ones, but was unable to. This frustrated Alberto, who saw the case as an example of the pervasiveness of semi-legal practices within the immigration system. In his criticism of the vice director, however, Alberto did not acknowledge that she was trapped in the same "system of delinquency" as his clients. It was not that the vice director necessarily believed in a system of false (if authentic) documentation. Rather, the inefficiency of the official system led her to believe that the best solution was for Stefano to procure a false domestic work contract. In the end, in order to fulfill Stefano's desire to not engage in semi-legal practices, the vice director *did* eventually accept his application, but only after considerable persuasion. In doing so the vice director herself acted outside of the official rules by making an exception. Paradoxically, therefore, Stefano's desire to be honest required the vice director to engage in discretionary and rule-*breaking* practices.

Similarly unusual in his approach to the immigration bureaucracy was Ivan, a Ukrainian citizen who was in a long-term relationship with an Italian woman. While renewing his permit, Ivan had engaged in discussion with Alberto and Maria (the new head of the center). Ivan told them that his Italian partner had suggested the couple get married in order for him to be able to hold more secure legal status, and possibly citizenship. He, however, was ambivalent: "I am happy the way things are now. I don't want the reason that I get married to be for documents. Things should take their own course." Ivan resented the way in which the documentation regime invaded his private life and affected important personal decisions. When Ivan left, Maria recounted his story to another staff member, saying, "Can you believe it? What a fool!" Chiara, commenting on a similar situation, agreed. She thought those who did not take advantage of the existing possibilities were arrogant and idealistic, thinking themselves above other migrants. In her opinion individuals in such a position did not want to *appear* as if they had married for documents.

Stefano and Ivan's unusual reactions highlighted the embeddedness of following the pragmatic rules in order to get by. Informal strategies, such as procuring a false domestic work contract, enabled the bureaucracy to work smoothly and the various actors involved to achieve their desired ends.[1] Stefano's and Ivan's attitudes, however, disrupted the usual system. In the case of Stefano the rules were broken, rather than merely bent, by the official when an exception was made and the center was required to do more work by negotiating with the vice director. All of this would have been avoided if Stefano had heeded the advice to obtain a false domestic work contract.

Stefano's and Ivan's dismissal of *il sistema paese* as corrupt and delinquent obscures the complex rationale for why such rule-bending practices exist in the Italian context, and people's motivations for engaging in them. Although Stefano and Ivan felt that they could reject the "real system," given its systemic nature others did not feel that they necessarily had the choice to opt out. Mistrust of the state, as well as the overly complicated nature of the legal system and its bureaucracy, creates a situation in which people feel they must bend the rules, since to follow them all would be impossible. In order to meet the requirements of the official system, which necessitates forms, stamps, and certificates, individuals were required to engage in semi-legal, personalistic, and creative strategies. Those who engage in forms of tax evasion or other rule-bending practices are not necessarily "scheming entrepreneurs" (Shore 1989: 69). Rather, these semi- or extralegal practices are ethically deliberated modes of action based on a hegemonic view of the imagined Italian state as inefficient, inchoate, and possibly corrupt. Social relations and a fear of losing out were important justifications for manipulating the official rules.

Social Relations

Engaging with the "real system" is intimately tied to social and kinship relations. By rejecting its logics, one risked alienating others. Agreeing with Alberto, both Chiara and Biniam frequently said they believed that the logics of *il sistema paese* made it possible for those who were sly and delinquent to succeed while those who were honest lost out. Yet, despite their strong opinions on the matter, they all also engaged in such practices. Biniam frequently criticized Italy as a "country of delinquents" where "illegality becomes legality" (*illegalità diventa legalità*). When the 2011 *decreto flussi* procedure was confirmed, however, he too became involved in *il sistema paese* by submitting an application to be the employer for his cousin in Eritrea. As he told me, he felt obliged to do so.

> I hate getting involved in all this stuff. But I really don't have a choice. They [friends and family] all know about the *decreto flussi* over there [Asmara, Eritrea] and expect us to help them. If it were up to me, I would just ignore them, but it is my parents who pay the price. Others will accuse them [his parents] of having selfish children who don't want to help anybody.

Chiara, his sister, had helped Dewat (their close friend) by acting as his employer in the 2009 amnesty, so it was Biniam's turn to help somebody in the 2011 *decreto flussi*. In the end, Biniam did submit the application. During the process he frequently discussed why the cousin he was "employing" in the procedure deserved help. "She's had it tough. She is a single mother and she has always worked hard." Viewing his cousin as in need helped Biniam justify his participation in *il sistema paese*.

Like her brother, Chiara was also highly critical of how she believed things were run in Italy. Still, she was a skillful player of *il sistema paese*. Over the many years she had spent in the city, making full use of her charming, lively, and flirtatious personality, Chiara had made contacts in various institutions that she could draw on to help people—her "social cases" (*casi sociali*), as Biniam called them. Countless times during my fieldwork she made phone calls to friends of hers who worked at the *questura* to request that somebody's application be viewed in a sympathetic light. She also had contacts at the *comune* and managed to speed up Mehdi's (a volunteer) friend's public housing application when he and his family faced eviction from their apartment. Other staff members at the center also took advantage of Chiara's contacts, frequently selecting cases for her to inquire about at a later date. Despite her criticism, therefore, Chiara was an apt and active player in *il sistema paese*. Like Alberto, she enjoyed the challenge of craftily navigating the system. Notwithstanding the satisfaction she took in skillfully eliciting favors, however, she was firmly motivated by her desire to help people, which, given her integrated position in Italian society she viewed as her responsibility. Her central objection to *il sistema paese* was that sometimes people's rule-bending tactics caused those who were more "deserving" to lose out. In her opinion, rule-bending was not morally problematic if people used it to obtain what they were entitled to. But it *was* problematic if people bent the rules for personal gain, such as by lying about their marital status in order to be eligible for public housing.

In her discussion of her respondents' practices of *raccomandazione*, which refers to clientelistic practices through which actors gain advantages such as jobs, jumping queues, or university places, Zinn (2001: xxi) has argued that such practices are situated within networks of emotional and affective relationships and are associated with ideas of personhood. Disengagement with them would communicate a change in one's subjectivity and a desire to declare oneself as an individual. I made a similar observation at my fieldsite. If he rejected the logics of *il sistema paese*, Biniam would be turning his back on his family and Chiara on her "social cases." Accordingly, a tension existed between disapproving of *il sistema paese* yet using it to help people. If Chiara did not draw on her contacts, ultimately she would alienate those she wished to help. She partially resolved this moral tension by using her contacts to indiscriminately help people she perceived to be in need (not just her friends and family), regularly volunteering at the center, and going the extra mile when doing so.

"La carta canta e villan dorme"

> (The paper sings and the villager sleeps. Or, the written paper cannot be contradicted.)

While bending the rules is socially acceptable, even condoned by officials, there are strict rules of rule-bending that must be followed if one is to be successful. These rules largely related to the correct documentation of circumstances, whether real or false. Successful navigation of the immigration bureaucracy required skill, knowledge, and finesse. In order not be caught out, one had to appear to follow the official rules: compliance with proceduralism was fundamental (see also Gupta and Sharma 2006: 12–16). Paperwork and its correct completion were essential elements in migrants' successful engagements with the immigration bureaucracy. It was not necessary for paperwork to represent migrants' "real" circumstances, but it needed to be authentic, even if false (Hull 2008: 513). Issues relating to migrants' false and inauthentic paper trails made up much of the center's work. Center staff needed to unravel clients' stories and to ascertain which parts of their narrative were true, false, authentic, and inauthentic. Domestic work contracts play a central role.

Many migrants needing to regularize their status or renew their permits took advantage of the possibilities that the informal nature of domestic work contracts offered. The regularization of domestic work involves drawing up a work contract and, in the case of migrant workers, a *contratto di soggiorno* (a work contract for migrant workers), registering the contract with the INPS (Istituto Nazionale della Previdenza Sociale, or National Institute for Social Welfare) and paying *contributi* (national insurance contributions), as well as providing the employee with an annual income statement. For migrants employed as domestic workers these documents are essential when renewing permits, as they attest to and document this work relationship. Because these contracts are between private individuals and the work takes place in households, the domestic work contract offers the possibility for many migrants without jobs or working in the informal market to regularize their status or to renew their permits. In order for this strategy to be fully successful, however, this work relationship must be authentically false (Hull 2008: 513). Much of the center's work dealt with cases in which migrants had not produced a sufficiently authentic paper trail and, as a result, faced problems when renewing their permits. Effectively managing one's paper trail was a sign of a long-term and integrated migrant.

In contrast to Alberto, whose empathetic manner enabled him to communicate with anyone, whatever their linguistic competence, Ginetta's mode of communication was unchanging and uncompromising regardless of the client at her desk. Her manner mirrored that found in any public office in Italy. She was formal and respectful, employing the formal third person *Lei* and speaking in bureaucratic language. Since *Lei* is also the third-person feminine singular pronoun, her clients were often confused, thinking she was referring to a third person rather than to them directly. Further, Ginetta's unmediated use of the *questura's* legalistic language, and the manner in which she cited articles of law word for word when explaining to clients why their applications had not been accepted, caused further confusion and misunderstanding.

One afternoon Ginetta was having particular difficulty communicating with a young woman and, as she often did, beckoned me over to mediate. The young woman had arrived in Italy through the 2007 *decreto flussi* and was now required to renew her permit. In order to renew this work permit the applicant is required to present a host of paperwork including, among many other documents, a work contract and the previous year's income statement. The conversation between the young woman and Ginetta went around in circles as Ginetta tried to ascertain whether this young woman had ever actually worked for the "employer" who had brought her to Italy via the *decreto flussi*. Ginetta was not necessarily asking if the young woman had been in a *genuine* employer/ employee relationship with this person, but whether such a relationship had been *authentically documented*. Authentic documentation for such a relationship would include pay slips, tax receipts, and income statements.

The young woman, however, was unable to understand Ginetta's questions because she did not understand her relationship with the person who was her "employer" in these terms. Through my asking of more direct questions, rather than Ginetta's more suggestive ones, we eventually discovered that the "employer" in this case was a family friend of the young woman who had "hired" her in the 2007 *decreto flussi* as a favor. It transpired that she had not genuinely worked for this "employer" and, more important, the "employer" had not authentically documented such a relationship. This young woman's paper trail, therefore, showed her entering Italy on the grounds of being employed by this "employer," but there was no subsequent documentation to evidence the actual employment. While her first permit, which she had obtained after entering the country, had enabled this young woman to legally reside in Italy for the past two years, because this work relationship had not been authentically documented since then, she now did not have the necessary requisites for renewal.

The communication difficulties that Ginetta and the young woman experienced highlight their different understandings of the bureaucracy and the way in which one navigates it. Ginetta was of course aware that many clients' documented lives were different from their real-life circumstances, but her formalistic manner conveyed an authentic falseness in her interactions with clients. In contrast, Alberto openly informed clients how to create authentic false paper trails. As a recent migrant to Italy and with relatively weak Italian language skills, Ginetta's client in this case, however, was unaware how she was engaged with the documentation regime and *il sistema paese.* In her eyes a family friend had helped her to obtain papers rather than employed her as a domestic worker in the 2007 *decreto flussi*.

Successful navigation of the documentation regime was usually a sign of a long-term, integrated migrant who was aware of the importance of authentic paper trails. For example, Chiara's hiring of Dewat in the 2009 domestic worker amnesty demonstrated skillful manipulation of the law's loopholes. Dewat, a close friend of both Biniam and Chiara, was also an Eritrean. He had unsuccessfully sought asylum in Italy ten years previously and had spent the intervening years as an illegal migrant in the country. Following failed attempts over the years to obtain legal status, Dewat and Chiara arranged for her to "hire" him as her *badante* (caregiver) in the 2009 domestic worker amnesty. Chiara has a registered disability, which made her eligible to hire a caregiver.

Although Chiara usually tried to avoid becoming involved in such situations, she felt some sense of responsibility for Dewat's predicament because she had recommended the lawyer he consulted when he first arrived in Italy. In Chiara's opinion, this lawyer had given Dewat poor advice, which had led to the rejection of his asylum claim. Taking care not to be caught out, Chiara ensured that their "work" relationship was properly documented. The *contratto di soggiorno* was drawn up and registered with INPS. *Contributi* were paid every three months (for which Dewat then reimbursed Chiara). And monthly pay slips as well as an annual statement of income were provided. Once Dewat had found an actual job, the contract was formally ended. When Dewat's permit expired, he renewed it without a problem, as his and Chiara's story was seamlessly documented in the required manner.

In the Italian immigration bureaucracy, by controlling their paper trails migrants can produce a new legal reality that enables them to effect concrete changes in their lives: legalize their status, renew their permits, or be reunited with family members. Becoming a documented domestic worker on paper transforms one's status from illegal to legal. Not effectively maintaining the paper trail, however, can lead individuals to lose control over the narrative that their documents recount. In such cases, paperwork—or the absence thereof— can also work against migrants and cause them to lose legal status or not to attain more secure positions. As Matthew Hull (2008) has similarly shown in relation to the expropriation of land in Islamabad, it was the *records* of home and land ownership, rather than the *actual circumstances* of home and land ownership, that determined compensation. Documents and paperwork are not merely representative of social and material relations that may or may not exist, but can have the power to affect those relations (Hull 2012b).

Paperwork and *bella figura*

The rules of rule-bending also encompassed the etiquette of discussing rule-bending. At the center, those who demonstrated understanding of *il sistema paese* and its nuances and details, were more likely to receive advice about the "pragmatic rules." Individuals' lack of knowledge about rule-bending was exposed when they failed to conform to the subtle rules for discussing how to manipulate loopholes and procure false documents. The following two contrasting case studies depict clients who wanted to find out how they could bend the rules. In the first, Biniam reacted in a hostile manner because he perceived the client to be arrogant and lacking in understanding. In the second, the client conveyed his understanding of *il sistema paese* and the appropriate ways to manage it, and thus received the advice he was looking for. The key to receiving helpful information on rule-bending was to demonstrate an understanding of the importance of the detail in paperwork and the limits to the system's flexibility.

Another tactic applicants employed in renewing permits or obtaining long-term permits was to present themselves as self-employed. Setting up a business enabled those who did not work, or worked in the informal labor market, to renew their permits by presenting authentically false paperwork that documented the business. This strategy was not without its risks. I came across many individuals who had set themselves up in this manner for the purpose of permit renewal, but because they lacked the appropriate documentation, the *questura* subsequently rejected their applications.

For those who *were* able to successfully set up and run their own businesses (genuine or not), being self-employed offered advantages in the documentation regime. Those who are self-employed are able to control the amounts on their annual declarations of income, which determine the amount of tax one pays. In the case of immigration applications, the amount of one's annual income dictates whether one can renew a permit or apply for the long-term permit. During my fieldwork, in order to renew a work permit, which lasted two years, one was required to declare an annual salary of at least 5,000 euros. In theory, the required amount was higher if one had dependents, but the *questura* was fairly lenient about this.

Officials were not lenient, however, with regard to applications for the long-term permit. Given this, those who were self-employed (or claimed to be self-employed) often adjusted their declared annual income according to whether or not they were submitting applications that year. With the help of their accountants (*commercialisti*), self-employed applicants were able to tweak the figures on their income declarations according to their needs, upping the figure when renewing a permit and lowering it in other years in order to pay lower taxes.

Having studied many applicants' declarations of income, Alberto was familiar with such tactics. Because they must manage various bureaucratic and tax institutions, the self-employed (and others) in Italy almost always employ a *commercialista. Commercialista* loosely translates as accountant and is considered necessary to ensure the correct navigation of Italian bureaucracy. A *commercialista* can aid both those who want to take advantage of loopholes in the system and those who do not want to bend rules but get caught out by trying to abide by them. *Commercialisti* are thus professional navigators of Italian bureaucracy, particularly in financial matters. They are not, however, experts on immigration law, and it was not uncommon for clients to arrive at the center having received incorrect information from their *commercialisti* or with errors on application forms that their *commercialisti* had completed.

Attempting to follow the strategy described above, one day at the welcome counter a Bangladeshi man with a self-employment permit asked Biniam and me how high his income should be in order to apply for the long-term permit. Biniam replied that he should put the amount he earned. The client then insisted, saying, "Yes but how much *is* the amount?" adding, "I can just get my *commercialista* to write the figure that I ask him to."

It was common for clients to inquire about minimum salary amounts required for different applications. However, the question would be phrased: "What is the amount needed in order to apply for the long-term permit?" This man, instead, asked: "What amount *should* I put . . . ?" The way in which he asked the question revealed that he was planning to falsify his document. Biniam's cold and obtuse response to the man was not because he disapproved of manipulating the system. As noted earlier, center staff members frequently advised clients to adjust the amounts on their declarations of income in order to be eligible for applications. Rather, as he told me, the fact that the man spoke about such things so directly made him appear arrogant and lacking in social knowledge. The way in which the man insisted on knowing the specific amount was objectionable to Biniam for three reasons. First, it made Biniam immediately complicit in this man's rule-bending activities. Second, it demonstrated that the man did not understand the nuances of rule-bending while at the same time attempting to seem knowledgeable. Third, the man's reference to his *commercialista* likely implied that he *did* have sufficient income for the long-term permit, but that he wanted to declare his income to be as low as possible in order to avoid paying higher taxes.

The documentation regime was a shifting terrain in which it was almost impossible to deliver concrete answers. In order to effectively respond to the man's question, Biniam would have had to make a series of inquiries about his previous years' income statements, how many dependents he had, and so on. The man's manner did not encourage Biniam to help him bend the rules, and instead he referred to the official rules, saying: "Put what you earn." Biniam thus feigned ignorance of the rule-bending practices and rejected the man's desire for collusion. His reaction was not due to his own belief that all rules needed to be followed. It was rather that he did not like the man's manner and, given the informal nature of the "real system," was not obliged to help him manipulate the rules.

This example shows that one's engagement with the "real" system must maintain an element of subtlety and nuance in order to avoid being perceived as arrogant or ignorant. The man in question had been too blatantly *furbo*, and thus not *furbo* enough. Although he possessed an implicit understanding of the gap between paper and practice, the image (*figura*) that the paperwork presents should not be so obviously exposed as false. The logics of *furbizia*, and of *il sistema paese*, are guided by their own norms, and actors must tread a fine line.

In contrast, the following case depicts actors *bonding* over their shared knowledge of bending the rules. On a quiet afternoon Biniam, Chiara, and I were sitting behind the welcome counter when a Moroccan man in his mid-twenties entered with his sister. He spoke Italian with a strong local accent and asked about the technicalities of hiring his sister, whose permit was expiring in several months' time, as the family's domestic worker. Employing her as the family live-in cleaner (*colf*) would enable her to renew her work permit. "As long as the family as a whole has a high enough CUD [declaration of annual income], that is fine," Biniam answered and passed him the leaflet for Home-Help,[2] telling him to go there to arrange a contract. He emphasized to them the importance that all the correct paperwork be completed and produced correctly. "Payslips, *contratto di soggiorno* [work contract], employer's declaration," he counted on his fingers. As the conversation continued, Chiara asked whether the man had citizenship. "No, you don't?" she responded, surprised. "That *is* a shame because if you had citizenship, she [his sister] would be eligible for a family permit and then you would not need to bother with all this." The man responded in a characteristically Italian manner saying, "*Ah beh*" (Oh well)," shrugging his shoulders and lifting his open-handed arms in resignation. "But when did you arrive here [in Italy]?" Chiara asked. He responded that he had arrived in Italy when he was fourteen years old, meaning that he was required to complete the usual procedure for citizenship applications. He had submitted the citizenship application three years ago, he told us. The conversation continued in a friendly and jovial manner as the three of them complained about the long waiting times for citizenship and discussed which official had interviewed him at the citizenship appointment.

Biniam's reaction to the man in this second case strongly contrasted with his reaction to the first man. While the Bangladeshi man in the first example had offended his sensibilities with his clumsy and forceful questions about income, the Moroccan man, although just as direct, managed to gain his trust. He achieved this partly thanks to his local accent and Italian manner of dressing and gesticulating, which immediately identified him as an insider and an integrated migrant, similar to Biniam. But he also earned Biniam's acceptance for the way in which he approached the situation. Although the Moroccan man *was* explicit about hiring his sister as a cleaner in order for her to renew her permit, he wanted to be informed about all the details rather than particular ones. Further, he was asking for information in order to help his sister, rather than for personal profit. Because the man wanted to know all the details about how to start a domestic work contract, he demonstrated his understanding of the importance that the paperwork must be in order: he was aware that there were rules to rule-bending. His manner and approach demonstrated this awareness, and Biniam was happy to openly advise him on manipulating the law's flexibility. Biniam and Chiara's shock that the man lacked Italian citizenship, and their shared moaning about the *questura* and *prefettura*, further illustrated their view of him as an insider.

Thus the manner in which individuals spoke about rule-bending demonstrated their understanding of the dual system of the "official" rules and the "real" rules. Crucial to this was the understanding that the paperwork *did* matter. False situations must be authentically documented.

The limits to rule-bending for migrants

Through their bureaucratic encounters and engagements in the unofficial rules of *il sistema paese* migrants come to partake in a collective imagination of the Italian state. Bureaucratic engagements are, then, forms of citizen-making. Yet the following case studies depict two individuals who were well integrated into *il sistema paese* but nonetheless ended up losing out. These cases demonstrate that although being *furbo* was necessary to get by, years of rule-bending could lead to migrants risking their own and their families' future security. This outcome reminds us of the limits and precarity that immigration law imposes on migrants alongside the cultural citizenship it might also engender.

As this book has described, strategic navigation of the bureaucracy was useful, perhaps even essential. Yet, given the documented nature of migrants' lives, rule-bending in one application can create problems in others. Rashid was a man from Pakistan who frequently waited in the center for hours on end hoping eventually to speak with Alberto. Alberto explained that Rashid came to the center so often because he had still not received any response to the citizenship application he had submitted several years ago. Through visits to the *prefettura* and the *questura* on Rashid's behalf, Alberto discovered why his application had been blocked. Background checks are carried out on citizenship applicants to ensure that the applicant does not have a record of criminal offenses and has paid taxes, fines, and so on. While conducting this research on Rashid's background, the *questura* discovered that his children had not been going to school. Rashid's children were born in Italy, but when they were still very young went with their mother to live in Pakistan.

I asked Alberto whether it would be helpful for Rashid to send the school certificates from Pakistan. Alberto shook his head and explained that migrants who are legally resident in Italy are not allowed to live permanently in another country. More seriously, because on paper his wife and children were living in Italy, Rashid had been receiving family benefits. Thus, if Rashid were to argue that his children were in Italy, he would be committing an offense by not sending them to school. If he proved they had been living in Pakistan, he risked being accused of benefit fraud. Alberto advised Rashid to renounce his application and hope that nobody followed up on either issue: in this instance, there was no way around the bureaucracy. Rashid had taken advantage of the relative leniency in the Italian system by managing to ensure that his daughters and wife, although now living in Pakistan, had the flexibility to return to Italy. Since on paper they lived in Italy, he was entitled to receive the family benefit allowance. His actions were the epitome of *furbizia*: taking advantage of bureaucratic systems where possible in order to personally benefit. However, Rashid's citizenship application had created a contradiction between paper truths and real-life circumstances. Although he may have had insider knowledge, legally he was not an insider, and his actions led to his losing the possibility of citizenship in the country where he had lived for over twenty years.

In the last week of my fieldwork Biniam asked me to fill out the *kit* for an update (*aggiornamento*) of the long-term permit for an Eritrean acquaintance of his named Sarah. The application form asked for information about the person's nuclear family and dependents (if applicable). Officially Sarah had one daughter and was a single mother. In reality she lived with Kidane, also an Eritrean, who was the father of her daughter. On paper, however, Kidane lived at his mother's house because holding residence in the same house as Sarah would have ruined her eligibility for public housing. Two weeks before I completed Sarah's application to update her long-term permit, I also met Kidane at the center. Kidane grew up in Italy and was about to obtain Italian citizenship, for which he applied several years previously. He came into the center concerned that his four-year-old daughter would not automatically obtain citizenship if they did not, on paper, share the same place of residence. If a parent obtains Italian citizenship, any children they have under the age of eighteen also automatically obtain citizenship. However, there is an assumption that the parent will reside with the child and, as in this instance, difficulties are encountered when this is not the case. This situation, reflecting a Catholic influence on ideas of rights, clearly creates problems for any family that may not have a traditional nuclear family setup. In Kidane's case it was not that he and the mother of his child were separated in reality, but rather that on paper they were in order for Sarah to have access to public housing as a "single mother." These two situations demonstrate that there were real consequences of manipulating paperwork. In this case, Kidane and Sarah's daughter stood to lose an opportunity for Italian citizenship, despite the fact that she had been born in Italy and her father had grown up there.

Kidane's mother worked as a cleaner in the central trade union offices, and after encountering her on our way to the center, Chiara told Biniam and me that she had little sympathy for Kidane's situation. "She [Kidane's mother] is acting like he is a victim. Sorry, but no, you can't have everything. People like them [Kidane and Sarah] are the reason those who actually *are* in need do not get housing—like Sami," she said, referring to the man she and I were helping to arrange his stillborn baby's funeral.

Living in a cramped one-bedroom flat with his wife and three daughters, Sami had told us he did not understand why the *comune* had informed him that he was ineligible for public housing yet acquaintances of his, who owned expensive cars, were. "We immigrants have become the mirror of Italians," Chiara continued. This was a comment Chiara made frequently. In her view, migrants' strategic navigation of the bureaucracy in order to achieve their desired ends was a sign they had absorbed the most negative aspects of Italian culture. Although she also engaged in rule-bending practices, in her mind the fact that her activities were not self-interested separated them from others. For Chiara, rule-bending in desperate situations was acceptable, but not when motivated by a desire to profit, especially financially.

In these cases, the fact that it was Italian citizenship that Rashid and Kidane risked through their rule-bending was not without irony. As Chiara noted, their actions showed that they had developed behavior fitting with the representation of Italians' attitudes toward law and the state. Yet it was this Italian-like attitude that prevented Rashid and Kidane from gaining citizenship. The mismatch between a migrant's social knowledge and embeddedness—which were required in order to navigate the bureaucracy—and exclusionary citizenship laws made such knowledge and embeddedness precarious. Paradoxically, the social and cultural learning that marked some migrants as more integrated into Italian life could be the very thing that endangered their right to live in the country.

Conclusion

This chapter has explored the way in which the immigration bureaucracy and migrants' navigation of it has a particularly Italian flavor. The dominant narrative, that the Italian state and its legal and bureaucratic institutions are inefficient, incompetent, and possibility corrupt, makes rule-bending and the manipulation of loopholes the expected mode of behavior. By exploring how migrants' strategic navigation of the immigration bureaucracy fits into this shared imagination of the Italian state, I argue that through their encounters with the documentation regime migrants develop what are deemed to be culturally appropriate forms of navigating it. In doing so, they become Italian cultural citizens.

Yet, alongside the system's openness to flexibility and manipulation there exists a strict sense of proceduralism. Paperwork must be in order and, whether false or not, circumstances must be authentically documented, a process that requires skill and expertise. The documented nature of migrants' lives, however, means that rule-bending in one application can create problems in others. Therefore, while encounters with the immigration bureaucracy produce migrants as cultural citizens, it is precisely this insider behavior that in other moments may prevent them from obtaining more secure legal status or actual juridical citizenship.

4 Becoming an Immigration Adviser
Self-Fashioning through Bureaucratic Practice

Extract from fieldnotes, January 2011

Chiara and I are on one of our usual Saturday afternoon walks around the city. We stop at John's internet café so that she can make a long-distance call to her parents in Eritrea. The café is alive with activity. Several customers are using the phone booths, while others are at desktop PCs checking their e-mail. As we enter, Chiara warmly greets John, a middle-aged Nigerian man, and they briefly exchange niceties, asking after each other's families. John is sitting in a large swivel office chair behind the counter. He is dressed smart casual in a shirt, sweater, and chino-style trousers with a hands-free earpiece attached to the side of his head. On the desk in front of him is a permit renewal application form that he is in the middle of completing for a man standing next to the counter clutching a plastic bag filled with paperwork.

I stand outside the booth as Chiara uses the phone, observing the comings and goings. It is a couple of weeks before "click day," when *decreto flussi* applications must be submitted online. Applications can be completed independently, but most applicants seek out help, such as at the advice center. John's internet café is clearly also offering a similar service. As I wait, two people come in to ask him for information about the application process. Chiara finishes her phone call, and as we leave we overhear John arranging an appointment to complete the online *decreto flussi* application for a client the following week. "Ha," Chiara snorts. "He is doing *decreto flussi* applications here as well. I wonder how much he is charging. Immigration, Anna, is big business," she tells me knowingly.

Ethnographic studies of law and bureaucracy have long highlighted the unintended consequences, what might be called "side effects" (Ferguson 1990) or "spillovers" (Cabot 2014: 2), produced by legal and bureaucratic processes. This chapter focuses on one such spillover: the emergence of immigration advisers, or community brokers, who assist migrants in their navigation of the documentation regime. When dealing with the Italian immigration bureaucracy, the assistance of some kind of adviser is essential for even long-term migrants. Here I examine the manner in which becoming an immigration adviser is a means through which individuals with migrant backgrounds are able to escape the low-status occupations to which migrants are usually restricted in Italy.

Anthropological work on law and bureaucracy has highlighted the affective potential of legal and bureaucratic processes to produce uncertainty, indeterminacy, anxiety, and hope for those involved within them (Kelly 2006; Navaro-Yashin 2007; Nuijten 2003). In relation to immigration law, scholars have shown how legal processes discipline subjects as "deportable" (De Genova 2002), create deep uncertainty in people's lives (Gonzales and Chavez 2012), or, paradoxically, produce cultural insiders (Tuckett 2015).

In this chapter I show how engagements with immigration law produce possibilities for self-fashioning and social mobility. By focusing on the role of community brokers, I show how styling oneself as an immigration adviser and expert enables these brokers to develop new subjectivities. Those I am grouping under the umbrella term "community broker" have various motives for doing assistance work, but one that is shared by most of them is the ability to fashion themselves in ways that suit them. These include fulfilling a desire to be professional, to gain standing in their community, to satisfy charitable impulses, or to fight for social justice. Crucially, being a community broker offers possibilities for gaining social status that are generally not otherwise available to migrants in Italy.

In the anthropological canon, brokers have been described as "synapses" (Wolf 1956: 1075). They mediate between smaller and larger structures, whether between local and national society (Silverman 1965), voters and politicians (Koster 2012; Lazar 2004), or development programs and local populations (Lewis and Mosse 2006). They bridge communication between persons, groups, structures, and even cultures (Boissevain 1974: 148). Relying on the gap between individuals and the resources they need access to, brokers are often depicted as morally ambiguous figures (James 2011; Lindquist 2015b): self-interested entrepreneurs who manipulate the multiple worlds they occupy for their own profit, ultimately entrenching and reproducing existing inequalities (Blok 1974; Boissevain 1974). Despite increased ease of communication and movement, recent work has shown that the demand for brokerage services has remained high in modern society (Lindquist 2015a). Contemporary migration regimes are areas in which this demand is particularly high.

Whether facilitating migrant mobility, easing communication channels, or enabling the production and completion of bureaucratic paperwork, brokers are key figures in the highly bureaucratized global migration regime. Despite the indispensable role migration brokers often play, however, they are frequently condemned by academics, policy makers, and development workers (Lindquist, Xiang, and Yeoh 2012). Usually framed as "traffickers" and "smugglers," migration brokers are portrayed as callous and cruel, exploiting migrants and their labor for their own self-interest (Andrijasevic 2010; Kyle and Liang 2001; Salt and Stein 1997). In particular, it is informal brokers rather than formal brokers, in the guise of lawyers or official labor recruitment agencies, who are deemed undesirable. At best the informal broker is described as "illegal" or "illegitimate," at worst as "criminal" and "immoral," but in both cases the broker's practices, relationships with clients, and connections to the "formal" system are often left unexamined (Bakan and Stasiulis 1995; Guevarra 2006; Guevarra 2009).

This broad-brush negative stereotype, however, overlooks a key fact: in an era in which migration regimes across the world are highly regulated and bureaucratized, the expertise of individuals who know how to navigate the "migration industry" (Lindquist 2010) is essential for migrants and migrant employers, as well as for sending and receiving states. Adam McKeown (2012: 21) argues that the demonization of migrant brokers is historically connected to liberalism and "the emerging ideal of the 'free' migrant as an atomized, self-motivated individual." Within the historical context of slavery and indentured labor, "brokerage came to be understood as a relic of pre-modern social organization, unsuited to the freedom and transparency of modern markets, personal liberty and the West" (23). This historical demonization, he argues, has meant ignoring the essential role brokers play in helping migrants to navigate unfathomable bureaucracy and paperwork, as well as "drawing attention away from working conditions, laws and public attitudes that are equally responsible for migrant suffering" (24).

Some recent ethnographic work on migrant brokers goes far in undoing these stereotypes and highlights how minute practices of brokerage are deeply intertwined with top-down legal and political processes. The flourishing of migration brokers and the demand for their assistance is directly related to the increased bureaucratization and regularization of migration (Alpes 2013, 2017; Lindquist 2012: 74). They cannot, therefore, be simplistically dismissed as illegitimate or illegal. Rodriguez (2010) and Guevarra's (2009) work on the Filipino state as a labor broker, and Xiang's (2012) work on private migrant recruitment agents in China, describe how, and the extent to which, states rely on and facilitate brokerage practices. As well as both sending and receiving states, brokers, migrants, and their social networks are all involved in brokerage systems (Spener 2009).

Further disrupting the stereotype of the broker as predatory is ethnographic work that shows how brokers and migrants are often fluid rather than distinct categories. Heng Leng Chee et al. (2012: 95, 112) challenge the stereotype of the marriage broker as an unscrupulous businessman by showing that it is often Vietnamese brides themselves who act as matchmakers between women and Malaysian men. Becoming a marriage broker offers opportunities for newly married wives to build social and economic capital. Sverre Molland's (2012) work on sex trafficking in Thailand also describes the blurred boundaries between broker and migrant. He shows that while anti-trafficking programs promote social networks as a means to create "safe" migration, it is within social networks that practices of coercion and deception take place, as the friends and kin of "victims"—who are possibly "trafficking victims" themselves—become complicit in the victims' trafficking. Finally, Johan Lindquist's (2012: 75) work on *petugas lapangan* (PL), who work as field agents in labor migration brokerage in Indonesia, also disrupts the dichotomies of "victims" and "perpetrators" that frame debates around transnational migration. In his account, brokers were migrants themselves in the past, and some become migrants again in the future (see also Fernandez 2013). In fact, in Lindquist's case study, as in all of the above examples, it is the brokers' shared experiences with their prospective clients and their ability to gain trust and credibility that ensure their success. Successful brokerage, therefore, relies on relationships of trust and friendship that may be instrumental but are not necessarily lopsided (Alpes 2017; Kyle and Liang 2001; Lindquist 2015b: 171; Spener 2009).

Accordingly, migration brokers are essential for migrants' successful navigation of immigration regimes, as well as the functioning of the system itself. Their practices highlight the inseparability between the formal and the informal, between the legal and the illegal, and between altruistic and profit-oriented networks (Lindquist, Xiang, and Yeoh 2012: 17). Many migration brokers facilitate mobility transnationally, often in the guise of some kind of recruitment agency; in contrast, the brokers featured here specialize in assisting migrants with the unwieldy immigration bureaucracy in the host setting. Migrants' dealings with documentation regimes begin rather than end with the crossing of borders. In Italy, as elsewhere, because immigration regimes are structured to prolong migrants' temporary and precarious status, those subject to them are continually required to deal with the cumbersome and highly complex documentation regime. Community brokers play a key role in this process.

Classical anthropological analyses of brokers have tended to prioritize either a political economy analysis or a methodological individualist approach (James 2011; Lindquist 2015b). In the former, the structural role of the broker as filling a gap between state and society is emphasized, while in the latter it is the broker's position as a cunning and creative cultural figure. In what follows I provide a synthesis of these approaches by contributing to, and building on, recent work on the socially embedded role of the broker that challenges the notion that they are amoral or immoral (James 2011; Lindquist, Xiang, and Yeoh 2012; Lindquist 2015b).

Focusing on four community brokers who acted as volunteers in the center, I show how brokers' activities are ethically motivated, both to diminish the exploitation of their own labor and to improve their own social and economic status. Ethical practices do not necessarily signify morally "good" or altruistically motivated behavior. Rather, ethics here refers to the Foucauldian conception of the term, in which a person's conduct is ethical in so far as it is shaped by attempts to make herself into a certain kind of person (Foucault 2003; Laidlaw 2002). By contextualizing the migrant brokers' activities within the Italian political, legal, and economic setting, I show how becoming a migration broker is rooted in personal projects of social mobility within a context in which migrants are legally and economically marginalized.

Advising in the documentation regime

An exploration of the role of the migration advice broker in Italy needs to address two points. First, as noted already, most migrants in Italian society have a very low social and economic status. Engaging in brokerage activities is a means for some former migrants to attempt to overcome the marginalized position migrants normally occupy. And second, the extreme ambiguity, changing rules, and discretionary decision-making that characterize the Italian immigration bureaucracy make the services of advisers essential for migrants navigating the regime.

Despite migrants' varied backgrounds, precarious and discriminatory legal, economic, and political circumstances unify their experiences in Italy. In line with other southern European countries, migrants are restricted to the lowest-status and poorest-paid jobs. Male migrants fill unskilled and semi-skilled manual labor shortages in the construction, agriculture, and manufacturing industries. Female migrants overwhelmingly work as domestic laborers in private homes as either live-in housekeepers or caregivers for the elderly, and often a mixture of the two. Research has shown that even well-educated migrants are unable to move out of these low-status and poorly paid work sectors and are almost entirely excluded from nonmanual jobs (Fullin and Reyneri 2011: 143). These circumstances reflect the structure of the Italian labor market, in which there are large labor shortages for jobs that native Italians will not do (144) but a shortage of higher status professional and managerial jobs (121). As a result, unemployment is high among young Italians because this increasingly educated group are not willing to do manual labor yet are unable to secure higher-status positions. Although young Italians are able to live with their parents and hope for improved job opportunities to arise, migrants are usually forced to accept and remain in these low-status jobs.[1] Immigration law, which ties legal status to employment, effectively traps migrants in these positions.

These dynamics explain why migrant unemployment remains low despite overall high unemployment in Italy (Fullin and Reyneri 2011). For the community brokers discussed here, becoming an immigration consultant is a means through to which to carve out a different employment trajectory. For example, by translating documents, interpreting at offices, and filling out basic applications, Mehdi, the Moroccan community broker and volunteer at the center, was able to eke out a basic living for himself and avoid employment as a fruit picker or other similarly poorly paid wage labor.

Immigration law is intrinsic to migrants' restriction to low-status and low-paid work sectors. Obtaining legal status requires presenting a regular work contract, and permits must be renewed every two years, thus ensuring that migrants stay in these poorly paid and low-status jobs or risk losing legal status. The long-term permit and citizenship offer possibilities for secure legal status, but both are notoriously difficult to obtain, and it is not uncommon for long-term migrants or even those born in the country to lose legal status. During my fieldwork I met several young adults who had arrived in Italy as infants but at the age of eighteen had fallen into "illegality," when they were no longer able to renew their permits as dependents of their parents. Without being in school full-time or holding a job contract, these young people who had grown up in the country had lost their right to live there. Calavita (2005a: 45) has described this as the "institutionalization of illegality," whereby legal status is precarious and "doled out in small increments" making "stints of illegality" inevitable. This institutionalization of illegality and precarity highlights the role of immigration law in sustaining migrants' vulnerability and tractability as workers (De Genova 2002: 439). As in other contexts, therefore, Italian immigration laws contribute to the overall marginal and subordinate position that migrants occupy in Italian society.

Like the top-down policies, the everyday workings of the immigration bureaucracy also produce uncertainty and indeterminacy in the lives of migrants and elevate the perceived need and desire for advice services. First, Italian immigration policies are set at the national level, but their implementation varies across space and time, making the immigration system confusing and unpredictable to navigate. Although technically the law is the same in all geographic areas, practice varies according to the city's *questura*. For example, the *questura* of one city may enforce the policy requiring applicants for the long-term permit to reside in accommodation of a particular size, but a neighboring city *questura* might not. Such small but important details mean that it is essential to receive well-informed advice when preparing and submitting applications.

Second, immigration policies are easily manipulated. This is relevant to the minutiae of applications as well as to entire policies. For example, migrants may falsify their self-certified declarations of domicile if for some reason the accommodations would not be acceptable to the authorities (such as when an applicant's place of residence is overcrowded). The 2009 amnesty for undocumented domestic workers is a good example (as discussed in Chapter 2). But in order to take advantage of such policies, applicants require advice, assistance, and sometimes contacts in order to complete the relevant paperwork.

A third characteristic of the Italian documentation regime that generates the need and desire for expertise and advice is the understanding that anything can be achieved if one has access to the correct resources and assistance. This notion that, in the words of one interlocutor, "the impossible is possible," feeds the demand for expertise and advice.

Fourth, and finally, the vast amount of paperwork documenting the minute details of applicants' lives, which is required for any application, intimidates most individuals into seeking out assistance. Most or all of this paperwork can be completed and prepared by the applicants themselves. The highly technocratic language of Italian bureaucracy, however, means that even literate and educated migrants seek the help of some kind of immigration expert.

The advice scene

Reflecting immigrants' need for assistance in navigating the documentation regime, there was a host of other immigration advice outfits across the city. These

Figure 11. Photograph of a shop that offers services to migrants related to their immigration applications. Photograph by author.

varied from costly lawyers situated in smart chambers to Pakistani-run internet cafés where, for 10 euros, a permit renewal application could be completed on the spot. The services they offered included general information about the requisites needed in order to complete applications and form-filling services.

Different organizations attracted different clients. HomeHelp, for example, was a co-operative that specialized in domestic work contracts for private employers. With an ever-growing elderly population and limited state provisions for care of the elderly, the employment of cheap live-in caregivers who usually also act as cleaners is very common. Officially, HomeHelp does not provide immigration advice–related services, but given the dominance of female migrants in the domestic work sector, as well as the need for legal status in order to work, specializing in work contracts *and* permit renewal was smart business for the co-operative. The clientele of HomeHelp, therefore, largely consisted of female domestic workers and their Italian employers. In contrast, the internet cafés that operated as immigration form-filling businesses on the side were used exclusively by migrants. The on-the-spot service that such establishments offered was particularly popular if an individual's permit was close to expiring and there was no time to wait for an appointment elsewhere.

Anyone can give immigration advice or complete applications; there is no special training or certification required. As a result, many people and organizations do so, and the quality of advice and services varies greatly.

Community brokers

Early in my fieldwork I conducted participant observation at the *questura*, joining the large numbers of people who arrived there early in the morning to submit applications and collect permits, or in a fruitless attempt to get information about their already submitted applications. After several days of observation I began to recognize the faces of individuals I had also seen at the advice center and other sites within the documentation regime. Dressed smartly and holding briefcases, these were self-styled immigration "experts" who acted as documentation brokers in their communities. They spoke good Italian and understood the basics of immigration law. Most of their clients were members of their own community with less cultural capital and weaker language skills. When I began fieldwork at the advice center I learned more about these self-styled brokers in the local context, several of whom volunteered there.

The services that these brokers provided were similar to those offered by the migrant advice center and other organizations, but also extended beyond what was available in more formal outlets. Mustapha and Naveed were two smartly dressed volunteers from Morocco and Pakistan respectively. At the center, volunteers worked exclusively at the reception counter. Mustapha, however, held an almost permanent position at one of the desks in the back office where he made phone calls and received people who asked for him. His clientele were exclusively Arabic-speaking, and he completed application forms for permit renewal, family reunification, and other applications on their behalf. He also offered more illicit services, such as helping clients to procure a *contratto di soggiorno* in order to renew a permit. During the process of permit renewal it is common practice for individuals to procure "false" work contracts. In these cases one individual would act as the "employer" for another. Whether or not one pays for this service depends on the relationship between the purported "employer" and "employee." Individuals such as

Mustapha act as a broker when the "employee" does not personally know somebody who could act as an "employer." In such cases there would certainly be a fee, from which the broker would take a cut. Although completing application forms for individuals without an appointment, providing information on immigration law, and offering general assistance with translation were acceptable tasks for volunteers at the center, brokering work contracts in exchange for financial remuneration was not.

Unlike Mustapha, Naveed usually worked at the reception counter, alongside the other volunteers, giving out information about requisites for applications, booking appointments, and checking the status of submitted applications online. He helped clients of all nationalities but was well known to those in the Pakistani community, who asked for him by name or as the "*ragazzo Pakistano*" (Pakistani guy) when they visited the center. He also took a particular interest in citizenship applications and helped Ginetta complete and submit clients' applications. Naveed told me that he had once been fairly affluent in Italy, but eighteen months earlier the metalwork factory where he worked had laid off many of its staff and he had since struggled to find another job. He was living off his unemployment compensation (*cassa integrazione*), as well as doing some translation work for the *tribunale* (courthouse), and he spent most days at the advice center. His current quality of life, he told me, was "not good." Reduced to receiving unemployment pay, he was now sharing a bedroom, whereas previously he had rented a private room in a shared apartment. The fact that he was receiving unemployment compensation confirmed his story; the unemployment benefit is fairly uncommon among migrants, who are usually on more precarious work contracts with fewer benefits (Pastore and Villosio 2011: 14).

As well as volunteering at the advice center, Naveed attended courses at the *centro del impiego* (job center), reflecting his active desire to improve his employment credentials. Like Mustapha, Naveed also completed permit renewal and other applications for a fee. Unlike Mustapha, however, Naveed did not use the center and its services as an outpost for his own immigration business or to recruit clients. Instead, in his spare time he offered form-filling services mainly to members of the Pakistani community who did not want to wait for an appointment at the center or, for some other reason, found it more convenient to pay Naveed 10 euros for an on-the-spot permit renewal application.

Once it was discovered that Naveed and Mustapha were exchanging advice on immigration-related matters for financial remuneration, both were asked to leave the center. Since the center in its official role as a *patronato* already received money from the state for the completion of applications, any payment for services was forbidden. When clients did want to make individual payments to the adviser that helped them—which they often did with a mixture of gratitude and an idea that it would help their application—they were told that they could make a donation to the trade union. Given this, the private payments Mustapha received for completing applications clearly contravened his role as a volunteer. He was using the center as an outpost for his own immigration business and charging clients for services that should have been free.

Naveed's case, however, is more complex and raises issues of who is expected to volunteer and who should be paid. He frequently hinted that he felt exploited in his role as a volunteer, essentially doing unpaid work while others were remunerated. On one occasion, he told me, "Staff members are so rude to volunteers, but there is no difference between what they [staff members] do and what I do." In the same conversation he insinuated that he had hoped to be employed at the center but had since given up on that idea. While staff members interpreted his behavior at the center as underhanded, Naveed seemed to have concluded that, since he could not find remunerative work at the center, he would use his time as a volunteer productively to acquire knowledge that he could use elsewhere. He did not charge people at the center itself, but was prepared to charge people for services outside of it, reasoning that had he not done so they would have paid someone else. More broadly, he saw his actions as justified in a milieu in which everybody seemed to be making money.

Similarly fed up with feeling unappreciated was Mehdi, another Moroccan volunteer who was in his early fifties. Mehdi, a university graduate, lived a somewhat nomadic lifestyle. He had lived in France not long before I met him in Italy and described himself as a "citizen of the world." He had an eccentric personality, at times becoming furious with clients if he felt they were rude while other times being gentle and affectionate. He was politically minded with an empathetic sensibility and a strong sense of social responsibility. For example, when the new head of the center attempted to restrict its services to trade union members only, Mehdi passionately resisted. He repeatedly exclaimed to me, "We need to help people, Anna. We are here to help." He was highly disapproving of Mustapha and others like him. In fact, it was pressure from Mehdi that pushed the center's head to eventually expel Mustapha. He frequently brought clients whom he identified as particularly vulnerable, and who otherwise might have remained under the radar, to the attention of Alberto. This was so in the case of Stephanie, a Nigerian woman, whose child had been taken away by social services, and Sami, a Bangladeshi man, struggling with bureaucratic arrangements after his baby was stillborn.

During my fieldwork, Mehdi was a regular presence at the center, except for a period of several weeks when he was employed by HomeHelp. Shortly after his employment there began, however, Mehdi resumed his volunteer work at the center, saying that he had resigned. He explained that he did not want to be part of an organization that charged for services that people could receive for free at the trade union–run advice center. His decision had economic consequences, reducing him to the slim pickings he gained from an informal certificate translation service and summer work as a fruit picker.

Throughout my fieldwork, Mehdi stuck to his principles in spite of his financial difficulties. He never charged for the advice he provided, other than for the translation of certificates. However, when I met him on returning to my fieldsite in November 2012, he had distanced himself from the center and was operating an informal immigration advice business himself. I learned of Mehdi's new venture when fellow volunteer Chiara and I ran into him in the city center. He was accompanied by a tall, disheveled-looking Moroccan man. As we walked together, Mehdi explained that he had been helping his companion, who was walking a couple of meters behind us. "*Poverino*" [poor thing], he has lost all his documents," he explained. Mehdi then proceeded to tell us that the man had paid him 150 euros for three days of help with replacing his permit, identity card, and the other lost documents. "We've been to the *carabinieri, comune, questura*, all over. He pays me 50 euros a day—and it has taken three days to sort everything out." Once we arrived in the center of town, Mehdi insisted on buying us coffees (in the past it would have been me or Chiara who paid) and went inside to order while Chiara and I sat down at an outside table. As we drank our coffees the conversation turned to the advice center. He told us:

> I never go there anymore. I am fed up with her [Maria—the new head of the center]. She keeps calling me, asking me to go back there to act as an interpreter, but I won't—she can learn Arabic herself. Comasco [the center's lawyer] is just as bad. He calls me in to translate, charges the client 500 euros, and what do I get? *Grazie!* [Thank you!] Well, my name isn't *Signore Grazie* [Mr. Thank You].

On our way home, I discussed his comments with Chiara. She was shocked that Mehdi, previously so opposed to charging people for assistance, was now doing so. "He has become like everybody else," Chiara said. "He is just exploiting other Moroccans who can't speak Italian. He is only providing a translation service. He's hardly an expert." In response I suggested that Mehdi was only filling a gap that someone else might have filled in his absence, and pointed to his financial need. Chiara found this rationale morally reprehensible. "If he needs money, he should go and work in a factory like everybody else [other migrants]. It is not an excuse!" In her eyes, community brokers who profited from navigating the complicated and time-consuming documentation regime were ultimately complicit in perpetuating migrants' structural marginalization.

It was certainly the case that Mehdi's decision to charge for interpreting was at odds with his previously espoused attitude. But something else was at play: the importance and due recognition of, and value attributed to, relevant skills. His rant about the new head of the center and the lawyer Comasco reflected his resentment about providing work voluntarily for which others were paid. Besides, Mehdi was not exactly contradicting his previous beliefs. The service he was now providing—accompanying a migrant from place to place and translating for him while helping to navigate the bureaucracy—was *not* available free at the center, or anywhere else.

Mehdi's statement that he was not *Signore Grazie* echoes arguments made about peer-educator programs in South Africa (James 2002; McNeill 2011). Those running HIV peer-educator schemes imagine the educators—a type of broker—to be inspired by community-minded sentiments. In practice, however, in a context of high unemployment, becoming a peer educator provides an opportunity for upward class mobility and other career options (James 2002; McNeill 2011: 150–151).

These cases highlight the way in which motivations to volunteer or to peer educate must be contextualized. The Italian migrant-advisers I worked with, in a similar vein, were seeking to improve their career opportunities, status, and material conditions in a context in which migrants are generally restricted to the lowliest work sectors. The fact that they charge for services is not evidence of amoral behavior, but rather an ethically informed critique of their own labor exploitation.

Self-fashioning through brokerage

Chiara's criticism of the activities of migrant advisers gives the impression that Mustapha, Naveed, and Mehdi were profiting at the expense of their clients. In some ways her position is reminiscent of Marxist analysts who understand brokers as amoral individualists who exploit the gap between the poor and the resources to which they need access for their own personal gain (James 2011: 320). In reality, however, the brokers' clients, most of whom were employed full-time with fairly secure incomes, were materially better off than the brokers themselves. The clients' salaries were low in comparison with national salaries, given the poorly paid jobs to which migrants are restricted in Italy; but in comparison with the community brokers, who were not formally employed, the clients were relatively financially secure. In fact these brokers, like many others in the Italian setting (both migrants and nonmigrants), were effectively employed in the informal labor market, which also put their legal status at risk (Reyneri 1998).

While some individuals choose to work "off the books" (sometimes entirely but frequently partially) to reduce the amount they owe in taxes, for migrants informal work carries risks since evidence of employment and salary are necessary for permit renewal. Those who do work informally, therefore, must produce false documentation of their work and salary in order to renew their permits. Mehdi, for example, was in a difficult situation when he needed to renew his permit. He had come to Italy as the "husband" of a Moroccan woman already resident in Italy, whom he described as a "dear friend." When this woman passed away, Mehdi needed to renew his permit on the basis of work rather than family, meaning he needed to provide documentation that he had a contract and a salary. As he did not have either of these, a friend from the trade union helped him by "employing" him as a domestic worker. These brokers were not, therefore, callous and greedy individuals motivated exclusively by financial gain. Rather, they too were in insecure positions, and providing immigration services was a way of resisting or avoiding the otherwise low-status work to which migrants are restricted, while also eking out a rather meager and precarious existence.

Despite her criticisms, Chiara too was carving out a higher-status identity for herself as an immigration expert. Her comments reflect part of her own ethical project of fighting for migrants' rights through solidarity, but they do not take into account the inequality within the hierarchy of brokerage in which she too was involved. Having lived in Italy for decades and holding Italian citizenship thanks to her Italian-Eritrean paternal grandfather, Chiara's situation was rather different from Mehdi's. Indeed, her fluent Italian, high-status job, secure legal status, and good connections meant it was significantly easier for her to be uncompromisingly motivated by the public good. Furthermore, while she strongly criticized those who profited from the documentation regime, she was engaged in processes of self-fashioning through her role as an immigration expert in a manner not totally different from the others.

Chiara's personal trajectory is unlike that of the other three community brokers discussed here. As noted in Chapter 1, she migrated to Italy from Eritrea when she was thirteen years old accompanied by her older brother and father, whose own father was an Italian national. She was schooled in Italy, growing up in the country in the 1980s at a time when there were very few migrants or nonwhite people in the country. She "feels" neither Italian nor Eritrean, while also identifying as both. Her younger brother, who migrated to Italy many years later, frequently teased her for the way she spoke her native Tigrinya, which had become a foreign tongue to her after many years of rarely speaking the language. Yet she also wrestled with her Italian identity, in large part because of the racialized discrimination that she has experienced throughout her life in access to work, housing, and everyday social encounters.

Chiara moved to the city where I met her in her twenties, and first worked as a dishwasher in restaurant kitchens. Some years after her arrival she came across the newly opened advice center, which at the time was a much smaller establishment run by the man who founded it and a small team of volunteers. She soon became a member of this first set of volunteers who, like her, held strong political views and were deeply motivated to improve migrants' rights in Italy. She has continued to volunteer at the center in some capacity ever since. Her occupational status has improved somewhat since her dishwashing days, and by the time of my fieldwork she was employed by the *comune*. Her employment trajectory contrasts with that of most migrants, having given her opportunities to work beyond the usual job sectors to which migrants are restricted. She explained that her employment at the *comune* owed much to her knowledge about and use of positive discrimination policies, which ensure that a certain quota of public servants are registered as disabled. Chiara has a registered disability that qualified her to be counted in such a quota. Such permanent public service jobs are highly coveted in Italy, and like other public servants Chiara benefited from the job security, good salary, and flexible hours that the position provides. Ultimately, however, she found her work boring and unsatisfying and spent much of her time dedicated to what she calls her "*casi sociali*" (social cases). Over the years spent as a public servant and volunteer at the center, Chiara has cultivated a huge network of contacts in various offices whom she calls on when assisting her *casi sociali*. She has contacts at the *questura*, *prefettura*, the *comune*, the trade union, and the center-left political party Partito Democratico. Her flirtatious and charismatic personality, sense of humor, and sharp intelligence make her contacts amenable to her various requests for favors and assistance.

Chiara came across many of her *casi sociali* while volunteering at the center, but she also assisted her neighbors and others she encountered in her daily life.

Her background made her in demand with the Eritrean community, among whom she was known as an immigration expert. But, like Mehdi, she was determined not to prioritize her co-nationals over others, and I assisted her in helping countless people from various backgrounds throughout my fieldwork. Depending upon the specificities of a client's problem, after listening to their account she would make a series of phone calls to her contacts to see if she could somehow resolve the issue. At other times she would visit the local *questura* in person, bringing trays of *pasticcini* (pastries) in order "to sweeten them up," she would say, while winking conspiratorially. While at the *questura* she would visit people she knew to get information about a case or to ask them to reconsider a decision. Her network of contacts was so wide that other staff members at the center often called on her to help them with their own clients.

Although Chiara was certainly motivated by her strong sense of social justice and desire to make the world a better place, she also visibly thrived in her role as charismatic broker, skillfully eliciting favors and promises from contacts in order to help her clients. In this sense, her behavior was not so different from that of those she condemned. Although she would never accept any financial reward for the work she did—even being bought a coffee made her feel compromised—the nature of the shifting, indeterminate, and unjust documentation regime enabled her to carve out a role for herself that gave her meaning, satisfaction, and high social standing. In addition, while Chiara's uncompromising critique of the others is partly due to her own suffering in the past, ultimately she had come to hold secure and prestigious employment of a kind that Mustapha, Naveed, and Mehdi could only dream about.

In differing ways, then, for each of these community brokers becoming an immigration expert was a means of creating possibilities that were usually not available to migrants in Italy. Mustapha was able to become a smartly dressed businessman and a point of reference in the Arabic-speaking community. Having been unsuccessful in securing a job at the center, Naveed nonetheless used his time there to learn the intricacies of Italian immigration law in order to develop his own mini-business during his period of unemployment. Mehdi, who struggled to hold down a normal work schedule, was able to make ends meet by offering assistance to individuals in navigating the bureaucracy. And Chiara was able to tolerate her boring job and fulfill her political desire to campaign for migrants' rights by dedicating much of her time to her *casi sociali*.

Although they differed in their knowledge and experience of immigration law, by learning the basics of Italy's immigration bureaucracy these individuals were able to carve out roles for themselves. In contrast to the usual accounts of immigration law and the manner in which it works to create vulnerable and de-portable subjectivities (Calavita 2005a; De Genova 2002; Gonzales and Chavez 2012), here immigration law has a different role. The shifting and opaque na-ture of the immigration bureaucracy was a means through which more expe-rienced migrants could fashion themselves as professional and authoritative experts—a role that, as a migrant in Italy, was otherwise almost impossible to develop.

Chiara may be correct in her assertion that Mehdi and others like him were ultimately profiting from the Kafkaesque documentation regime that created the need for an "expert's" assistance. But they were also challenging the condi-tions that migrants endure in the Italian context and were using their knowl-edge of the immigration bureaucracy as a way to refashion themselves and resist marginalization. If immigration bureaucracies function as mechanisms to ensure migrants' continual marginalized and insecure position in society (Calavita 2005a; De Genova 2002), then these brokers were turning the mecha-nism on its head, using the immigration bureaucracy as a tool with which to overcome such marginalization and create alternative life opportunities.

Conclusion

In increasingly bureaucratized immigration regimes migration brokers, who are experts in "the politics of micro-documentation" (Lindquist 2012: 88), are in high demand. In Italy, where becoming and staying a "documented" migrant involves the production of paper trails across state institutions, private com-panies, employers, trade unions, and landlords, individuals and organizations that offer assistance are indispensable in migrants' successful navigation of the immigration bureaucracy. In this chapter I have presented four community brokers who fill the gap produced by the documentation regime's simultane-ous creation of uncertainty and possibility. These brokers play key roles in both assisting migrants in their navigation of the regime and enabling the system to function, supporting the classical anthropological finding that "the formal order is always parasitic on informal processes" (Scott 1998: 310).

Exploring these four community brokers' trajectories, I have shown that their brokerage practices go beyond filling a gap in the market. Whether moti-vated by a desire to gain prestige or to fight for social justice, their activities are imbued with meaning and the pursuit of ethical value (Foucault 2003). These observations firmly dispel the common characterization of brokers—and in particular migration brokers—as corrupt or immoral. As Chiara's strong opin-ions make clear, and in line with anthropological work on brokerage, however, such community brokers are morally ambiguous. They help migrants navigate unfathomable bureaucracy, but at the same time enable the exclusionary and Kafkaesque immigration bureaucracy to function. They gain some prestige and social mobility through their fellow migrants' need of assistance, but are also often in more materially insecure positions than their clients.

The anthropological record has tended to define brokers as either exploitative profiteers or creative hustlers, but Deborah James (2011: 319) argues that we should instead understand the broker as both product and producer of the society in which she or he emerges. This assessment rings true here. As migrants, community brokers emerge from the marginalized political and economic contexts in which they are situated and are motivated by a desire for social mobility. By acting as brokers they are producing a critique of their own labor exploitation as well as carving out alternative possibilities for themselves. In this case, therefore, brokerage practices should be understood as ethically imbued acts in which knowledge of immigration law makes it possible for individuals to engage in projects of self-fashioning.

5 Disjuncture in the Documentation Regime
The Second Generation's Challenge to Citizenship Law

Extract from fieldnotes, July 2010

We've closed the advice center and are waiting outside while Alberto locks the door. Stepping into the hot summer's evening feels almost refreshing in comparison with the stuffy atmosphere inside. I unlock my bike and we walk slowly round the corner toward Bar Marco, our usual haunt for an after-work *aperitivo*. Alberto makes his obligatory stop at the *tabaccheria* to restock on Marlboro Lights while I wait outside chatting with Bilal. I have met Bilal several times since I started volunteering at the advice center. He now lives in Finland but regularly visits Italy to see his parents. He used to volunteer at the center and always comes by when he is in town. Tall with dark hair and eyes and olive-colored skin, Bilal's manner is jokey, flirtatious, and confident. He also speaks with a strong local accent. Chiara has already told me Bilal's story and explained why he now lives in Finland.

He arrived in Italy from Morocco as a child with his parents and two siblings. After reaching the age of eighteen, Bilal was unable to find a work contract and had no desire to carry on with his studies. Two years ago his permit expired and, lacking the necessary requirements to renew it as an adult, he fell into illegality. When his girlfriend invited him to move to Finland with her, Bilal decided he had had enough of living the life of an illegal migrant in Italy and joined her there.[1] As we wait outside the *tabaccheria*, he says to me, "No matter how culturally and socially integrated you feel here, no matter how much you love it, the bureaucracy always excludes you and makes you feel *straniero* [like a foreigner]."

Bilal and others like him live with the paradox of existing in, or risking, illegality in a country in which they have grown up. Bilal also embodies another paradox:

he is both Moroccan and Italian. In this chapter I analyze the way in which immigration and citizenship laws create disjunctures for such people and explore the dynamic tensions that shape experiences of migration, citizenship, and belonging in Italy. Profound contradictions exist, such that while migrants are made "other" and different through a political and media discourse fueled by anti-immigrant sentiment, they are simultaneously being created as "new" Italians. In the Italian context, understandings of citizenship and membership are highly racialized, and ethnicity and nationality are conflated. This conflation, which is rooted in a "biopolitics of otherness" (Fassin 2001), not only excludes the possibility of "genuine" citizenship for those who do not "look" Italian, but also assigns those who appear as "other" the status of a low-level worker with associations of criminality and poverty.

Yet despite this, and despite the marginal position that migrants have been structurally and socially assigned in Italy, second-generation migrants are actively challenging and helping to reshape ideas about insiders, outsiders, citizenship, and Italianness. Stories like Bilal's show that, through everyday sociality, second-generation migrants are contesting embedded categories of identity and nationality and, in doing so, are creating the potential for a lasting transformation of how migrants are perceived in Italy. I suggest, however, that Italy's bureaucratic treatment of immigration and citizenship remains out of sync with these "ground-level" shifts. The exclusionary bureaucratic system effectively blocks a gradual process of inclusion that might otherwise occur in Italian society. The disjuncture between the integrated lives that migrants build for themselves and the repeated hurdles that immigration and citizenship laws put in their way is at the heart of the lived experience of migration and exclusion that my interlocutors faced.

The 1.5 generation

Recent work on the so-called 1.5 generation—those who migrated as young children—has explored the way in which, on reaching the age of eighteen, those who are undocumented must learn to be illegal (Gonzales 2011). This literature explores the contradictions inherent in being an illegal migrant in the county where one has grown up and challenges ideas about citizenship and legality. On reaching legal adulthood those in this group experience trauma as they become illegal subjects overnight. Writing about the 1.5 generation in the United States, Roberto Gonzalez and Leo Chavez (2012: 267) describe how their interlocutors dreamed of futures that, given their upbringing, were in accordance with the values of the American Dream, but on turning eighteen realized they were different from their peers: no matter how hard they worked "they were to remain on the sidelines."

In a political climate in which the citizenship policies of migrant-receiving countries are becoming increasingly restrictive, the production of "illegal citizens"—those who have grown up in a country but hold no juridical right to stay there—is rapidly growing. With antiterrorism laws establishing the terrain, it has become increasingly common for young people who have grown up in Europe and North America to be sent back "home" following encounters with the police—often to a country to which they have no or few links (De Genova and Peutz 2010; Drotbohm 2011; Peutz 2006). The situations of these young people, who may have multiple senses of identity and belonging, contradict the passport and other documents that imply unambiguous identification with one singular place (Coutin 2003; Drotbohm 2011; Mandel 2008). In these situations the ambivalent and tense relationship between belonging and citizenship comes to the fore.

The situation of the 1.5 and second generations in Italy, which is characterized by precarious legal status and racialized ideas about citizenship, offers important comparative contributions to this subject (Andall 2002; Bianchi 2011; Colombo, Domaneschi, and Marchetti 2011; Colombo and Rebughini 2012; Riccio and Russo 2011; Zinn 2011). Specifically, my focus on everyday encounters with the bureaucracy of immigration law highlights the disjunctures at play when cultural insiders are made into structural outsiders. The current Italian citizenship law, passed in 1992, is based on the principle of *jus sanguinis*, the right to citizenship based on one's ancestry. For those newly arriving with no ancestral links, or even for those born in the country, naturalization is the only option.

To become a naturalized Italian citizen, among other bureaucratic requirements applicants must document ten years of continuous legal residence in Italy (five years for EU citizens). In Italy residency refers to one's place of address but is also an official bureaucratic status for citizens and noncitizens alike. Residency is distinct from legal status, and noncitizens are not obliged to hold residency: registered domicile is sufficient for the purpose of permit renewal, family reunification, and other applications. The official status of residency, however, is necessary for citizenship applications. The requirement of ten years of documented *continuous* residency (not just domicile) was a frequent stumbling block for long-term migrants who desired to submit citizenship applications. Loss of residency, caused, for example, by an eviction following a problem with one's landlord, means that applicants are required to rebuild ten years of documented residency. This is the case even if the period of absence is very short. Given these bureaucratic requirements, those I knew who did hold Italian citizenship had usually been living in Italy for much longer than the required ten years in order to have become eligible to apply.[2] Considering these difficulties in obtaining citizenship, it is unsurprising that the number of migrants who are naturalized as Italian citizens is lower than in other European countries (Bianchi 2011: 324)

Because the citizenship law favors Italian ancestry, attaining citizenship is a lengthy and difficult process for those who were merely born or grew up in Italy. Minors can obtain citizenship through their Italian parents, and anyone who is born in Italy can apply for citizenship within one year of their eighteenth birthday. The latter, however, is a bureaucratic procedure that is far from straightforward. If, for example, a child's parents fall into illegality after losing employment, the child is no longer eligible to apply for citizenship on turning eighteen. Instead, he or she is required to meet the same requirements as any adult migrant. In addition, if one who is born in Italy does not submit the citizenship application within a year of turning eighteen, the right to apply for citizenship is lost. After reaching eighteen, in theory, young people no longer have the right to a family permit and thus must either work or study full-time to avoid losing their legal status. Accordingly, many young people face legal precarity on reaching adulthood and certainly do not have the same possibilities as their peers with native parents.

As noted in previous chapters, although in the Italian context it is very easy to fall into illegality, regularization procedures are offered fairly frequently. It was common for migrants to fall into "illegality" and then regain "legality" at a later stage. As for migrants in general, so too for the 1.5 and second generations: I met several young people who had lost legal status at eighteen and then later regained it in a regularization procedure. Also, being an illegal migrant, or being issued a deportation order, did not necessarily preclude possibilities for attaining legal status in the future. The experiences of the 1.5 and second generations, therefore, demonstrate that definitions of legality and illegality are unstable and shifting categories.

Conflating ethnicity and nationality

Anthropological literature has explored the way in which racism has become increasingly conceptualized through notions of "cultural fundamentalism" (Stolcke 1995). This contemporary anti-immigrant rhetoric "emphasizes differences of cultural heritage and their incommensurability" (4), moving away from an emphasis on race and biology. Discourses and attitudes based on cultural fundamentalism were evident in the advice center, as well as in other everyday spaces such as bars, shops, and people's homes. At the center, some staff members engaged in discriminatory discourses based on cultural mores, such as food, breastfeeding, or religious practices. Mehdi's fiery behavior, for example, was often explained in relation to his "Muslim" cultural background which, according to some staff members, fostered "male aggression." In other spaces, such as shops and bars, people's conversations about migration regularly turned to the risk of losing local dialects or other cultural traditions. Migrants and their children were deemed to threaten and dilute local culture.

Racism was not only expressed, however, through discourses of incommensurable cultural differences: episodes of discrimination based on bodies, skin, and appearance were also at the heart of my interlocutors' experiences. As Bruno Riccio and Monica Russo (2011: 362) point out, the racialized divisions that exist in Italy are "not a matter of mere cultural racism; phenotypic characteristics have also become more and more relevant in fostering Italian internal boundaries." As a result, a "biopolitics of otherness" is produced in which skin color and supposed origin overwhelm the legal definition of the "other" (Fassin 2001: 6). Through the identification of complexion, skin color, dress, *tracce* (referring to facial features), language, and other indicators, migrants were automatically identified as *extracomunitario*, meaning non-Italian, immigrant, and noncitizen.

The assignment of this status is closely tied to exterior appearance and to the assumption that Italianness can be detected through a particular kind of racialized body. Flavia Stanley has argued that this is because in Italy ethnicity and nationality are conflated, meaning that anyone who is not considered to be Italian (or a tourist) is demarcated as *extracomunitario*:

> In a culturally pluralistic society, nationality can also have a similar connotation to "ethnicity," which exists entirely outside the issue of citizenship ... While the use of "ethnic" does reveal a person's deviation from the norm of whiteness in the United States, one who is ethnic is not necessarily assumed to be a noncitizen. The reverse seems to be true in the context of increasing immigration and the existence of more culturally diverse populations in Italy. (Stanley 2008: 55)

This is different from the processes of subjectification that migrants may undergo in other contexts. Taking poor Cambodians and rich Chinese immigrants as contrasting examples, Aihwa Ong (1996) shows that in the United

States "dominant ideologies clearly distinguish among various Asian nation-alities, assigning them closer to the white or the black pole of American citizenship (753), illustrating how "racial hierarchies and polarities continue to inform Western notions of cultural difference" (751). As poor welfare recipients, Cambodians are "blackened," while the Chinese immigrants' wealth has a "whitening" effect. Unlike traditional receiving countries, such as the United States and the United Kingdom, in Italy, where ethnicity and nationality are conflated, there is not a discourse that acknowledges the existence of Asian or black Italians as a cultural category. Rather, "being black and being Italian [are] perceived as mutually exclusive categories in Italy" (Andall 2002: 400). Given this, my respondents were not placed on a pole of Italian citizenship. Instead, through discourses of either criminalization or victimization they were constructed as poor, low-status, and other.

Being defined as other in such stereotypical and negative terms was a frequent cause for complaint by my respondents with migrant backgrounds, who experienced racism on a daily basis. They described with anger the way in which presumptions about their identity were made solely on the basis of their appearance. Al Badisi, an Italian citizen originally from Morocco, said:

> Just this morning I was at the post office in Rosetta [a small town north of the city]. I was filling in my *bolletta* [bill] and the woman working there was chatting away to two *carabinieri* who happened to be there. The *carabinieri* turned to leave, calling out to the woman that they were leaving but that they would pass by in a little bit. Then, I tell you, they turned their heads and looked pointedly in my direction. I know that they meant it in reference to me, I was the only person in there and they were trying to say I was a threat to the woman.

Biniam, also an Italian citizen, originally from Eritrea, told me: "When you get on a bus, people look at you suspiciously, as if you are going to rob their bag or something. Next time you're on the bus, look around. The immigrants are at the back and the Italians are at the front." In the case of women, assumptions about criminality were expanded to include presumptions about prostitution. Chiara asked me: "Do you know how many times men have pulled up in their cars on the side of the road while I'm waiting for the bus and asked 'How much?' In broad daylight!"

These statements echo the way in which *extracomunitari* are portrayed in the media according to racialized stereotypes. Al Badisi and Biniam were perceived to be "*maghrebini*" (Moroccan; from the Maghreb) and thus dangerous (though Biniam was Eritrean, he was constantly mistaken for a Moroccan), while Chiara, as a black woman, was equated with prostitution. Such discrimination against presumed *extracomunitari* also affected access to work and housing. Chiara described to me her long and depressing processes of searching for an apartment to rent. On meeting her, prospective landlords, who had been enthusiastic to rent to her over the phone, quickly made up excuses for why the property had suddenly become unavailable.

While it is fair to state that the term *extracomunitari* classifies migrants into an inferior and discriminated-against category, there are also subcategories based on nationality within this classification. Stereotypical discourses about particular nationalities included judgments about the temperament, ability to integrate, and type of employment the migrants were expected to hold. Sweeping generalizations were prominent in judgments made about clients in the day-to-day workings of the center. Bangladeshis were "*teste dure*" (hard-headed or slow), meaning they were to be pitied and ignored as they tried to sell you roses and various light-up plastic goods in bars; Ukrainian women were tough and difficult, but also made the perfect *badanti* (caregivers) for elderly Italians; Moldovan women were gentle domestic workers and, because of their reputation as well integrated and attractive, seemed appropriate for work in bars. Senegalese were good-natured and strong, with the men regarded as good workers in engineering factories; Indians were intelligent; Pakistanis were corrupt and misogynistic and were said to rip each other off through dubious loans used to set up grocery shops. The Chinese were hard-working and entrepreneurial; Moroccans were deviant and, along with Tunisians, considered likely to be drug dealers; Filipinos were sweet and unthreatening, with both men and women expected to work in the cleaning services.

Similar stereotypes prevailed in society at large. On my second day in the city my Italian flatmate, Paolo, who was sporting a faded red "I did not vote for Berlusconi" t-shirt, narrated to me the goings-on in the noisy little piazza below our apartment. The noise, Paolo informed me, was caused by the groups of people that hung out there, usually "*extracomunitari.*" Apparently, until recently, groups of Senegalese men had populated the *piazzetta* who, according to Paolo, were "big and jovial." They were "harmless to others," he told me, but they did end up "arguing and fighting with each other after drinking every day from noon." Currently, he informed me, eastern European men frequented the area, also drinking continuously: "They are problematic and can become very aggressive, especially the Polish men." However, none were worse than the Moroccans, who "cause more problems than the Tunisians or Algerians," he explained. This type of discourse was common in discussions about *immigrati* and came up frequently when I told people about my research project. These stereotypes tended to be similar across different people's narratives and were also reflected in—and possibly partly created by—the media (Mai 2002; Maritano 2002; Riccio 2002).

In this conflation of ethnicity and nationality, those who do not *look* Italian are not considered to *be* Italian. Furthermore, those deemed to originate from the global South or post-Soviet countries are singled out for special discrimination, and described in terms that identify them as inferior "others." In the next section I explore issues related to "authentic" and "inauthentic" citizenship, which arose when *extracomunitari* became Italian.

Authentic and inauthentic citizenship

Notwithstanding their actual citizenship status, in my fieldsite migrants were indiscriminately placed in the category of *extracomunitario*. The cultural category "black Italian" did not exist, but one could be an *extracomunitario* with citizenship. In this context Italian citizenship was stripped of any significance other than its formal legal meaning. Most of my newly Italian interlocutors— migrants who had acquired citizenship—considered citizenship to have no more significance than a piece of paper: they viewed it as akin to a *permesso* and as serving solely instrumental ends. Other studies of migrants in the Italian context make a similar observation (see Andall 2002; Bianchi 2011; Colombo, Domaneschi, and Marchetti 2011; Zinn 2011) .

All of my "new Italian" friends had accounts of times they had been stopped by the police either on the street or at some kind of security checkpoint. On such occasions the presentation of their Italian identity card had caused confusion and suspicion, and had elicited a demand to see a *permesso di soggiorno* (a document that an Italian citizen would not have). Once their citizenship status was eventually and grudgingly acknowledged, it was nonetheless considered "inauthentic" (Gilroy 2002: 50). Which is to say that, in the view of the officials, having an Italian passport did not mean that someone was "really" Italian.

These ideas about authentic and inauthentic citizenship were evident in the everyday workings of the advice center. Clients were asked if they had Italian citizenship rather than if they were Italian. When staff members or center users affirmed that they were Italian, it was voiced as a political statement rather than a neutral comment. Someone who claimed Italian citizenship in this way did so as if responding to a disbelieving official. Alternatively, the affirmation was made in a tongue-in-cheek tone; these neo-citizens were sardonically communicating that they knew they would never be considered really Italian, but were also simultaneously challenging this assumption.

Reflecting this attitude, my friends and colleagues Al Alami and Al Badisi did not take offense when Ginetta gently teased them about their ultimately inauthentic citizenship. In summer 2010 they both finally gained their Italian citizenship after five and four years of waiting, respectively. During that period there was lighthearted joking in the center when either one turned up. Ginetta called Al Alami, the first to obtain citizenship, Italo1, and Al Badisi Italo2. Ginetta's name-calling was received with ripples of laughter from Al Alami and Al Badisi, as well as the others in the center. Her comments made it clear that although Al Alami and Al Badisi were now officially Italian citizens, it was a joke to think that they could ever be really Italian.

The case of Rose and her lack of awareness of the rights that citizenship bestowed on her elucidates the understanding of citizenship as nothing more than a bureaucratic process—the final stage in the documentation regime. Rose, a Nigerian woman, came in to the center to ask if it would be possible to bring her sister to Italy through family reunification. She was initially told this was not possible before the staff member thought to ask if she had Italian citizenship. It turned out that she did, and therefore, on grounds of family reunification, her sister would be able to obtain a permit in Italy. Rose then asked if she could bring her mother and husband. "No problem," she was told. By this point the staff member had left, and she and I were speaking in English together. She was beaming and said, "I had no idea I could do all this. It's not bad, this Italian citizenship!"

Two points are highlighted by this encounter. First, despite the large number of clients who passed through the center who *were* Italian citizens, staff members often immediately assumed the clients were *extracomunitari*. And second, clients who were Italian citizens still self-identified as *extracomunitario* and were often not aware of the rights they had gained by obtaining citizenship. Rose's ignorance about her newly acquired rights revealed her attitude about her procurement of Italian citizenship. For her it was like the renewal of her last ever permit, a bureaucratic step that meant she no longer had to deal with the *questura*. She did not view her Italian citizenship as giving her the same rights as a "real" Italian. Similarly, people did not consider her to be Italian.

Others I knew understood their new citizenship in the same way, although their attitude was more critical. Indeed, the most common statement in conversations about obtaining Italian citizenship was: "It doesn't change anything, but it is good not having to queue at the *questura* anymore." When stating that it doesn't change anything, my interlocutors were referring to the fact that, despite their citizenship status, they were still treated like *extracomunitari*. Those who were particularly angry about the discrimination they experienced distanced themselves from their Italian citizenship, emphasizing that they did not "feel" Italian or did not want to be considered so. Those who were more critical felt disheartened that no matter how long they spent in Italy they would always be considered *extracomunitario*. As Chiara told me:

> Italians who know me will say "you're different, you're not a real immigrant," because I speak perfectly and "play the Italian." But, if they saw me on the bus, in an office, or on the street and did not know me, they would be just like everyone else. They would presume I am an *immigrata di merde* [immigrant of shit]. That is what Italians think when they see an *extracomunitario*.

People's acceptance of Chiara due to her "playing the Italian" with her accent, clothes, and manner, challenges these seemingly clear-cut assumptions about authenticity.

In this context, then, legal citizenship was not considered to confer equality or to be an instrument to create common sociality. Rather, there was authentic citizenship and inauthentic citizenship. The inauthentic citizenship of migrants was a legal document and nothing more. Although the new citizens were entitled to all the formal rights of citizenship, they were still considered *extracomunitari*: that is, poor, low-status noncitizens.

In recent decades, studies have critiqued T. H. Marshall's (1950: 15) influential definition of citizenship as a "status bestowed on those who are full members of the community," which includes civil, political, and social rights, as well as obligations. This analysis, however, obscures the fact that in reality citizenship is unequally experienced by members across society (Kymlicka and Norman 1994; Yuval-Davis 1991). Differentiating factors include age, gender, ethnicity, sexuality, class, and economic status. Of particular note, in a setting where market participation increasingly sets the tone for full membership in society, the capacity to accumulate wealth and to spend it is central. As Calavita (2005a: 159) has noted, since migrants' poverty is a key factor in their stigmatization and marginalization within Italian society, "consumer" may be a more appropriate term to denote inclusion in that society than "citizen." She writes: "To be a legitimate participant you must be, if not an actual consumer, at least perceived to be capable of consumption . . . It is because of the nature of immigrants' participation in the marketplace—as discounted labor—that they can never be full members of this community of consumption" (163). According to this logic, migrants face forms of exclusion similar to those faced by a large number of poor citizens (164).

The 1.5 and second generations, however, are challenging these logics that dismiss migrants as second-class citizens. With their regional Italian accents, fashionable clothes, and nonchalant attitudes, this young group is not as easily demarcated as *extracomunitario*. Instead, they look like consumers. After presenting two case studies that demonstrate the possible risks that current citizenship laws create for this group, I analyze the challenges that the 1.5 and second generations are posing to these outdated understandings of Italianness.

Performance and appearance

Migrants who speak Italian with a strong foreign accent seemed to be easily demarcated as inauthentically Italian. In contrast, those who come to Italy as children, or those born in the country to foreign parents, come to embody an Italian "habitus" (Mauss 1973) that disrupts ideas about authentic and inauthentic citizenship and Italianness. The literature on the second generation in Italy has explored the challenges of daily racism and difficult access to citizenship that this cohort of young people face (Andall 2002; Bianchi 2011; Riccio and Russo 2011). In particular, scholars have explored second-generation associations and this group's attempts to further their political agenda and challenge racist and discriminatory attitudes (Riccio and Russo 2011; Zinn 2011). This section examines similar themes, but instead of looking at political arenas in which the 1.5 and second generations challenge attitudes, it focuses on everyday encounters and the apparent disjunctures that they embody in the incongruity between their bodies and bodily performances.

Although these processes of "othering" imply a straightforward understanding of what makes an Italian "Italian," both the historically weak sense of nationhood and the lived reality of the 1.5 and second generations suggest that the notion of a clearly demarcated national identity is not as strong as it may seem. Ideas about Italianness are increasingly being challenged by the second generation, who effectively perform Italianness but may not look or be Italian. This uncertainty and curiosity about those who are considered non-Italians yet behave like Italians was evident in the advice center. Most staff members could be described as liberal and open-minded, yet they treated even long-term migrants who spoke perfect Italian in a patronizing manner as charming and novel subjects.

More surprising still was "foreigners" speaking with regional accents. The first time I met Tesfay, the leader of the Young Eritreans' Association, he was teased by Claudio, an Italian volunteer at the center. Claudio is from Lecce in Puglia (in southern Italy), and Tesfay grew up in Bari, which is Lecce's rival city. As Tesfay was leaving the center one day, he and Claudio well-meaningly heckled each other with partisan banter. After Tesfay had left, those at the reception counter said, "God, it is such a shock when he speaks. A Barese Eritrean!" Here Claudio and the others were referring to Tesfay's strong Barese accent. A black man speaking with a the southern regional accent was "matter out of place" (Douglas 1970: 36), and Tesfay's manner of speaking destabilized Claudio's and others' rigid understandings of identity.

The importance of regionalism in Claudio's comment was significant. As noted, because of Italy's regional character and late national unification, people often feel closer to their region than to the country as a whole. Thus for a migrant to identify with a particular region is a strong indicator of Italianness (see also Zinn 2011: 380). Italian natives' shocked reaction to apparent "outsiders" speaking in local accents is not unique to the Italian context, but two issues make such a reaction noteworthy. First, in Italy, notwithstanding class, everybody has an accent that betrays their regional background, and accents are common topics of conversation. To speak fluently in Italian is to speak with a regional accent (I was teased for, and also confused strangers with, the local accent I developed during my fieldwork). In addition, migrants' presence is fairly evenly distributed across Italy, meaning that there is not a particular Italian accent that would be deemed acceptable for a migrant to have.[3] And, second, because migrants are automatically assigned to the category of *extracomunitario*, being identified as non-Italian is to be identified as somehow inferior.

Not all migrants feel cowed by such assumptions and prejudices. As previously noted, my friend Chiara is an Eritrean by birth who has lived in Italy since she was thirteen years old. She is called Chiara Mariotti—thanks to her paternal grandfather's ancestry—and speaks perfect Italian, yet she has dark skin and long braided hair that reveal her Eritrean origins. Her gesticulations and ways of speaking, eating, and walking all demonstrate her embeddedness in an Italian "habitus," but in the Italian context her dark skin automatically makes her *extracomunitaria*. When she was younger she would run home crying after episodes of racism in which she was mistaken for a prostitute or heckled in the street. On other occasions she struggled to find a job and to secure a tenancy from a landlord. And at her workplace, she is frequently mistaken for the cleaner and asked to refill the toilet paper in the bathroom. "Black person equals cleaner," she commented wryly. In recent years, she told me, she has learned to deal with the prejudice in different and more empowering ways, mainly through humor and her strong sense of irony.

She recounted to me that while she cleaned the stairs of the building in which she lived, she allowed people to think that she was Signora Chiara Mariotti's *colf* (cleaner) and then reveled in their discomfort when she turned up at her building meetings as *the* Signora Chiara Mariotti: no one would match the Italian name with her dark skin. She laughingly told me about how, when she goes to public offices, officials often speak slowly to her, thinking that perhaps she does not understand Italian. I witnessed this myself when I accompanied her to offices to run errands: a moment's delay between when the official first saw her and then heard her speak was typically followed by a slightly bemused expression. She told me that she enjoyed this moment of tension when the official was left looking rather foolish.

Playing on prejudices, she questions and challenges people's views by embodying the contradiction of dressing, speaking, and behaving like an Italian while not looking like one. Chiara is fully aware that people are often surprised and perplexed by her "immigrant" looks and contrasting "Italian" behavior and language skills. Playing dialogically with the signifiers that are foisted upon her as a black woman in Italy, through irony and joking Chiara is able to mock prejudice and subtly challenge the discriminatory assumptions of those around her.

As early members of the 1.5 generation, Chiara and Tesfay embody what Paul Gilroy (2002: 69) terms "ideological contradictions." Like the black athletes Gilroy describes as challenging ideas of Britishness, Chiara's and Tesfay's embodied Italianness, expressed through language, dress, and body movements, seemed to contradict their black skin—and vice-versa. The contradictions that Chiara and Tesfay embody correspond to Stanley's (2008: 56) observation that "those seen as physically distinct from Italians, regardless of their performativity, also carry the assumption that they are not citizens of the Italian state." As has been argued, judgments about who is (or could be) Italian are based on a very limited notion of Italianness. Identity is expressed and practiced according to body politics, where difference from the physical "Italian look" immediately demarcates somebody as not Italian.

Stanley may be correct in her analysis of people's immediate judgments, but both Chiara and Tesfay unsettle these naturalized assumptions. Claudio's joking with Tesfay and Chiara's teasing of her neighbors reveal the discomfort and ideological contradictions that the tension between "body" and "body techniques" create. Gilroy's black athletes represented an ideological contradiction when he was writing; since then, the perception of blackness has changed significantly in contemporary Britain.[4] Accordingly, though there is not yet a mainstream discourse about the possibility of a hybrid Italian identity, ideas about Italian-ness, race, and belonging are perhaps—or perhaps are becoming—more open to disruption and subject to temporal change. Chiara and Tesfay are not easily made other, but rather cause uncomfortable and perplexed reactions through the ideological contradictions that they embody.

Despite the extent to which "body techniques" disrupt understandings of Italianness and being *extracomunitario*, the bureaucracy remains an exclusion-ary force that produces a disjuncture whereby an apparent insider is at risk of becoming a structural outsider. These processes of othering and structural marginalization need to be understood as working in tense and contradictory relationships with actual social relations, notwithstanding the lack of a dis-course on hybridity. This group complicates the division and hierarchy between "formal citizenship" and "substantive cultural identity that defines genuine membership" (Gilroy 2002: 50). In this way, documents, citizenship, appear-ance, body techniques, and habitus can work at diverse tangents to one another and must often be negotiated simultaneously by the migrants themselves.

"But I have an identity card": Italians without citizenship

In the last few days of my fieldwork, a seventeen-year-old named Lindita came in to the center for advice. Her citizenship was "almost ready," she said, but her *permesso* had expired. The *permesso* had expired over a year ago and thus was theoretically unrenewable. Since a valid permit is a requirement for concession of citizenship, this could have created serious problems. Lindita was born in Italy, and when she turned seventeen years old the *comune* had written to her, informing her of the possibility of applying for Italian citizenship within a year of her eighteenth birthday. Receiving such information from the *comune* was rare, and ignorance of the fact that one must apply within a year after turning eighteen leads to many young people losing out on the possibility of attaining Italian citizenship.

Fortunate to have received the letter, Lindita and her mother followed the instructions and completed the appropriate paperwork for the application. However, they were unaware that obtaining citizenship required one to have a valid permit at the moment of the *giuramento* (swearing of the oath). Lindita was very relaxed about the situation, and when I met her she seemed as though she had entered the advice center on a whim. On hearing about her situation, Alberto became concerned about her losing this possibility for citizenship.

Lindita, however, remained calm, saying, "It's fine, I have a *carta d'identità*" (identity card, which is a valid identity document for an Italian but useless for a noncitizen). Her ignorance about the details of the procedure revealed her liminal status. Although by law she was considered a migrant, she did not inhabit a "migrant world;" which might have bestowed her with the appropriate knowledge. Further, her calmness and certainty of the power of her identity card demonstrated that she felt she belonged in Italy.[5]

In a similar situation was Aurelie. Her father was well known in the center, having been back and forth in his efforts to sort out her permit. He had told staff in the center that Aurelie's permit had been "blocked" in the *questura* for two years, although his had already been issued. According to staff members this situation was strange, as children are dependent upon their parents: if Aurelie's father had the correct requirements to renew his permit, then hers should automatically have been renewed. Unable to fit all the pieces of the story together to create an understandable narrative, Alberto finally asked him to send his daughter to the center. A few days later, Aurelie came in. She stood out from many of the other people in the center. She was dressed in the manner typical of Italian teenagers, wearing tight jeans and brand new Converse sneakers. Her accent and fluency in Italian gave away her local upbringing. When she showed me an old photocopy of her father's permit, a ragged sheet of paper with a photo of her six-year-old self stapled on, I realized who she was and told her to wait while I went to find Alberto.[6] Since Alberto was going for his weekly meeting at the *questura* with the vice director the following Friday, he asked Aurelie for all her identity documents so that he could present her situation and find out what had happened. Accordingly, on Alberto's request, I photocopied Aurelie's documents. When I asked her for her identity card, she presented me with a flimsy paper document with the details written in French. "It is from the Ivory Coast's consulate," she informed me, as I quizzically turned it over in my hands. I told Alberto that she did not have the usual Italian identity card (to which all legal residents are entitled), and the reality of Aurelie's situation dawned on Alberto as he put together the pieces of the story. Alberto realized that there was no blocked application for renewal of a permit. Instead, Aurelie possessed no valid permit at the current time and had not possessed one for the three years since her father's renewal.

The problem lay in her father's lack of awareness about the need for children to acquire their own, independent, legal status. When Aurelie's father had renewed his permit, she had already turned fifteen, at which age, although still dependent upon her father, she ought to have applied for and been issued her own permit. But since she had never submitted an application, Aurelie had technically slipped into the limbo of illegality.

Passing Aurelie back her Ivory Coast embassy-issued identity card, Alberto asked, "So you haven't had a permit for three years?" She shrugged her shoulders with a curious look, apparently totally oblivious to the significance of, or unbothered by, this information. As I chatted with her later she told me that she had arrived in Italy when she was six months old: "I was practically born here," she said. Later that evening I saw her with a group of young people, giggling on the arm of her boyfriend. She may have been technically undocumented, but like Lindita she did not seem to feel disenfranchised or concerned; her sense of belonging in Italy overrode the technicalities of her legal status. Both girls' reaction to the news that they were illegal and at risk of being denied citizenship was met with a kind of casual bemusement. For these young women the world of immigration bureaucracy was one from which they felt disconnected, and one that was completely out of sync with their sense of belonging. Chiara often said that the 1.5 and second generations were in some ways the most vulnerable group in immigration politics (see also Riccio and Russo 2011: 363). It was precisely because of their cultural capital and embodied sense of integration that many young people, out of sheer ignorance—theirs and their parents'—risked their legal status.

The second generation were not all strangers to the immigration bureaucracy. In fact it was common for children to accompany their parents or other members of their communities to the advice center to act as interpreters. Notwithstanding their familiarity with the immigration bureaucracy, however, for those without citizenship the contradiction between holding precarious legal status in the country where they had grown up and citizenship in their parents' land was common to all. Lindita's and Aurelie's rather indifferent reactions to the news of their precarious legal status differs from that reported in research conducted in the United States, which emphasizes the second generation's feelings of abjection on realizing their illegal status (Gonzales and Chavez 2012). Instead, the young women seemed to hold what Jacqueline Andall (2002) has called a "second-generation attitude." Perhaps over time Lindita and Aurelie would also feel like they had "awoken to a nightmare" (Gonzalez and Chavez 2012). For the moment, however, their seemingly nonchalant attitudes highlighted the contradiction that immigration and citizenship laws pose for the 1.5 and second generations: being socialized by their host country through their education and environment while simultaneously holding the status of undocumented migrant (Gonzales and Chavez 2012).

Like migrants in other settings, Lindita and Aurelie challenge our assumptions about who an undocumented migrant is. Their experiences offer insights into the disjuncture that exists when state practices simultaneously produce the same individual as both "cultural citizen" and undocumented migrant. These young people are culturally socialized as Italians or Americans but as adults become subject to the same laws that tactically produce a vulnerable and tractable work force (De Genova 2002).

Individuals such as Lindita, Aurelie, Chiara, and Tesfay undoubtedly challenge ideological assumptions concerning race, belonging, and citizenship. Moreover, as a growing body of literature on second-generation associations has explored, the 1.5 and second generations in Italy are becoming politically active and demanding more nuanced recognition of Italianness and citizenship (Riccio and Russo 2011; Zinn 2011). Despite these changes, however, the structural obstacles that exclusionary immigration and citizenship laws create entrench the marginalization of migrants and their children, fundamentally limiting possibilities for change. Exclusionary citizenship laws, economic marginalization, low-level work opportunities, and racial stigmatization interact to produce and reproduce migrants as inferior and other. As Calavita (2005a: 165) notes, "With this powerful economics of alterité, and the legal infrastructure that supports it," integration policies and initiatives demanding equal recognition face considerable challenges.

Conclusion

This chapter has explored the tensions in the pervasive discourse of othering in Italy. This discourse has set up a powerful division between Italians and *extracomunitari* that has been understood in a particular social and historical setting. The result of this othering, together with exclusionary immigration and citizenship laws, is the conflation of ethnicity, nationality, and citizenship (Stanley 2008). Those who do not *look* Italian are not considered to *be* Italian. In line with Fassin's (2001) discussion of biopolitics, racialized discourses based on skin color and appearance are used to dichotomously characterize non-Italians as either tourists or *extracomunitari*. Being identified as *extracomunitaro* is to be made into a low-status worker other with associations of criminality and poverty. However, examining the situation of the 1.5 and second generations shows how unstable and contestable these racialized assignments are.

Inflammatory media reports that emphasize entry and flows of immigrants have dominated the political discourse on migration in Italy, making immigration appear to be in a permanent state of emergency (Cole and Saitta 2011: 528). In spite of this, and the structural marginalization that migrants and their children are subject to, however, the 1.5 and second generations are challenging ideas of insiders, outsiders, and citizenship in everyday encounters simply by being. Yet those who challenge still remain potentially structurally and legally marginalized because immigration and citizenship regimes are out of sync with everyday social contexts and encounters. The exclusionary bureaucracy, as well as the lack of an alternative political discourse about migration and hybridity, blocks any real change that could occur over time in Italy.

These young migrants have cultural capital but do not necessarily have the legal right to remain in the country. Worse still, they run the risk of being permanently excluded from citizenship if they fail to closely attend to their legal status. Although being a legal citizen would not necessarily diminish the racism or processes of othering they experience, it could encourage changes in society over time so that, for example, being black and Italian need no longer be considered mutually exclusive categories (Riccio and Russo 2011: 370). This analysis challenges and contributes to our understanding of citizenship and the ways in which inclusion in a society is multifaceted, precarious, and temporal. What it means to be a citizen exists in law and on paper, and also in everyday encounters that create new and unexpected meanings.

Possibilities for change in Italy lie with the 1.5 and second generations, whose situations are profound evidence of the injustices that the Bossi-Fini law creates. While Italians were sometimes shocked or bemused by the existence of black or Chinese Italians—those who through their dress, speech, and gesticulations embodied Italianness yet did not look Italian—they were equally shocked to realize that many of these young people were in fact at risk of becoming undocumented migrants. While immigration laws successfully naturalize migrants' otherness, making their social, legal, and economic marginalization seem acceptable (Calavita 2005a; De Genova 2002), when those who appear less other—such as the 1.5 and second generations—are also subject to such processes, these injustices are brought into sharp focus.

Such laws create injustices not only for the 1.5 and second generations, but also for those who may be considered other but are also human. This reality is pertinent not only to Italy but also in different host settings, where members of the second generation are deported back to their "home" nation-states, parents are unable to legally enter the country where their children have citizenship, and husbands and wives struggle to live within the same borders. Examining the 1.5 and second generations' everyday experiences of the documentation regime underscores the profound difficulties, contradictions, and injustices that immigration law creates in the lives of *all* migrants.

6 Stepping-Stone Destinations
Migration and Disappointment

Extract from fieldnotes, April 2011—"The Arab Spring"

The center has plummeted into chaos in the past couple of weeks. Fresh crowds of young Tunisian men arrive daily from Lampedusa. Their deeply tanned faces, sports caps, designer t-shirts, and sneakers make them easily identifiable. Every evening the news channels screen the island's daily events, depicting crowds of young men exiting boats and hanging around languidly. Cameras focus on individuals being interviewed. "Let us leave the island," they demand. "We're treated like dogs here! Let us go. I don't even want to stay here. I want to go France where my family are."

Politicians and the media treat the arrival of these thousands of mainly young men as akin to a natural disaster, something completely out of the state's control. Their arrival has sparked bedlam as Berlusconi's government grapples with what action to take while attempting to communicate to the rest of the world that this is not only Italy's problem. The news channels report that Berlusconi, in an act of solidarity, has offered tax cuts to all Lampedusa islanders and has bought a mansion on the island. Meanwhile Roberto Maroni, the interior minister, has passed a law giving all those who arrived between January 1, 2011, and April 5, 2011, a temporary permit. Once identified and documented, the young Tunisians gladly leave the island, seeking out friends and relatives in Italy and beyond.

Through word of mouth, those who have arrived in my fieldsite city quickly discover the advice center, which is inundated with queries about how to acquire the temporary permit. Chaos ensues because the rules and regulations for obtaining emergency permits are unclear. The holders of these permits are not entitled to work, and there are few housing options or other forms of assistance available to them. "Well we'll just have to go and steal then," these young men respond provocatively when told that these permits do not allow them to work. "We need to eat," they say. Most of them intend to leave Italy. France is the most popular planned destination, since many have friends or relatives there. The Tunisians' desire to leave Italy is welcomed by the Italian government, and the newly invented temporary permits allow them to travel within the Schengen Area. France, however, does not view these migrants as its problem, and on April 17 Nicolas Sarkozy, the French president, stalls the progress of trains arriving from Ventimiglia on the Italian-French border. In response, the Italian foreign minister angrily announces that Sarkozy's action is "illegitimate and in clear violation of general European principles."

This chapter centers on migrants' oft-stated desire to leave Italy. It was a commonly held view that Italy was inferior to other northern and western European countries, which were perceived as being better organized and less racist, as well as providing improved employment opportunities. After arriving in their European destinations, migrants are usually depicted as remaining in them (unless they are removed against their will through deportation). An analysis of desired or actual migration onward, however, reveals that migrants' trajectories continue to be mobile. Freedom-of-movement acts, changing labor markets, and diasporic networks of communication add to migrants' mobility as destination countries shift and change. Imagining better opportunities elsewhere shapes migrants' experience of life in Italy and highlights the differences and inequalities between host countries.

The disappointment of those who aspire to migrate but ultimately never leave their homelands has been extensively discussed in the anthropological literature on migration (Carling 2002; Gaibazzi 2014; Jansen 2009; Vigh 2009). In this examination of migrant experiences in Italy, I focus on those who *have* migrated but who still feel as though they have failed owing to their lack of onward mobility. My aim is to show that this sense of disappointment is largely due to the limited opportunities that Italy offers migrants for upward mobility (Fullin and Reyneri 2011; Reyneri and Fullin 2011; Reyneri 2004b). In large part these limitations stem from the racialized discrimination discussed in Chapter 5 and a deep concern that, despite having grown up in the country, their children would also face limited opportunities due to their migrant status. These limitations are also related to an imaginary migration trajectory in which moving on from Italy is thought to be the only way to success.

A sufficient number of rumors and accounts of "successful" migrants who have managed to take advantage of Italy's relatively flexible permit system, and the possibilities offered by the Schengen Area, circulate in order to create a sense that onward migration is possible if only one has the wherewithal to do it. These narratives and imaginations of on-migration play an important role in shaping the understanding of life trajectories for those who remain. Drawing on Ong (1999), I label those who did manage to migrate onward from Italy as "flexible citizens." This theorization underscores several key points that I develop throughout the chapter. First, it demonstrates the embeddedness of nonelite migration projects within contemporary logics of capitalism. Second, it underlines how this logic, which places success and failure on the shoulders of individuals rather than on broader structures and migration policies, infuses the experience of migration. And last, it shows how this logic prioritizes the process of migration as the only route to life improvement, thereby eclipsing alternative avenues for social betterment that migrants might otherwise pursue.

Studies conducted in places with high levels of emigration show that understandings and imaginations of "home" and "away" are structured by unequal global power relationships in which material success and personal development are thought to be achievable only through migration (Bal 2013; Gaibazzi 2014; Gardner 1993; Gardner 2008; Vigh 2009). The disappointment and sense of personal failure among those who have already migrated illuminate the "hierarchies of globalization" (Carling 2002: 37) that mean most are incorporated into a globalizing world market but not everybody is able to benefit from it (Bal and Roos Willems 2014: 255). Although studies have usually focused on those who are excluded from the migration process, it is also those who have left their homelands but still feel "unsuccessful" that experience this differentiated inclusion in the global market.

There is no future here

Most of the migrants I knew who remained in Italy felt a lingering sense of failure and disappointment. Analogous to the motivations that spurred their initial migration, the desire to leave Italy was commonly framed in terms of trying to create a better future. Explaining why they did not want to remain, people described the racial discrimination they faced in Italy, as well as the associated lack of higher-status job opportunities and the concern that their children would also face discrimination. This interweaving of economic, legal, and social marginalization with limited possibilities for upward mobility for migrants or their children shape and fuel their desire to leave Italy and produce it as an inferior country in migrant imaginaries.

Such disappointment with the migration project is not unique to migrants in Italy. The literature on migration frequently emphasizes migrants' disappointment on arriving in their host destination countries (Gardner 2002; Mahler 1995; Vigh 2009). Disappointment is often related to the economic realities of low-paid jobs and expensive living costs—the realization that the streets are not paved with gold (Mahler 1995: 92). Thus, while feelings of disappointment are not unique to Italy's migrants, in the Italian case migrants' disappointment was dialogically related to the perception that there were greater, if still limited, possibilities for success elsewhere.

Khalid, a Tunisian man who frequently visited the center, told me that he desired to migrate to France. Currently he lived in Italy with his wife and two Italian-born children, but before his marriage he had lived in France for a year and a half. One morning in the center while waiting for his appointment, he described to me his belief that in France migrants do not confront the same barriers and difficulties they face in Italy—difficulties that he believed were purposefully propagated by Berlusconi's government's politics. He told me that in France the process of obtaining documents was a simple bureaucratic procedure—"They don't try and make life difficult, you know?"—while in Italy it felt like a struggle through a maze of documents for which the migrant was personally responsible.

After a bogus marriage with a French woman fell through, Khalid was forced to return to Italy, where he still had a valid permit. After returning, he applied for his wife to join him through family reunification, and later his two children were born. He said that in Italy his main concern was that he could not envision a future and was worried for his children who would grow up in a country where they had no citizenship and faced daily prejudice. I asked him if he intended to return to France, to which he responded that he would like to, as would his wife, who constantly laments that there is no real life in Italy. Given his financial situation, however, he could not see how he would be able to. "She's the one I am sorry for," he said, pointing to his seven-year-old daughter.

It is concern for their children's future that migrants cited as one of the central reasons to leave Italy. As Jeffrey Cole and Pietro Saitta (2011: 528) observe in a poignantly titled afterword, "Italy, Dreams of a Monochrome Society?," the "master narrative emerging from opinion polls, political rhetoric and government policy and practice, is that Italy remains a white, Catholic nation rooted in Italian soil." This narrative, they write, is contradicted by the fact that a large number of migrants who now live in Italy make significant contributions to society. Most of all, it denies the emergence of a new Italian—"the youth of foreign origins" (528).

Within this context, parents were deeply concerned that, despite their hard work and sacrifice, their children would grow up as second-class citizens. The chance of being professionally successful in the country seemed to feel unrealistic even for migrants born and bred in Italy. Concerned for his baby daughter, Livia, Biniam frequently half-joked about sending her to the U.K. for university. "There is no future here," he would say seriously. Further shaping this sense of dissatisfaction was the notion that there were improved possibilities elsewhere. This belief was closely related to the fact that some people *did* manage to move on from Italy—either temporarily or permanently—which compounded the sense of personal failure and disappointment for those who were unable to.

Migrants developed these imagined lives in other countries through electronic media and contact with family and friends. When referring to life in other European countries people would exclaim, "Black people are doctors and lawyers!," or "There are shops where you can buy all the Eritrean ingredients," or "Your permit gets sent to you in the post." They contrasted such positive images of accepting, cosmopolitan, and efficient countries with Italy, which they viewed as discriminatory, inefficient, and backward. The conditions that pushed migrants into marginalized positions in Italian society, and created them as the subaltern other, led to their disparagement of the country for its perceived lack of cosmopolitanism, multiculturalism, and development. Although these opinions had a defensive use, they also fueled migrants' sense of failure: many ultimately blamed themselves for their lack of mobility.

Italy as a stepping stone

The disappointment and sense of personal failure among those who remained was compounded by the continuously circulating stories and rumors of those who had managed to migrate onward. Although most encounters with the Italian immigration bureaucracy are characterized by uncertainty, arbitrariness, and delay, its ambiguous nature also creates scope for flexibility and manipulation. In the stories that follow, Italy was often represented as a kind of "soft option," as migrants took advantage of the country's relatively flexible permit system in order to scope out opportunities in other European countries (Schuster 2005). With the freedom to cross borders enabled by the Schengen Agreement, migrants could use Italy as a place to acquire and renew permits while working elsewhere and eventually permanently migrating onward. Migrants were also aware of the benefits offered by particular host countries. They favored Scandinavian states because of their reputation for strong social welfare systems and high levels of employment. On the other hand, decisions about where to on-migrate were also determined and constrained by diplomatic and legal frameworks. Thus social imaginations (Appadurai 1996) about migration destinations were shaped by, and constructed on, the basis of stories, rumors, and experiences, as well as pragmatic knowledge about laws.

For those who did manage to migrate onward, their individual stories varied significantly. Some on-migrated almost immediately after arriving in Italy, as part of a prearranged plan. Others did so years later, sometimes even after acquiring Italian citizenship. Still others left Italy several times before finally moving back to Italy and settling there. The differences in people's trajectories depended on various factors, such as their "home" country, whether they had family members or contacts in Italy or elsewhere, or the location for which they had managed to procure visas. On the other hand, there were many migrants who may have desired to on-migrate at some point in the past but who had since established themselves in Italy and no longer wished to uproot.

Cases of successful on-migration were not uncommon, but they also held a mythic quality. People who had done so were frequently the subject of conversation at the center. They were good fodder for gossip, but they also held a practical function for clients who wanted to know how they could emulate aspects of a particular case they had heard about. These stories circulated within communities at social occasions, as well as between communities in workplaces and at sites within the documentation regime where people were forced to wait around for appointments. Their circulation shaped imaginaries about future possibilities and provided practical guidance. The following cases illustrate two different types of on-migration trajectories. The first case study involved members of the Eritrean community who migrated onward from Italy. The second focuses on another typical trajectory: migrants' use of Italy as a legal stopping base while traveling to other European countries in search of better employment opportunities.

Through my close connection with Biniam and Chiara, I came to know many members of the Eritrean community. Conversation and gossip over coffees, as well as during meals at people's houses and at Eritrean bars, frequently revolved around the migration trajectories of community members. Through my exposure to these stories of Eritreans' on-migration two impressions stood out. First, Eritreans were more likely than other groups to successfully migrate onward from Italy. Second, and relatedly, because on-migration stories (both successful and unsuccessful) were so common, their importance in shaping people's imaginaries of future migration trajectories, or their lack of mobility, was apparent.

Given the allegations of human rights abuses against Eritrea's president, which include denying his citizens human and democratic rights, forbidding freedom of speech, and legally obliging them all to undertake indefinite military service, Eritrean citizens have relatively good chances for successfully claiming asylum. In addition to being eligible for asylum, Eritreans have two further incentives to leave Italy. First, they have possibilities to gain legal status that others would not (although, as will be detailed below, the Dublin Regulation means that traversing through Italy is risky). And second, those countries that offer welfare provisions for refugees—which Italy does not—are understandably more desirable to this group. Decisions about where to migrate after Italy are heavily influenced by the trajectories of those who have gone before. "For the Eritrean community, Italy is just a stepping stone," Biniam told me one quiet afternoon in the center sitting at the counter:

> No one ends up staying here. Of the group I arrived with [other Eritreans who arrived in the same year], there were eight of us, and now there is only me left. Eritreans are like sheep: they all follow each other. It used to be Great Britain, but now Sweden is the country of choice. I would say about 95 percent of Eritreans who come to Italy these days move on elsewhere.[1]

In recent years, Biniam informed me, Eritreans have been less successful in claiming asylum in the U.K., whereas their chances were perceived to be higher in Sweden, where refugees also enjoy a more generous social welfare system than in Italy, receiving housing and benefits.[2] When I asked him who remained in Italy and why, Biniam responded that those who have family or other obligations may be forced to remain, while others were "*deficienti*" (half-wits) and unable to migrate elsewhere.

The prevalence of on-migration among Eritreans was confirmed by the countless numbers of such nationals I met in my nineteen months of fieldwork, many of whom were about to leave or had already done so. There was the *professore*, as Biniam called him, who had previously been a university lecturer in Asmara. After several years of saving money in Italy, he decided to move to the United States, where he would try to claim asylum. He undertook a dangerous journey that involved traveling from Italy to El Salvador and Mexico before entering the United States as an asylum seeker. While the United States was often discussed as the desired destination for many Eritreans, the risks and costs involved in getting there were too high for most.

In other cases, migrants tried to ensure that their children migrated onward. Several parents I knew successfully applied for their children to join them in Italy through family reunification, only to swiftly send them away to other European countries. Fekle spent months struggling to apply for her sixteen-year-old son Simon to come to Italy from the Sudan through family reunification. Weeks after he arrived, Simon hid in a truck and crossed the channel to the U.K., where he claimed asylum as a fourteen-year-old. His application was successful, and an English family has since adopted him. Although Fekle was again separated from her son, she considered his on-migration a success and was comforted by the belief that he faced a brighter future.

Also keen for his children to live elsewhere in Europe, Johan, an Italian citizen himself although originally from Eritrea, frequently came to the advice center to check the status of his teenage children's permits. They had recently arrived in Italy through family reunification. But as soon as the permits were issued they flew to Sweden where, after discarding their Italian permits before going through passport control, they claimed asylum. When I left the field their asylum claims were being processed. In both of these cases the parents placed a higher priority on their children living in countries perceived to offer better opportunities than they did on living near them. Their decisions reflect the extent of people's beliefs that their children would be better off living outside of Italy.

Not all Eritreans' attempts at on-migration were successful, however. In July 2010, Biniam's cousin Emanuel left his job in Genoa to fly to Sweden. From there he would attempt to fly to Cancun in Mexico in an effort eventually to reach the United States. He knew of several others who had attempted such a route with success. It was not to be for Emanuel, however, who returned soon after his departure, having been stopped in Stockholm for not holding the correct visa. When I said to Biniam that Emanuel must be very disappointed, Biniam shrugged his shoulders saying, "There is a very high risk of being stopped. He wasn't surprised." "But what about all the money he must have lost on the ticket?" I asked. "Well that's what it costs," he replied, again shrugging his shoulders.

Although the frequency and normality with which such journeys are spoken about made them appear almost mundane, such attempts were highly risky and likely to fail. This is largely because the asylum seekers' eligibility for asylum or humanitarian protection is severely curtailed by the Dublin Regulation, which dictates that would-be refugees should remain in the first country they arrive in.[3] Therefore, asylum seekers arriving on the shores of Italy must claim asylum in Italy. This means that those who had on-migrated elsewhere, and who had successfully been granted asylum, were risking future deportation back to Italy. Unaware of such laws, many Eritreans have claimed asylum in the

U.K. and other countries after originally passing through Italy. Those who fall victim to an efficient immigration bureaucracy may have their asylum revoked, sometimes even years later, after it is discovered that records of their fingerprints already exist in Italy.

In this respect, migrating to the United States or other countries not involved in the Dublin Regulation is safer because records of claimants' fingerprints will not be on a shared database. One way to reduce the risk of discovery was to avoid claiming asylum in Italy altogether. Indeed, many of those I knew who had successfully claimed asylum elsewhere in Europe had previously been living in Italy, not as refugees but rather with family or work permits, and some even had citizenship. Although the fingerprint databank for asylum claimants was likely to be crosschecked, the border agency of the new destination countries cannot feasibly crosscheck asylum seekers' fingerprints with those of all legal migrants living in countries that have signed the Dublin Regulation. Therefore by *not* claiming asylum in Italy and instead obtaining a permit through other means, these Eritreans were effectively remaining beneath the radar and were unlikely to be caught out when they eventually did claim asylum in the U.K., Sweden, or elsewhere.

An Eritrean woman named Yanet had adopted this strategy (see figure 12). She was the partner of Dewat, a close friend of Biniam and Chiara. Dewat had lived without papers in Italy for ten years. As detailed in Chapter 3, he eventually obtained a permit during the 2009 domestic worker amnesty. This amnesty in theory gave undocumented domestic workers who had been working in Italy before April 2009 the opportunity to gain a permit through their employer. In reality, however, the law gave the opportunity to be regularized to anybody who was able to find, and usually pay, an "employer." Luckily for Dewat, Chiara was able and willing to "hire" him, and in 2010 he received a permit.

Yanet had lived in Italy for over five years, where she held the long-term permit, lived in public housing, and had a job in a cleaning company. Several years previously, during the time Dewat's "illegal" status had trapped him in Italy, Yanet had moved to Sweden, where she had claimed and been granted asylum, and was now living as a refugee with their two young children. Living in Stockholm she received the full benefits to which she was entitled as a refugee. Meanwhile, in Italy, she remained, on paper, a legal resident. Her public housing was still in her name (where Dewat lived), and she continued to receive contributions for maternity leave. In Sweden, Yanet lived under a different name and, because she had never claimed asylum in Italy, was very unlikely to be discovered.

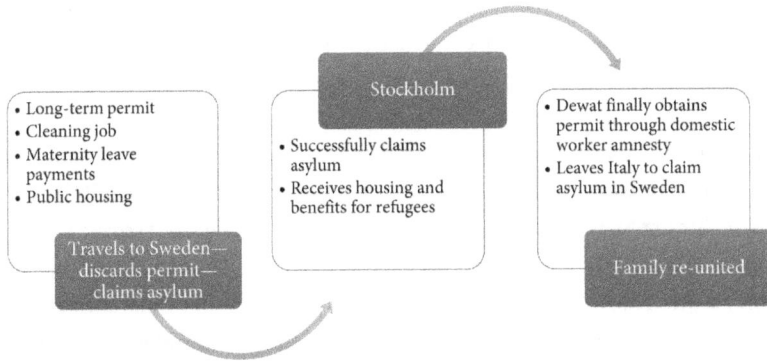

Stockholm

- Long-term permit
- Cleaning job
- Maternity leave payments
- Public housing

- Successfully claims asylum
- Receives housing and benefits for refugees

- Dewat finally obtains permit through domestic worker amnesty
- Leaves Italy to claim asylum in Sweden

Travels to Sweden— discards permit— claims asylum

Family re-united

Figure 12. Immigration experience of Yanet, a multiple permit holder.

I met Yanet when she made a return trip to Italy in order to organize the paperwork related to her resignation from the cleaning company. Eventually her paper existence in Italy would fade, as her documents relating to her legal status, public housing, and employment, among others, expired. Since she was happily living in Stockholm, this was not a problem. The key to Yanet's success was her foresight to not claim asylum in Italy, where her fingerprints would have been recorded in the database that EU member states share. In 2011, after Dewat received his permit through the amnesty in Italy, he joined Yanet in Sweden. Paradoxically, while his previously illegal status had confined him within Italy's borders for over ten years, his permit to stay in the country enabled him to leave it. Two weeks after arriving in Sweden under a different identity, Dewat claimed asylum: his claim has since been accepted. Although he had previously attempted to claim asylum in Italy, he was unlikely to be caught out by the Dublin Regulation. More than ten years had passed since he had made the original claim, at which time the electronic database for fingerprints did not exist. Without this technology it would be very difficult for Dewat's double claim to be discovered.

Italy as a legal base

It is not only by claiming asylum elsewhere that migrants migrate onward from Italy. The long-term permit also offers possibilities for starting a life in a new destination, as it is technically valid for work purposes in all Schengen member states. Ironically, for many the motivation to obtain this permit is to leave Italy. Those who held the long-term permit, or desired to, frequently visited the center to ask which countries it was possible to work in and how. Some did permanently migrate to other countries if they found work, and others lived elsewhere for a period of time before returning to Italy and on-migrating again if they could.

Sharif, the husband of a Pakistani woman I knew, was mostly absent from family life. For weeks at a time he went to different Schengen member countries, including Norway, Sweden, and others, in attempts to find secure employment. While away he worked on short-term contracts doing manual labor or factory work. Sharif's wife told me that her husband thought there were better employment options outside of Italy, and once he had found something permanent the whole family intended to migrate. The long-term permit gave him the freedom to follow employment opportunities across borders because it did not require renewal and therefore did not necessitate presenting evidence of income in Italy.

Whether individuals permanently migrated elsewhere or left Italy only briefly, Italy could be used as a platform to enter Europe or as a base where legal status was more easily obtainable and from where other opportunities in Europe could be scoped out. Since "illegal" status immobilizes migrants, Italy's easily manipulated rules and access to permits made it a country migrants could use as a legal base until they were securely set up elsewhere or until they made Italy their final destination country.

Flexible citizens

For those who took advantage of Schengen freedom-of-movement laws or cheap flights to travel to Sweden in order to claim asylum, the motivation to leave Italy ran parallel to the logic that had originally compelled them to migrate: that of moving to places that offered better opportunities for life improvement. Leaving Italy was also bound up with decisions based on families and networks, which were often situated in a historical context of colonialism. However, while recognizing the complexity and nuances in migrants' decisions to on-migrate, I suggest that we can view my respondents' stories as revealing a wider discourse situated within the "cultural logics of accumulation" (Ong 1999: 6) in which improved social and material capital were desired.

While the high-flying and elite Chinese respondents that Ong (1999) writes about faced significantly different concerns from those that preoccupied my interlocutors, her arguments surrounding flexible citizenship have relevance here:

| Enter Italy and obtain "legal" status | → | Apply for long-term permit | → | Travel to Schengen member states in search of work opportunities | → | Eventually settle elsewhere or remain in Italy |

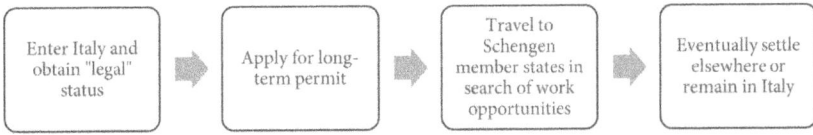

Figure 13. Italy as a stepping stone to legal residence.

> Flexible citizenship refers to the cultural logics of capitalist accumulation, travel, and displacement that induce subjects to respond fluidly and opportunistically to changing political-economic conditions. In their quest to accumulate capital and social prestige in the global arena, subjects emphasize, and are regulated by, practices favoring flexibility, mobility, and repositioning in relation to markets, governments, and cultural regimes. (Ong 1999: 6)

She further notes that "those most able to benefit from participation in global capitalism were those able to celebrate flexibility and mobility" (19). As I have shown here, flexibility and mobility are also valued by migrants from more humble backgrounds, who, although lacking elite status, nonetheless aspire to the "good life." Therefore, whereas Ong views flexible citizens as part of a global elite whose mobility is enabled by their wealth, the stories presented show how the marginal and seemingly immobile can also be considered flexible citizens in the contemporary global marketplace.

The long-term permit is intended to confer secure legal status in Italy, but my respondents used it, with varying degrees of success, as a means of gaining access to more profitable labor markets elsewhere. By taking advantage of the Schengen Area, those with long-term permits and good networks of contacts were able to engage in Europe's diverse labor markets and accumulate capital. They did not perceive Italy as the ideal destination country but, given the relative ease of procuring documents, for flexible citizens it served as a legal base when opportunities elsewhere were more restricted.

On-migrating was not rooted solely in economic instrumentalism. Migrants hoped that in the future their children would be able to enjoy better circumstances for capital accumulation and that they would be free from racist and xenophobic discrimination. As observed by Calavita (2005b), migrants' experiences of racism, legal precarity, and economic marginalization in Italy are deeply intertwined. Among my respondents, many felt frustrated by the fact that, regardless of their citizenship status, integration, or wealth, they would nonetheless continue to be considered "*immigrati*," with all of the negative associations and limitations for social mobility that the term implies. Of course, my interlocutors' ideas about racial equality elsewhere may have been idealistic. Indeed, Ong (1999: 91–92) notes that in the United States her rich Chinese respondents struggled to be recognized as holding cultural capital, since there was a "mismatch . . . between the symbolic capital and its embodiment." Despite this mismatch, however, my respondents held firm to their conviction that outside of Italy their opportunities for social and economic mobility would be better. As such, their desire to leave Italy was embedded in their aspiration to gain social and economic capital for themselves and their children, as well as to escape racialized discrimination.

In labeling those who left as "flexible citizens" I do not wish to romanticize their on-migration. Those who migrated onward took up subordinate positions in other societies, either in low-level jobs or as welfare-dependent refugees. Analytically situating nonelite migrants as flexible citizens, however, highlights the ways in which they are as equally embedded in the cultural logics of capitalism, transnationalism, and globalization as the high-flying investors that Ong describes. This is important, not only in framing the practices of those who leave Italy, but also to accurately understand the situations of those who remain, who acutely experience the inequalities created by the uneven nature of globalization and capitalism.

Feelings of failure

The previous section largely described people who actually left Italy, but for most such mobility is not possible. In reality, the standard permit (in contrast to the less easily acquired long-term permit) allows little freedom. Permit renewal is a time-consuming process, contingent on evidence of salary and employment (Tuckett 2015). An individual who has spent most of the year outside Italy would be unlikely to hold the requisites needed for renewal and would be required to maintain a domicile and employment in Italy or risk becoming an "irregular" migrant elsewhere.

Despite these realities, there were sufficient accounts and rumors of successful on-migration stories to create a feeling among those who remained that it was their own personal inability to take advantage of opportunities that had forced them to remain in Italy and—as they perceived it—live a less successful life. Feelings of disappointment around staying in Italy were, therefore, dialogically related to the sense that there were better possibilities elsewhere and that others were managing to take advantage of them.

This dialogical relationship is akin to that between "home" and "destination" countries so often explored in the anthropological literature on migration. As noted earlier, this body of work has focused on the experiences of those who remain in a locality from which there is a large amount of migration (Gaibazzi 2014; Gardner 1993; Gardner 2008; Vigh 2009). In relation to this, drawing on Bourdieu, Steven Vertovec (2004) has coined the phrase "transnational habitus" to describe the extent to which transnationalism structures the experience, dispositions, and practices of even those who never migrate. Within this habitus, geographic movement and economic success are inextricably linked, since, in the minds of both migrants and nonmigrants alike, "connectedness to the global labor market is seen as virtually the only avenue for success" (Gardner 2008: 488). Transnationalism is not, therefore, about equal global flows, but rather about dialogical relationships of power between localities (Gardner 1993, 2008) within which "mobility is the most powerful and most stratifying factor" (Bauman 1998: 9).

The circumstances of those who *have* migrated but who nonetheless still feel immobile add another layer to the "transnational habitus" in which geographic movement is hierarchically ranked, with certain destinations imagined as more powerful than others. The following narratives call attention to these "hierarchies of globalization" (Carling 2002: 37) in which individuals are differentially incorporated into the global market and benefit unequally, if at all, from it (Bal and Roos Willems 2014: 255). They show how this transnational habitus, which dictates that the only way to get ahead is to migrate (Gardner 2008: 479), continues to structure and stratify the experiences of those who already have migrated. Those who remained in Italy and did not become flexible citizens felt like failures. Drawing on Chiara's alternative view of "getting ahead," which is premised on the potential of group struggle to improve migrants' conditions, I argue that the grounding of the transnational habitus within the logics of the global labor market restricts people's imaginaries of how to achieve life betterment.

Contributing to the sense of failure and despondency among those who remained in Italy was the commonly held view in different communities that those who stay are either *deficienti* (half-wits) and thus incapable of leaving the country, or *delinquenti* (delinquents) profiting from the country's supposed flexible and clientelistic systems. Regardless of whether or not this stereotype is true, the negative portrayal of those who remained in Italy was contrasted with the positive depiction of those who had left.

During evenings out with volunteers and staff members from the center, the conversation frequently turned to those who were no longer around. I learned the names and characters of a set of volunteers who, with Chiara, had been part of the advice center's original team. These people were described as political, bright, ambitious, and keen to fight for migrants' rights. Chiara would sigh nostalgically as she recalled events and struggles that they had experienced together. "But now he is in your parts," she would say, referring to different individuals who had since migrated to the U.K. If not living in the U.K., they were in France, Belgium, or Germany. "Why did they leave?" I inquired of her. "To find better opportunities elsewhere . . . and because they were smart," she answered. In this sense, the center acted as a microcosm for a wider pattern in Italy, in which the supposedly best and brightest moved on.

People from many different communities emphatically told me that those migrants who had settled in Italy—be they Moroccans, Tunisians, Eritreans, or some other nationality—were not representative of that national group. Although he did occasionally go to Eritrean bars, Biniam always complained about those who frequented them: "Only those with *teste dure* [hard heads—fools] are here [in Italy]. There is nobody to have a serious conversation with." On other occasions, when he did meet someone he liked, he would enthusiastically and positively discuss how this individual was different from the others and how he had been able to have an intelligent conversation about the political situation in Eritrea. Similarly, Mehdi frequently warned me not to speak to certain of his countrymen: "They are delinquents, Anna, stay away from them." Like Biniam, he told me that in Morocco many people were intellectual and political but that here [in Italy] the majority were delinquent.

On one of our regular Saturday night dinners at her house, Chiara told me that there were four different kinds of migrants who remained in Italy. First, there were those who were unable to change their circumstances. This category referred to those who lacked the skills, resources, or language to improve their situation. Second, there were those who were content with their situation and therefore lacked the drive to dramatically change their circumstances. This category referred to those who might have originally planned to leave the country but had since settled with their families and were relatively securely employed. She cited Al Alami as an example of such a migrant. He held a fairly stable job in the trade union, lived in a public housing apartment in a good neighborhood with his three children and wife, and had recently obtained citizenship. Third, Chiara noted, there were those who effectively engaged in *il sistema paese* (system of the country; discussed in Chapter 3). This category referred to those who have taken advantage of what she considered to be a corrupt system. She specifically referred to individuals she knew who were involved in community associations and had embezzled funds from the *comune*. Last, she said, are those who do not have the courage to start again. In a rare moment of dejection, she said, "I'm in that category. It's true. I don't have the courage to start somewhere new, from zero."

Such a discourse about the "low caliber" of migrants who remain in Italy further compounded individuals' own sense of failure. As such, my interlocutors' denigration of Italy, adulation of countries they perceived to be superior, and damning opinions of the type of migrant that remained in Italy made their own trajectory appear more negative than it was. Although they attributed their situations to their own failures, their circumstances in fact challenged such sweeping statements about Italy and the kind of migrant that remained there.

If my respondents viewed staying in Italy as indicative of their own failure, it did not mean that they did not get on with their lives or enjoy them. Furthermore, despite the frequent lamentations regarding the country, some people told me that they preferred life in Italy to that in countries such as Sweden or Norway. As I was told by Ahmed, an Algerian man, "Life in Italy is better than in Norway. It is so cold there, and everybody just stays in their houses."

Migrants' experiences were related to their personal circumstances, their country of origin, and the particularities of onward migration for those who shared those origins. For Biniam and other Eritreans, it was the sheer scale of on-migration from Italy that made for the sense of failure among those who remained. In contrast, individual achievement and economic success were reasons for migrants to become more sedentary. Among the Chinese people I spoke to, for example, there was a much lower degree of on-migration—and of dissatisfaction as well. This difference could be related to the fact that Chinese people were more likely to own businesses, which gave them better long-term options. Idris, Biniam's fifty-year-old best friend who had previously lived in the United States, owned a cleaning business and did not wish to on-migrate. He worked long hours but had become relatively financially successful and, unlike Biniam and other Eritreans, was relatively satisfied with his life in Italy. Economic success or belief in such a possibility was, therefore, a motivating factor to remain in Italy, even if it was not a reality for most.

Chiara held a different and uncommon view of migrants who left Italy and what their departure signified for those who remained. Her moment of somber reflection about her own reasons for staying was rare. Despite her highly critical opinion of Italy, she firmly believed that migrants should not on-migrate. Her

Figure 14. Photograph of a Chinese migrant–owned shop. Photograph by author.

brother advised those who could do so to leave Italy, but Chiara passionately argued that it was the responsibility of today's migrants to make Italy a better country for the future. Although she wholeheartedly agreed that the quality of life was better for migrants elsewhere, she did not think that leaving the country was the solution. During an argument with her brother over this topic, she stated: "It is our responsibility to stay here. Do you think it was easy in England or France when immigrants first arrived? They struggled for the way it is now."

Chiara believed that time and commitment were needed from the first generation in order for the situation to improve for the next. She passionately argued against what she regarded as Biniam's defeatist "jump-ship" attitude, reasoning that it was difficult to imagine a better future if the most intelligent and hard-working migrants continued to leave the country. She compared the situation to a "brain drain" in which the most ambitious and promising people migrate, meaning that the situation in the "home" country never improves. Chiara thus held those who had left partly responsible for the lack of development of migrants' rights in Italy. In her opinion, it was precisely those individuals who were needed in order to create change. Demonstrating her strong sense of social responsibility and justice, she argued that it was up to individuals like her to make the system better. "We immigrants also have to take responsibility for the situation in this country. We can't only blame the politicians. If we want things to get better we have to work for it, like people have done before in other countries."

Discussing the steep rise in the cost of permit renewal, Chiara exclaimed: "We [immigrants] have to get pissed off! We cannot accept this situation, we need to react. People like me can be the *portavoce* [spokesperson], but we need the masses behind us." For Chiara, collective action and solidarity were needed to improve the situation. Yet her views were not commonly shared. Instead, possibilities for betterment were seen to lie elsewhere. This widespread understanding of Italy as a stepping-stone country added to migrants' sense of disappointment and infused the experience of those that remained.

Chiara's views about on-migration also highlight the limitations of Arjun Appadurai's (1996) theory of social imagination. His acknowledgment of the power and widespread nature of social imagination is pertinent, but as Ong (1999: 11) notes, "He gives the misleading impression that everyone can take equal advantage of mobility and modern communications." For those such as Biniam, whose financial difficulties prevented him from migrating onward, access to the benefits of capitalism are far from equally distributed. And, rather than identifying "the processes that increasingly differentiate[d] the power of mobile and nonmobile subjects" (Ong 1999: 11), those who remained in Italy attributed their immobility to personal failure. Indeed, Biniam's opinion that those who remained were *deficienti* was accompanied by an acute sense of his own failure to improve his life conditions by on-migrating. Moreover, as Chiara's assertions suggested, the social imaginary based on mass media and transnational connections, which posits migration as the only means of achieving success, is ultimately guided by the "cultural logics of accumulation" (6) that, by their very nature, neglect other kinds of future imaginaries. Chiara argued that this neglect of collectivist imaginaries among those remaining in Italy impeded the country's ability to build greater equality for migrants and their children in the future.

Conclusion

Like the social imaginary that drives initial migration flows, my respondents' desire to on-migrate from Italy are a consequence of the uneven and hierarchical nature of globalization, in which not all destination countries are considered equal. The low-status and low-paid work to which migrants are restricted, and the racialized discrimination they suffer, accentuates their unequal incorporation into the global labor market, from which they scarcely benefit. Like their initial migration, mobility and on-migration from Italy were seen as the only way to improve their life conditions. Italy's relatively malleable immigration laws, as well as the European Union's freedom-of-movement agreements, allow migrants a certain amount of mobility, which encourage and concretize such imaginations of life elsewhere.

Situating my interlocutors' desires to on-migrate within the cultural logics of accumulation, I have shown that nonelite migrants can also be considered flexible citizens. Yet the flows and flexibilities celebrated by capitalism are also intimately connected to the global inequalities it creates. For those who do manage to move on, their position as the most marginalized in society continues in a new setting, while those who remain wrestle with the enduring belief that they have failed. Imaginaries of better futures, meanwhile, are restricted to individual and family-oriented projects rather than collective struggles to create a fairer and more equal society.

Conclusion

Extract from fieldnotes, October 2013

In the past two weeks, two shipwrecks off the coast of Lampedusa have left over six hundred dead. The first boat was mainly occupied by Eritreans and Somalis, the second by Syrians and Palestinians. All are referred to as "refugees" in the media, although of course the survivors' asylum claims are yet to be processed. I speak to Chiara on the phone, who wryly asks if I have heard what Prime Minister Enrico Letta has announced. On visiting the island, he promised that the hundreds who lost their lives "are Italian citizens as of today" and would be given a state funeral. Like commentators in the press, Chiara is highly skeptical of Letta's gesture, and she echoes a journalist's comments that "such measures are grotesque and will only reinforce the idea, among would-be refugees and their advocates, that a dead migrant is preferable . . . to a live one" (Dejevsky 2013). "They don't give citizenship to the children who are born in the country, but they will give it to dead migrants at Lampedusa. What hypocrisy!" Chiara exclaims. Later I learn that the Lampedusa dead received neither posthumous citizenship nor a state funeral.

Despite the initial outpourings of sympathy and compassion, in the end the victims and survivors of this tragedy were treated in the usual manner: the dead were buried quietly with only numbers to mark many of the graves, and the survivors were detained in immigration centers. The publicity in the immediate aftermath, however, highlights many of the contradictions surrounding discourses about migration and migration flows.

Harrowing images of those who have died trying to enter Europe garner universal sympathy and a call for more humane border regulations. Yet business-as-usual soon resumes, with the loudest voices calling for stricter immigration controls and more deportations. The border spectacle (De Genova 2002) is a key component of these discourses around migration, at some moments acting as a symbol of migrant suffering, and at others as a symbol of state control (or lack thereof). This focus on the border produces a lopsided view of migration that obscures the way in which immigration policies relate to broader political and economic processes—of contemporary migration and economic globalization—in which we are all included. In this final chapter I analyze how migrants' navigation of the documentation regime, and the playing out of immigration policies on the ground more generally, must be situated in relation to such processes.

As analysts have consistently pointed out, the number of migrants who attempt to arrive in Europe "clandestinely" is a tiny fraction of the total number who enter "legally" on some kind of visa for tourism, work, study, or family purposes (Andersson 2014: 5; de Haas 2017). Despite this fact, however, academics, policy makers, NGOs, and the media continue to focus their attention on the site of the border itself, symbolized by the image of small, overcrowded boats making perilous journeys across the Mediterranean in which so many tragically lose their lives.

It is unsurprising that NGOs, journalists, and academics are interested in this sharp end of immigration law, where not only legal status but life itself is precarious and at risk. The "illegality industry" is, after all, productive (Andersson 2014), and it is not only migrants' illegality that is produced. "As a 'problem' to be solved, [illegality] sparks new security 'solutions,' NGO projects, professional networks, activist campaigns, and journalistic and academic engagements that might otherwise remain unfunded and ignored" (Andersson 2014: 274). Meanwhile, for immigration policy makers who face multiple and conflicting pressures in what has become a highly politicized environment, focusing on "symbolic policy instruments to create an appearance of control" (Massey 2009: 35) can divert attention away from the reality of immigration policies within the borders of the nation-state: policies that are often less restrictive than politicians' anti-immigrant rhetoric suggests (see also de Haas, Natter, and Vezzoli 2014).

The border spectacle (Andersson 2014; De Genova 2002), and border enforcement more broadly (Feldman 2012; Heyman 1995), have been largely demystified by scholars. But less attention has been given to the internal legal and administrative borders *within* host states where "legality" and "illegality" are likewise produced and experienced. By closely examining migrants' everyday interactions with the immigration bureaucracy as they seek to "legalize" their status, renew permits, bring over family members, and apply for citizenship, this book focuses on the less visible and less sharp end of immigration law. In doing so, it points to the complex and contradictory processes of inclusion and exclusion produced through encounters with that law. Close ethnographic attention to migrants' encounters with the documentation regime supports established arguments about how immigration law produces migrants' precarious and marginalized status, which ultimately works to subordinate their labor (Calavita 2005b; De Genova 2002; Kearney 1991; Portes 1978).

The Kafkaesque process of permit renewal, as well as the requisites for renewal itself, regularly place migrants in legal limbo and can transform even long-term migrants or those born in the country into "illegal" subjects. The dominant role of migrants in low-status work with little hope for social mobility, combined with the everyday racism to which they are subject, recalls Calavita's (2005b: 64) point that temporary and insecure legal status continuously reproduces migrants as "other." This is a "critical ingredient of their flexibility" and ensures that they remain in low-level and poorly paid jobs.

Yet alongside this structural effect of immigration law—which consistently marginalizes migrants and their labor—everyday interactions with the immigration bureaucracy produce other outcomes and affects that simultaneously engender both inclusion and exclusion. In the Italian context, strategic navigation enables migrants to bend the rules and have applications accepted: individuals "legalize" their status, family members are reunited, and permits can be renewed. In addition to these tangible results, engagement with the documentation regime also produces affective outcomes. Learning how to complete permit renewal applications and other basic paperwork provides an opportunity for savvy migrants to become informal immigration advisers, acquiring both material gain and social status. Strategically navigating the immigration bureaucracy through rule-bending and loophole-finding, meanwhile, is a means through which migrants become Italian-like cultural insiders.

Yet this close attention to encounters with immigration law highlights the paradoxical nature of the processes of inclusion and exclusion they produce. While culturally learned rule-bending was necessary for migrants in their successful navigation of the immigration bureaucracy, it was precisely migrants' socially embedded modes of behavior that could lead to their applications for citizenship and other forms of secure legal status being refused. Immigration law and bureaucracy, therefore, work to create more than migrants' labor subordination. Indeed, it is the dynamic coexistence of both inclusionary and exclusionary processes, which encounters with the documentation regime generate, that most poignantly reproduces migrants' precarious position in Italian society.

Immigration policy contextualized

Examining what immigration law does, and how it works out on the ground, shows how immigration policy is deeply intertwined with broader policymaking (Czaika and de Haas 2013: 489). This is true both for both immigration policies that determine migration flows and for those targeted at migrants already on host territory. The domestic work contract—which relates to labor market, migration, welfare, and family policies—is a case in point. Italian immigration law is relatively lenient toward domestic workers, providing them with frequent opportunities to enter the country and legalize their status. But it is not only genuine domestic workers and their employers who are able to benefit from this leniency integrated into immigration law. The domestic work contract enables large numbers of migrants who do quite different jobs to regularize and maintain their legal status, benefiting a range of employers and the economy more generally. The private and relatively unregulated nature of the domestic work contract in Italy makes it possible for any migrant with the appropriate resources and knowledge to regularize his or her status if someone is willing to act as their "employer."

It is thus important to acknowledge that immigration policy is inseparable from other forms of policymaking. Despite the polarized rhetoric that increasingly characterizes the issue of migration, migration policy is a "mixed bag" (de Haas, Natter, and Vezzoli 2014: 4) made up of conflicting policies aiming to satisfy a host of competing individuals and organizations. "Border spectacles" attempt to produce coherent and "strong" images of migration management, but in reality immigration control is complex and contradictory. And, as this book has shown, it is migrants, advisers, brokers, low-level officials, and others who navigate its contradictions and enable the policies to function.

What do migrants' strategies of navigation achieve?

Illegal street sellers who legalized their status in the 2009 domestic worker amnesty, or aunts who "hired" their nephews in the 2011 *decreto flussi*, may seem, on the face of it, to prove that Italy's immigration policies have failed because they have not achieved their intended aims. Yet if we consider how these policies actually play out on the ground, and the diverse actors that they end up satisfying, their lack of success is less apparent. Rather, like all policies, they are the result of a "compromise between multiple competing interests" (Czaika and de Haas 2013: 491) and therefore are inevitably riddled with contradictions. It is revealing, however, to explore what these policies actually do. This book's close examination of the documentary processes within the immigration bureaucracy points out these policies' side effects and what they ultimately achieve (Ferguson 1990: 254).

The 2009 domestic worker amnesty managed to realize multiple and conflicting aims. In large part it did so by allowing large numbers of illegal migrants to use the amnesty to legalize their status, despite not being technically eligible to do so. These included: individuals who had entered on a tourism visa (or some other short-term visa); those who had once held a permit to stay but for some reason (usually unemployment) had been unable to renew it; members of the second generation who, in a post–high school limbo period, had lost their legal status; and those who did not want to work but needed to appear employed in order to renew their permits. These individuals' manipulation of the amnesty's loopholes enabled multiple and conflicting aims and interests to be reconciled. Much-needed domestic workers were able to be regularized and would now pay taxes and national insurance contributions. The demands of families in need of domestic workers were met. Illegal migrant workers (both domestic and nondomestic) already on Italian territory—who would be expensive and difficult to deport—were able to be regularized. And, thanks to the latter, a fresh supply of legal migrant labor was made available to a variety of employers.

The 2011 *decreto flussi* is a further example of the way in which the execution of individual policies met the desires and demands of different institutions, organizations, and actors. In previous years the *decreto flussi* procedure had been used by migrants in a similar manner to amnesties—as a way to regularize the status of illegal migrants already on Italian territory; but the 2011

decreto flussi largely served a different purpose. Because of the short time period between the September 2009 amnesty and the January 2011 *decreto flussi*,
at the time of the *decreto flussi* many of those who needed to regularize their
status had already done so in the amnesty. Therefore, instead of functioning as
a type of regularization, the 2011 *decreto flussi* was used as a means of family
reunification.

Again, various groups and individuals were placated by the introduction
of the *decreto flussi*. Businesses and families were supplied with much needed
legal migrant labor. Trade unions and NGOs that lobby the government to enable legal migration achieved their aims. Potential migrants still in their home
countries were given an opportunity to migrate. The services of migration brokers, who organize contracts between migrant "employees" and "employers,"
were in demand. And migrants already on Italian territory who either needed
to legalize their own status or wanted to bring over somebody from abroad
were able to do so.

In addition to reconciling these competing and conflicting interests, migrants' strategies of navigation also produced an accidental, but beneficial, effect for the Italian state and public perception of border control by concealing
both the number of illegal migrants on Italian territory and the fact that Italian
immigration law *itself* produces illegal immigration (Calavita 2005b). First, the
mass use of the 2009 domestic worker amnesty by any illegal migrant disguised
the large number of what would be considered "undesirable" illegal migrants
(that is, nondomestic workers) on Italian territory, while periodic *decreti flussi*
obscured the overall number of illegal migrants in Italy, as those legalized
would officially appear as new migrants from abroad.

Second, migrants' use of the regularization procedures masked the fact
that the country's immigration law increases the number of illegal migrants
on Italian territory (Calavita 2005b: 43). It was not only new illegal migrants
who took advantage of regularization policies. Those policies were also used
by migrants who had lived in Italy for years, or who were born in the country,
but had fallen into illegality, usually through unemployment. This unofficial
regularization of illegal migrants covered up the way in which immigration law
produces illegal immigration itself, in some cases even causing members of the
1.5 and second generations to become illegal. Migrants' tactical manipulation
of different regularization policies obscured this production of illegality, which
would be viewed highly unfavorably by the voting public, as well as by fellow
EU member states concerned about border security.

The introduction of both the amnesty and the *decreto flussi*, therefore, benefited a large and diverse number of institutions, organizations, and individuals in various ways. These included officially recognized stakeholders, such as businesses desiring foreign labor and trade unions (whose membership is increasingly made up of migrant workers), as well as unofficial stakeholders, such as illegal migrants or brokers organizing contracts between "employers" and "employees" for a profit in what would be technically an illegal transaction.

How policies play out on the ground shows how very different actors—from the elderly needing caregivers to profit-seeking brokers—play a role in the policies' introduction and implementation. In addition to satisfying the various pro-legal migration stakeholders, the official format of the policies—as an amnesty to regularize much needed domestic workers or as a *decreto flussi* that allows employers based in Italy to hire named employees from abroad—is deemed acceptable by those who would not normally support an increase in migration.

This "covering up" of migrant illegality and the pacification of competing stakeholders are not the result of policy makers' strategic design. Rather they are the "side effects" (Ferguson 1990) produced through the playing out of multiple and often conflicting laws and policies on the ground. Crucial to the side effects produced, and the various actors' appeasement, however, is the role played by migrants themselves. For it is their strategic navigation that silently reconciles the policies' contradictions and enables these outcomes to be realized. Though not designed, the outcomes achieved must not be dismissed as merely accidental or unintentional. Rather, immigration policies' execution takes place within a broader political-economic system that determines the reproduction of particular power relations.

Basic rewards

What, then, do migrants' strategies of navigation do for the migrants themselves? The benefits migrants reap through their interactions with immigration law and bureaucracy hold limited advantages. Strategic navigation produced only basic rewards, such as legalizing their status or reuniting them with family members, and did not help migrants and their children build secure and profitable lives. The particularities of Italian immigration law make long-term secure legal status and citizenship difficult to obtain. Many long-term migrants are unable to demonstrate ten years of continuous documented residency due to precarious working and housing conditions and are therefore not eligible to apply for citizenship. In addition, the interpretation of laws by the *questura* made it very difficult for a migrant to secure a long-term permit. "You have to be *perfetto* [perfect] to obtain the *carta*," Chiara once said at the reception counter. "No, *furbetto* [diminutive of *furbo*, meaning a little bit cunning]," a client waiting interjected.

In the case studies in Chapter 3, I described how over-bending the rules could lead to the loss of citizenship. Rashid and Kidane craftily exploited the gap between paper and practice, but in doing so left themselves vulnerable to exposure. In Rashid's case, because he received family benefits for his children who lived in Pakistan he was forced to withdraw his citizenship application. In Kidane's case, his partner's concealment of his presence on their family residence certificate, in order to secure public housing, made their daughter ineligible for naturalization. While their adept navigation of the welfare system demonstrated both individuals' integration into *il sistema paese*, as noncitizens there were limits to their rule-bending practices.

Given the extent to which migrants must document their lives for the submission of applications, people like Rashid and Kidane are at risk of becoming entangled and trapped within the different truths that their papers depict. These circumstances are evidence of the paradoxical disjunctures produced by the system. By learning to navigate the immigration bureaucracy, migrants become cultural insiders, yet exclusionary laws can transform this social and cultural learning into the very thing that endangers their right to live in the country.

In a similar situation were Aurelie and Lindita of the 1.5 and second generations who, in some respects, were in the most vulnerable positions of all. They did not view themselves as immigrants, yet were not legal citizens. Their obliviousness to the world of immigration bureaucracy put them both at risk of losing citizenship and even legal status. In fact, at the time of our meeting, Aurelie was unaware that she was technically an illegal migrant.

Thus, while the flexibility within the Italian immigration bureaucracy provides opportunities to migrants, overall the system is not designed to enable migrants to build secure lives for themselves and their families. On the one hand, therefore, Italian immigration law can be said to be fairly lenient despite the hardline rhetoric of many policy makers, but on the other, the leniency it provides ultimately benefits not migrants but their employers, as well as others profiting from the "migration industry" (Gammeltoft-Hansen and Sørensen 2013).

Limits of a neoliberal subjectivity

Notwithstanding their creative engagement with the documentation regime, my interlocutors' migration trajectories were tinged by feelings of disappointment and failure expressed through their conviction that better opportunities were available beyond Italy. Yet, even for those who did manage to leave Italy, prosperity remained elusive. Their setting may have changed, but their low status and inability to find well-paid work did not. Migrants were differentially included in the global marketplace, wherever the mobility of neoliberal globalization might take them.

It is within this context of the neoliberal global marketplace that the outcomes of migrants' strategies of navigation should be situated. Migrants' occupation in low-status, poorly paid, and often physically demanding jobs can be described—in Saskia Sassen's (1982) words—as "peripheralization at the core." Migrants from poorer countries—often former European colonies—are undertaking the work shunned by richer natives. Immigration policy, Calavita (2005b: 158) argues, doubly ensures the "peripheralization" of this subordinated migrant labor force, as these global inequalities are "*reproduced within* through the law and the economic marginality it helps constitute." Although economically peripheral, low-paid and low-status work is just as essential to the functioning of contemporary capitalism as financial and other specialized services are: software is delivered by truckers, office workers' buildings are constructed and cleaned, and care for the elderly and young is provided (Sassen 2012: 9). Yet those who undertake this work are not included in the wealth they help to produce.

In the neoliberal era, low-status migrant workers' marginalization, Ong (2006: 17) argues, is related to the notion that they lack neoliberal potential. By not demonstrating self-governing, self-entrepreneurship, and calculative practices (16), they are "treated as less-worthy subjects" (17) and are excluded from the benefits produced by neoliberalism.

Yet the stories of the migrants featured in this book highlight the limits of the possibilities offered by embodying a neoliberal subjectivity. Chapter 4 focused on the role of the migrant broker—the ultimate self-governing entrepreneur—but the everyday migrant, faced with the individual responsibility of organizing a plethora of documents, is similarly required to act in a broker like way. Laws have to be learned, contacts gained, and loopholes found by *all* migrants in their navigation of the regime. Often the help of advisers is needed, but gaining access to that help also requires strategic behavior. Migrants' tactical maneuvering, however, did not ultimately facilitate their social mobility and sometimes even precluded opportunities to gain more secure legal status. Notwithstanding their demonstration of entrepreneurial and self-governing characteristics, therefore, migrants were excluded from the wealth produced by contemporary capitalism. Their embodiment of these neoliberal values but ongoing exclusion from the benefits of capitalist developments (Ong 2006: 4) reflects the unequal structural conditions on which capitalism depends. As Ong points out, "populations governed by neoliberal technologies are dependent on others who are excluded from neoliberal consideration" (4).

These others are excluded whether or not they exhibit the desirable characteristics of a neoliberal self. In fact, it is the neoliberal-like characteristics of wily and crafty navigation that in the Italian case can also serve to sustain the mechanisms that produce and reproduce migrants' marginalization. By strategically navigating the ambiguous and Kafkaesque immigration bureaucracy, migrants' actions enable its policies to function. In doing so, immigration law's contradictions are silently reconciled and a host of diverse stakeholders are placated, including both those advocating for migrants' rights as well as those who profit from the exploitation of their labor.

Immigration law and migrants' navigation of it, therefore, produces a variety of outcomes: from the reproduction of the Italian family, labor markets, and welfare systems to the production of cultural citizenship among migrants themselves. These diverse and unexpected outcomes are evidence of the unpredictability and contradictions with which law and policymaking are riddled. Although policy makers do not "design" these outcomes, they cannot be dismissed as merely accidental: they take place within, and are determined by, the political and economic system in which they are situated. The constant focus on international borders and the conceptualization of migration as permanently in crisis act to depoliticize issues surrounding immigration and, crucially, separate them from nonmigrants' lived realities. Shifting our focus away from the border to the legal and bureaucratic processes that construct and structure migration within a specific nation-state reveals how everyday encounters with immigration law and bureaucracy—from acts of brokerage and advice to the production of "authentic but fake" work contracts—are deeply embedded in broader political and economic processes that ultimately reproduce the binary dynamics of inclusion, exclusion, marginalization, and privilege created by contemporary neoliberal capitalism.

Looking to the future

This book explores the dynamic tensions created by the divergent affects and meanings produced through encounters with Italian immigration law. The contradictory and paradoxical effects generated by immigration regimes are most striking in the circumstances of the second generation and those who have been long settled in the country but nonetheless hold precarious documentation status. The mismatch between these individuals' local accents, gesticulations, and styles of dress and their uncertain legal status are indications of the disjunctures that immigration laws create in the lives of all migrants. As noted, in the Italian context those born in Italy are, in theory, able to apply for citizenship within one year of their eighteenth birthdays, but bureaucratic obstacles frequently prevent individuals from doing so. Those who have grown up in the country but were born elsewhere, meanwhile, are subject to the same immigration and naturalization laws as adult migrants. And last, immigration laws, which make status contingent on employment, mean that even those long settled in the country are always potentially at risk of losing legal status if they lose their job.

In contrast to the difficulty in attaining secure residency, temporary and provisional legal status is relatively easy to obtain, if one has the right resources. This is in large part because amnesties are the defining characteristic of Italian immigration policy (Ambrosini 2008: 567). Therefore, while it is relatively easy to enter Italy and to obtain basic legal status, it is difficult for migrants to build secure and comfortable lives in the country. This dynamic impedes meaningful integration and continuously produces immigration as an emergency problem. A first step toward ameliorating this situation would be to guarantee citizenship to the second and 1.5 generations (removing bureaucratic obstacles that currently exist) and improve the rights of long-term residents of Italy, so that losing one's job does not result in the loss of legal status after decades spent in the country. Although such measures would not be sufficient for integration (Bianchi 2011: 331), they are the necessary basis for any future development of a fairer Italian society in which migrants and their children might be recognized as equal and permanent members.

Thanks to the work of second-generation associations (Riccio and Russo 2011; Zinn 2011) and the everyday practices of the 1.5 and second generations, such changes are already under way. Exclusionary immigration laws that prioritize temporary legal status rather than the development of long-term integration, however, act as blocks to any significant changes in Italian society. As a result, migrants continue to imagine successful lives for themselves outside of

Italy, mainstream attitudes toward migrants continue to be negative (Armillei 2016: 35; Mannheimer 2016), and immigration remains a policy issue managed with emergency solutions. Solving these problems will require shifting attention to the situation inside the border and replacing emergency solutions with policies that guarantee secure legal status both for those who have grown up in Italy and for those who have made their lives there.

Notes

Introduction

1. *Questura* is the police headquarters where the immigration office is located. *Questura* is the singular, *questure* is the plural.

2. *Decreto flussi* is an accord between the Italian state and "sending" countries. It allows for the legal entry of workers who are desired by employers in Italy. How these agreements function on the ground is discussed throughout the book.

3. The name of the city is not disclosed in order to protect my interlocutors' anonymity.

4. All names have been changed in order to protect my respondents' anonymity.

5. The permit renewal procedures were similar for all immigrants and asylum seekers. However, the process of obtaining asylum is distinct from other immigration processes and is not discussed in this book.

Chapter 1

1. There are three central trade unions in Italy. The trade union in which I conducted fieldwork had other migration advice centers across the province and in the rest of Italy. Many of these centers were much smaller, situated within the trade union building, and open only a few hours a week. The other trade unions also had migration advice centers in the city and throughout Italy.

2. I never saw a female police officer inside this cabin.

3. During my research period the process for family members of Italian citizens changed, and they were also required to submit their applications via the postal system, rather than directly to the *questura*.

4. See Dubois (2009; 2010) for examples of welfare recipients interacting in various ways (flirtatiously, angrily) with welfare officials.

5. The subject of residency vs. domicile is further discussed in Chapter 5. Residency is a beneficial, but not essential, bureaucratic status for people (both citizens and noncitizens) living in Italy. With it one has access to various entitlements, ranging from parking spaces to welfare. However, while residency offers advantages, it is not essential for

migrants to hold. For permit renewal and family reunification applications, registered domicile is sufficient. As in the case of Carla, it was common for people to hold residency in one place and domicile in another. Thus, on some occasions individuals either did not have an official place of residence or did not reside in their place of residence, and instead held only domicile. As we will see in Chapter 5, this became problematic when applying for citizenship.

6. At the center, staff members referred to clients as "*utenti*" (users).

7. See Dubois (2010: 9–10) for a similar discussion surrounding terminology.

Chapter 2

1. I assume that this is because officials in other countries presume that all holders of Italian identity cards are Italian nationals.

2. *Indeterminato* and not *indeterminata* because its official term was "*permesso di soggiorno di lungo periodo*." However, people continued to call it the *carta*, as it had been previously known, which explains the grammatically incorrect "*carta indeterminato*"

3. When I use the term "residency" here I am referring to simply living in Italy. In Italy residency is a bureaucratic status independent of domicile and is unrelated to immigration matters. It was five years of domicile, not residency, that was required in order to apply for the long-term permit. The subject of residency is discussed in Chapter 5.

4. These cohorts did not fit the racialized stereotype of what kind of migrant makes an appropriate domestic worker. The overwhelming majority of domestic workers are female. Although Filipino men were considered acceptable domestic workers, Pakistani, Moroccan, and Tunisian men were likely to be associated with drugs, violence, and corruption; see Chapter 5.

5. Article 14 of the Bossi-Fini law.

6. "Trieste—Falsa sanatoria, vere espulsioni," http://www.meltingpot.org/Trieste-Falsa-sanatoria-vere-espulsioni.html#.Ud_mpWWstt4, accessed October 15, 2013.

7. See Sarat (1990) for an analysis of the dual dynamics of both oppression and resistance in relation to welfare recipients' navigation of the legal and bureaucratic system in the United States.

8. It was common for Chinese migrants to informally adopt traditional Italian names.

9. This is not to suggest that the 2011 *decreto flussi* was not also oversubscribed. There were more than 411,000 applicants for 98,080 places.

10. If parents guarantee their maintenance, young people in school full-time who are over the age of eighteen can hold family permits. Spouses can hold family permits if their partners can provide evidence of income. Yasmina was not married or in school; therefore neither of these options was available to her.

11. Depositing the application at the *questura* was also unusual practice. This kind of application would usually be sent to the *questura* via the post office.

Chapter 3

1. The employment of informal strategies facilitating the functioning of the bureau-

cratic institutions has been documented elsewhere. See, for example, Anderson (1990: 60) and Ledeneva (1998: 85).

2. A co-operative that deals with domestic work contracts (see Chapter 4).

Chapter 4

1. It should be noted that high levels of unemployment, as well as the implementation of austerity measures, are pushing many young Italians to leave the country and become migrants themselves.

Chapter 5

1. In Finland, Bilal is entitled to a permit as the live-in partner of a Finnish citizen.

2. Most people I knew who had obtained citizenship had been living in Italy for twenty years or more before submitting the application.

3. It should be noted, however, that it is a common trajectory for migrants in Italy to start their journey in the south of Italy and to then travel north in search of better paid and more secure employment.

4. This is not to suggest that British society or sport is free of racial issues. See the 2017 Race Disparity Audit for a recent report on the deep seated racial inequality that exists in the UK. https://www.gov.uk/government/uploads/system/uploads/attachment_data/file/650723/RDAweb.pdf, accessed January 4, 2018.

5. Lindita's situation was very common among young people in her position. There is currently a joint campaign between Save the Children Italia, G2 (a second-generation association), and ANCI (National Association of Italian Municipalities) aiming to raise awareness in *comuni* about the right of those born in Italy to apply for citizenship within one year after their eighteenth birthday. It was not uncommon for young people who were eligible to apply for citizenship to lose this opportunity because they were unaware of the procedure and their *comune* (through which the application is completed) did not alert them to this possibility.

6. Before the introduction of electronic, credit-card-sized permits, the permit was printed on a standard letter-sized sheet of paper.

Chapter 6

1. Earlier generations of Eritrean refugees were more likely to stay in Italy owing to perceived ties created through the shared colonial history (see Arnone 2008: 325).

2. In Italy those who have been granted asylum do not automatically receive housing or any kind of financial support.

3. The Dublin Regulation (previously the Dublin Convention) was originally set up in 1990. The goal of the regulation is to ensure that asylum seekers apply for asylum in the first EU member state to which they arrive.

References

Agnolotto, Stefano. 2012. Trade Unions and the Welfare State in Italy: CISL, INAS and the Italian "Fourth Way" (1945–1960). California Italian Studies 3(2): 1–24.

Alpes, Maybritt Jill. 2013. Migration Brokerage, Illegality, and the State in Anglophone Cameroon. DIIS Working Paper Series, 7: 1–18. Danish Institute for International Studies. Copenhagen.

———. 2017. Why Aspiring Migrants Trust Migration Brokers: The Moral Economy of Departure in Anglophone Cameroon. Africa 87(2): 304–321.

Ambrosini, Maurizio. 1999. Utili Invasori: L'inserimento Degli Immigrati Nel Mercato Del Lavoro Italiano. Milan: Franco Angeli.

———. 2001. La fatica di integrarsi: immigrati e lavoro in Italia. Bologna: Il mulino.

———. 2008. Irregular Immigration: Economic Convenience and Other Factors. Transfer: European Review of Labour and Research 14(4): 557–572.

———. 2015. Irregular but Tolerated: Unauthorized Immigration, Elderly Care Recipients, and Invisible Welfare. Migration Studies 3(2): 199–216.

Andall, Jacqueline. 2002. Second-Generation Attitude? African-Italians in Milan. Journal of Ethnic and Migration Studies 28(3): 389–407.

Anderson, Benedict R. O'G. 1990. Language and Power: Exploring Political Cultures in Indonesia. The Wilder House Series in Politics, History and Culture. Ithaca, NY: Cornell University Press.

Andersson, Ruben. 2014. Illegality, Inc: Clandestine Migration and the Business of Bordering Europe. Oakland, CA: University of California Press.

Andrijasevic, Rutvica. 2010. Migration, Agency and Citizenship in Sex. Basingstoke, U.K.: Palgrave Macmillan.

Appadurai, Arjun. 1996. Modernity at Large: Cultural Dimensions of Globalization. Minneapolis: University of Minnesota Press.

Armillei, Riccardo. 2016. Reflections on Italy's Contemporary Approaches to Cultural Diversity: The Exclusion of the "Other" from a Supposed Notion of "Italianness." Australian and New Zealand Journal of European Studies 8(2): 34–48.

Arnone, Anna. 2008. Journeys to Exile: The Constitution of Eritrean Identity through Narratives and Experiences. Journal of Ethnic and Migration Studies 34(2): 325–340.

Audisio, M., and N. Colombo. 1995. The Law-Making Process. In. Law Profile of Italy, ed. David Cole. London: The British Council.

Auyero, Javier. 2012. Patients of the State: The Politics of Waiting in Argentina. Durham, NC: Duke University Press.

Bailey, F. G. 2002. Stratagems and Spoils. In Anthropology of Politics: A Reader in Ethnography, Theory and Critique, ed. Joan Vincent, pp. 90–96. Oxford: Blackwell.

Bakan, Abigail, B., and Daiva K. Stasiulis. 1995. Making the Match: Domestic Placement Agencies and the Racialization of Women's Household Work. Signs 20(2): 303–335.

Bal, Ellen. 2013. Yearning for Faraway Places: The Construction of Migration Desires among Young and Educated Bangladeshis in Dhaka. Identities 21(3): 275–289.

Bal, Ellen, and Roos Willems. 2014. Introduction: Aspiring Migrants, Local Crises and the Imagination of Futures "away from Home." Identities 21(3): 249–258.

Bauman, Zygmunt. 1998. Globalization: The Human Consequences. Cambridge: Polity Press.

Bianchi, Georgia E. 2011. Italiani Nuovi O Nuova Italia? Citizenship and Attitudes towards the Second Generation in Contemporary Italy. Journal of Modern Italian Studies 16(3): 321–333.

Bloch, Alice, Nando Sigona, and Roger Zetter. 2011. Migration Routes and Strategies of Young Undocumented Migrants in England: A Qualitative Perspective. Ethnic and Racial Studies 34(8): 1286–1302.

Blok, Anton. 1974. The Mafia of a Sicilian Village, 1860–1960: A Study of Violent Peasant Entrepreneurs. Pavilion Series. Social Anthropology. Oxford: Blackwell.

Boissevain, Jeremy. 1974. Friends of Friends: Networks, Manipulators and Coalitions. Pavilion Series. Social Anthropology. Oxford: Blackwell.

Boswell, Christina, and Andrew Geddes. 2010. Migration and Mobility in the European Union. 2010 ed. Houndmills, Basingtoke, Hampshire, U.K.: Macmillan Education.

Cabot, Heath. 2012. The Governance of Things: Documenting Limbo in the Greek Asylum Procedure. PoLAR: Political and Legal Anthropology Review 35(1): 11–29.

———. 2014. On the Doorstep of Europe: Asylum and Citizenship in Greece. Philadelphia: University of Pennsylvania Press.

Cachafeiro, Margarita Gómez-Reino. 2002. Ethnicity and Nationalism in Italian Politics: Inventing the Padania: Lega Nord and the Northern Question. Aldershot, U.K.: Ashgate.

Calavita, Kitty. 1989. The Contradictions of Immigration Lawmaking: The Immigration Reform and Control Act of 1986. Law & Policy 11(1): 17–47.

———. 2004. Italy: Economic Realities, Political Fictions, and Policy Failures. In Controlling Immigration: A Global Perspective, ed. Wayne A. Cornelius, Takeyuki Tsuda, Philip L. Martin, and James F. Hollifield. Stanford, CA: Stanford University Press.

———. 2005a. Immigrants at the Margins: Law, Race, and Exclusion in Southern Europe. Cambridge, U.K.: Cambridge University Press.

———. 2005b. Law, Citizenship, and the Construction of (Some) Immigrant "Others." Law & Social Inquiry 30(2): 401–420.

Caritas. 2010. Dossier Statistico Immigrazione 2010 XX Rapport. Caritas/Migrantes.

Carling, Jørgen. 2002. Migration in the Age of Involuntary Immobility: Theoretical Reflections and Cape Verdean Experiences. Journal of Ethnic and Migration Studies 28(1): 5–42.

Chee, Heng Leng, Brenda S. A. Yeoh, and Thi Kieu Dung Vu. 2012. From Client to Matchmaker: Social Capital in the Making of Commercial Matchmaking Agents in Malaysia. Pacific Affairs 85(1): 91–115.

Cole, Jeffrey. 1997. The New Racism in Europe: A Sicilian Ethnography. Cambridge, U.K.: Cambridge University Press.

Cole, Jeffrey E., and Pietro Saitta. 2011. Final Remarks: Italy, Dreams of a Monochrome Society? Journal of Modern Italian Studies 16(4): 528–530.

Collyer, Michael. 2012. Migrants as Strategic Actors in the European Union's Global Approach to Migration and Mobility. Global Networks 12(4): 505–524.

Colombo, E., and P. Rebughini. 2012. Children of Immigrants in a Globalized World: A Generational Experience. 2012 ed. Basingstoke, U.K.: Palgrave Macmillan.

Colombo, Enzo, Lorenzo Domaneschi, and Chiara Marchetti. 2011. Citizenship and Multiple Belonging. Representations of Inclusion, Identification and Participation among Children of Immigrants in Italy. Journal of Modern Italian Studies 16(3): 334–347.

Coutin, Susan Bibler. 2000. Legalizing Moves: Salvadoran Immigrants' Struggle for U.S. Residency. Ann Arbor: University of Michigan Press.

———. 2003. Cultural Logics of Belonging and Movement Transnationalism, Naturalization, and U.S. Immigration Politics. American Ethnologist 30(4): 508–526.

Czaika, Mathias, and Hein de Haas. 2013. The Effectiveness of Immigration Policies. Population and Development Review 39(3): 487–508.

De Genova, Nicholas. 2002. Migrant "Illegality" and Deportability in Everyday Life. Annual Review of Anthropology 31(1): 419–447.

De Genova, Nicholas, and Nathalie Peutz. 2010. The Deportation Regime: Sovereignty, Space, and the Freedom of Movement. Durham, NC: Duke University Press.

Dejevsky, Mary. 2013. The Lampedusa Hypocrisy: Italy Prefers Migrants Dead on Arrival. The Spectator. https://blogs.spectator.co.uk/author/marydejevsky/, accessed April 14, 2017.

Douglas, Mary. 1970. Purity and Danger: An Analysis of Concepts of Pollution and Taboo. New ed. Pelican Books. Harmondsworth: Penguin.

Dreby, Joanna. 2015. Everyday Illegal: When Policies Undermine Immigrant Families. Berkeley: University of California Press.

Drotbohm, Heike. 2011. On the Durability and the Decomposition of Citizenship: The Social Logics of Forced Return Migration in Cape Verde. Citizenship Studies 15(3–4): 381–396.

Dubois, Vincent. 2009. Towards a Critical Policy Ethnography: Lessons from Fieldwork on Welfare Control in France. Critical Policy Studies 3(2): 221–239.

———. 2010. The Bureaucrat and the Poor: Encounters in French Welfare Offices. Burlington, VT: Routledge.

Eule, Tobias G. 2014. Inside Immigration Law: Migration Management and Policy Application in Germany. Aldershot, U.K.: Ashgate.

Fassin, Didier. 2001. The Biopolitics of Otherness: Undocumented Foreigners and Racial Discrimination in French Public Debate. Anthropology Today 17(1): 3–7.

Favell, Adrian, and Randall Hansen. 2002. Markets against Politics: Migration, EU Enlargement and the Idea of Europe. Journal of Ethnic and Migration Studies 28(4): 581–601.

Feldman, Gregory. 2012. The Migration Apparatus: Security, Labor, and Policymaking in the European Union. Stanford, CA: Stanford University Press.

Ferguson, James. 1990. The Anti-Politics Machine: Development, Depoliticization, and Bureaucratic Power in Lesotho. Cambridge, U.K.: Cambridge University Press.

Fernandez, Bina. 2013. Traffickers, Brokers, Employment Agents, and Social Networks: The Regulation of Intermediaries in the Migration of Ethiopian Domestic Workers to the Middle East. International Migration Review 47: 814–843.

Finotelli, Claudia, and Giuseppe Sciortino. 2013. Through the Gates of the Fortress: European Visa Policies and the Limits of Immigration Control. Perspectives on European Politics and Society 14(1): 80–101.

Foot, J. M. 2003. Modern Italy. Basingstoke, U.K.: Palgrave Macmillan.

Foucault, Michel. 2003. The Essential Foucault: Selections from The Essential Works of Foucault, 1954–1984. New York: New Press.

Freeman, Gary P. 1995. Modes of Immigration Politics in Liberal Democratic States. International Migration Review: 881–902.

Fullin, Giovanna, and Emilio Reyneri. 2011. Low Unemployment and Bad Jobs for New Immigrants in Italy. International Migration 49(1): 118–147.

Gaibazzi, Paulo. 2014. Visa Problem: Certification, Kinship, and the Production of "Ineligibility" in the Gambia. Journal of the Royal Anthropological Institute 20(1): 38–55.

Galt, Anthony H. 1974. Rethinking Patron-Client Relationships: The Real System and the Official System in Southern Italy. Anthropological Quarterly 47(2): 182–202.

Gammeltoft-Hansen, Thomas, and Ninna Nyberg Sørensen. 2013. The Migration Industry and the Commercialization of International Migration. Abingdon, U.K.: Routledge.

Gardner, Katy. 1993. Desh-Bidesh: Sylheti Images of Home and Away. Man 28(1): 1.

———. 2002. Age, Narrative and Migration: The Life Course and Life Histories of Bengali Elders in London. Oxford, U.K.: Berg.

———. 2008. Keeping Connected: Security, Place, and Social Capital in a "Londoni" Village in Sylhet. Journal of the Royal Anthropological Institute 14(3): 477–495.

Geddes, Andrew. 2008. Il Rombo Dei Cannoni? Immigration and the Centre-Right in Italy. Journal of European Public Policy 15(3): 349–366.

Geddes, Andrew, and Peter Scholten. 2016. The Politics of Migration and Immigration in Europe. 2nd ed. Thousand Oaks, CA: Sage.

Gilroy, Paul. 2002. There Ain't No Black in the Union Jack: The Cultural Politics of Race and Nation. New ed. Routledge Classics. London: Routledge.

Ginsborg, Paul. 1990. A History of Contemporary Italy: 1943–80. London, U.K.: Penguin.

———. 2003. Italy and Its Discontents 1980–2001. London, U.K.: Penguin.

Giordano, Cristiana. 2008. Practices of Translation and the Making of Migrant Subjectivities in Contemporary Italy. American Ethnologist 35(4): 588–606.

Gonzales, Roberto G. 2011. Learning to Be Illegal: Undocumented Youth and Shifting Legal Contexts in the Transition to Adulthood. American Sociological Review 76(4): 602–619.

Gonzales, Roberto G., and Leo R. Chavez. 2012. Awakening to a Nightmare. Current Anthropology 53(3): 255–281.

Good, Anthony. 2007. Anthropology and Expertise in the Asylum Courts. Abingdon, U.K.: Routledge-Cavendish.

Gordillo, Gastón. 2006. The Crucible of Citizenship: ID-Paper Fetishism in the Argentinean Chaco. American Ethnologist 33(2): 162–176.

Grillo, Ralph D., and Jeff C. Pratt. 2002. The Politics of Recognizing Difference: Multiculturalism Italian-Style. Aldershot, U.K.: Ashgate.

Guano, Emanuela. 2010. Taxpayers, Thieves, and the State: Fiscal Citizenship in Contemporary Italy. Ethnos 75(4): 471–495.

Guevarra, Anna. 2006. Managing "Vulnerabilities" and "Empowering" Migrant Filipina Workers: The Philippines' Overseas Employment Program. Social Identities 12(5): 523–541.

———. 2009. Marketing Dreams, Manufacturing Heroes: The Transnational Labor Brokering of Filipino Workers. New Brunswick, NJ: Rutgers University Press.

Gupta, Akhil. 1995. Blurred Boundaries: The Discourse of Corruption, the Culture of Politics, and the Imagined State. American Ethnologist 22(2): 375–402.

———. 2012. Red Tape: Bureaucracy, Structural Violence, and Poverty in India. Durham, NC: Duke University Press.

Gupta, Akhil, and Aradhana Sharma. 2006. The Anthropology of the State: A Reader. Oxford, U.K.: Blackwell.

de Haas, Hein. 2017. Myths of Migration: Much of What We Think We Know Is Wrong. http://heindehaas.blogspot.com/2017/03/myths-of-migration-much-of-what-we.html, accessed April 14, 2017.

de Haas, Hein, and Katharina Natter. 2015. The Determinants of Migration Policies: Does the Political Orientation of Governments Matter? IMI Working Paper Series, 117. University of Oxford.

de Haas, Hein, Katharina Natter, and Simona Vezzoli. 2014. Growing Restrictiveness or Changing Selection? The Nature and Evolution of Migration Policies. IMI Working Paper Series, 96. University of Oxford.

Herzfeld, Michael. 1992. The Social Production of Indifference: Exploring the Symbolic Roots of Western Bureaucracy. Global Issues. New York: Berg.

Heyman, Josiah. 1995. Putting Power in the Anthropology of Bureaucracy: The Immigration and Naturalization Service at the Mexico–United States Border. Current Anthropology 36(2): 261–287.

Heyman, Josiah, and Alan Smart. 1999. States and Illegal Practices: An Overview. In States and Illegal Practices, pp. 1–25. New York: Berg.

Hoag, Colin. 2010. The Magic of the Populace: An Ethnography of Illegibility in the

South African Immigration Bureaucracy. PoLAR: Political and Legal Anthropology Review 33(1): 6–25.

Hollifield, James, Philip Martin, and Pia Orrenius, eds. 2014. Controlling Immigration: A Global Perspective. 3rd ed. Stanford, CA: Stanford University Press.

Hull, Matthew S. 2008. Ruled by Records: The Expropriation of Land and the Misappropriation of Lists in Islamabad. American Ethnologist 35(4): 501–518.

———. 2012a. Government of Paper: The Materiality of Bureaucracy in Urban Pakistan. Berkeley: University of California Press.

———. 2012b. Documents and Bureaucracy. Annual Review of Anthropology 41: 251–267.

James, Deborah. 2002. "To Take the Information Down to the People": Life Skills and HIV/AIDS Peer Educators in the Durban Area. African Studies 61(1): 169–191.

———. 2011. The Return of the Broker: Consensus, Hierarchy, and Choice in South African Land Reform. Journal of the Royal Anthropological Institute 17(2): 318–338.

James, Deborah, and Evan Killick. 2012. Empathy and Expertise: Case Workers and Immigration/Asylum Applicants in London. Law & Social Inquiry 37(2): 430–455.

Jansen, Stef. 2009. After the Red Passport: Towards an Anthropology of the Everyday Geopolitics of Entrapment in the EU's "Immediate Outside." Journal of the Royal Anthropological Institute 15(4): 815–832.

Joppke, Christian. 1998. Why Liberal States Accept Unwanted Immigration. World Politics 50: 266–293.

Kearney, Michael. 1991. Borders and Boundaries of State and Self at the End of Empire. Journal of Historical Sociology 4(1): 52–74.

Kelly, Tobias. 2006. Documented Lives: Fear and the Uncertainties of Law during the Second Palestinian Intifada. Journal of the Royal Anthropological Institute 12(1): 89–107.

King, Russell, and Jacqueline Andall. 1999. The Geography and Economic Sociology of Recent Immigration to Italy. Modern Italy 4(2): 135–158.

King, Russell, and Nicola Mai. 2002. Of Myths and Mirrors: Interpretations of Albanian Migration to Italy. Studi Emigrazione 39(145): 161–200.

Koster, Martijn. 2012. Mediating and Getting "Burnt" in the Gap: Politics and Brokerage in a Recife Slum, Brazil. Critique of Anthropology 32(4): 479–497.

Kyle, David, and Zai Liang. 2001. Migration Merchants: Human Smuggling from Ecuador and China. Center for Comparative Immigration Studies. http://escholarship.org/uc/item/5h24b7j6, accessed January 4, 2017.

Kymlicka, Will, and Wayne Norman. 1994. Return of the Citizen: A Survey of Recent Work on Citizenship Theory. Ethics 104(2): 352–381.

Laidlaw, James. 2002. For an Anthropology of Ethics and Freedom. The Journal of the Royal Anthropological Institute 8(2): 311–332.

Lazar, Sian. 2004. Personalist Politics, Clientelism and Citizenship: Local Elections in El Alto, Bolivia. Bulletin of Latin American Research 23(2): 228–243.

Ledeneva, Alena V. 1998. Russia's Economy of Favours: Blat, Networking and Informal Exchange. Cambridge, U.K.: Cambridge University Press.

———. 2006. How Russia Really Works: The Informal Practices That Shaped Post-

Soviet Politics and Business. Culture and Society after Socialism. Ithaca, NY: Cornell University Press.

Lewis, David, and David Mosse, eds. 2006. Development Brokers and Translators: The Ethnography of Aid and Agencies. Bloomfield, CT: Kumarian Press.

Lindquist, Johan. 2010. Labour Recruitment, Circuits of Capital and Gendered Mobility: Reconceptualizing the Indonesian Migration Industry. Pacific Affairs 83(1): 115–132.

———. 2012. The Elementary School Teacher, the Thug and His Grandmother: Informal Brokers and Transnational Migration from Indonesia. Pacific Affairs 85(1): 69–89.

———. 2015a. Brokers and Brokerage. In International Encyclopedia of the Social and Behavioral Sciences. 2nd ed., pp. 870–874. Amsterdam: Elsevier.

———. 2015b. Of Figures and Types: Brokering Knowledge and Migration in Indonesia and Beyond. Journal of the Royal Anthropological Institute 21(S1): 162–177.

Lindquist, Johan, Biao Xiang, and Brenda S.A. Yeoh. 2012. Opening the Black Box of Migration: Brokers, the Organization of Transnational Mobility and the Changing Political Economy in Asia. Pacific Affairs 85(1): 7–19.

Mahler, Sarah J. 1995. American Dreaming: Immigrant Life on the Margins. Princeton, NJ: Princeton University Press.

Mai, Nicola. 2002. Myths and Moral Panics: Italian Identity and the Media Representation of Albanian Immigration. In The Politics of Recognizing Difference: Multiculturalism Italian Style, ed. Ralph Grillo and Jeff Pratt. Aldershot, U.K.: Ashgate.

———. 2003. The Cultural Construction of Italy in Albania and Vice Versa: Migration Dynamics, Strategies of Resistance and Politics of Mutual Self-Definition across Colonialism and Post-Colonialism. Modern Italy 8(1): 77–93.

Mandel, Ruth. 2008. Cosmopolitan Anxieties: Turkish Challenges to Citizenship and Belonging in Germany. Durham, NC: Duke University Press.

Mannheimer, Renato. 2016. L'opinione Degli Italiani Sull'arrivo Degli Immigrati. Eumetra Monterosa. https://www.eumetramr.com/it/lopinione-degli-italiani-sullarrivo-degli-immigrati, accessed August 3, 2017.

Maritano, L. 2002. An Obsession with Cultural Difference: Representations of Immigrants in Turin. In The Politics of Recognizing Difference: Multiculturalism Italian Style, ed. Ralph Grillo and Jeff Pratt. Aldershot, U.K.: Ashgate.

Marshall, T. H. 1950. Citizenship and Social Class and Other Essays. Cambridge, U.K.: Cambridge: University Press.

Massey, Douglas. 2009. The Political Economy of Migration in an Era of Globalization. In International Migration and Human Rights: The Global Repercussions of U.S. Policy, ed. Samuel Martinez. pp. 25–43. Berkeley: University of California Press.

Mauss, Marcel. 1973. Techniques of the Body. Economy and Society 2(1): 70–88.

McKeown, Adam. 2012. How the Box Became Black: Brokers and the Creation of the Free Migrant. Pacific Affairs 85(1): 21–45.

McNeill, Fraser G. 2011. AIDS, Politics, and Music in South Africa. Reprint ed. New York: Cambridge University Press.

Menjívar, Cecilia. 2006. Liminal Legality. American Journal of Sociology 111(4): 999–1037.

Mitchell, J. Clyde. 2006. Case and Situation Analysis. In The Manchester School: Practice and Ethnographic Praxis in Anthropology, ed. T. M. S. Evens and Don Handelman. New York: Berghahn Books.

Molland, Sverre. 2012. Safe Migration, Dilettante Brokers and the Appropriation of Legality: Lao-Thai "Trafficking" in the Context of Regulating Labour Migration. Pacific Affairs 85(1): 117–136.

Navaro-Yashin, Yael. 2007. Make-Believe Papers, Legal Forms and the Counterfeit Affective Interactions between Documents and People in Britain and Cyprus. Anthropological Theory 7(1): 79–98.

Nuijten, Monique. 2003. Power, Community and the State: The Political Anthropology of Organisation in Mexico. London: Pluto Press.

Ong, Aihwa. 1996. Cultural Citizenship as Subject-Making: Immigrants Negotiate Racial and Cultural Boundaries in the United States [and Comments and Reply]. Current Anthropology 37(5): 737–762.

———. 1999. Flexible Citizenship: The Cultural Logics of Transnationality. Durham, NC: Duke University Press.

———. 2003. Buddha Is Hiding: Refugees, Citizenship, the New America. Berkeley: University of California Press.

———. 2006. Neoliberalism as Exception: Mutations in Citizenship and Sovereignty. Durham NC: Duke University Press.

Pardo, Italo. 1995. Morals of Legitimacy in Naples: Streetwise about Legality, Semi-Legality, and Crime. European Journal of Sociology 36(1): 44–71.

Pastore, Ferruccio, and Claudia Villosio. 2011. Nevertheless Attracting . . . Italy and Immigration in Times of Crisis. LABORatorio R. Revelli Working Papers Series, 106. Turin.

Però, Davide. 2002. The Left and the Political Participation of Immigrants in Italy: The Case of the Forum of Bologna. In The Politics of Recognizing Difference: Multiculturalism Italian-Style, ed. Ralph Grillo and Jeff Pratt, pp. 95–113. Aldershot, U.K.: Ashgate.

Peutz, Nathalie. 2006. Embarking on an Anthropology of Removal. Current Anthropology 47(2): 217–241.

Pini, Domenic. 1995. Introduction. In Law Profile of Italy. London: The British Council.

Polchi, Vladimiro. 2008. Immigrati, l'Italia Riapre Le porte "Entro L'anno Nuovo Decreto Flussi." La Repubblica, August 5. http://www.repubblica.it/2008/08/sezioni/politica/immigrazione-flussi/immigrazione-flussi/immigrazione-flussi.html, accessed April 26, 2017.

Portes, Alejandro. 1978. Introduction: Toward a Structural Analysis of Illegal (Undocumented) Immigration. International Migration Review 12(4): 469–484.

Pratt, Jeff C. 2002. Political Unity and Cultural Diversity. In The Politics of Recognizing Difference: Multiculturalism Italian-Style, ed., Ralph Grillo and Jeff Pratt. Aldershot, U.K.: Ashgate.

Reeves, Madeleine. 2013. Clean Fake: Authenticating Documents and Persons in Migrant Moscow. American Ethnologist 40(3): 508–524.

Reyneri, Emilio. 1998. The Role of the Underground Economy in Irregular Migration to Italy: Cause or Effect? Journal of Ethnic and Migration Studies 24(2): 313–331.

———. 2004a. Immigrants in a Segmented and Often Undeclared Labour Market. Journal of Modern Italian Studies 9(1): 71–93.

———. 2004b. Education and the Occupational Pathways of Migrants in Italy. Journal of Ethnic and Migration Studies 30(6): 1145–1162.

Reyneri, Emilio, and Giovanna Fullin. 2011. Labour Market Penalties of New Immigrants in New and Old Receiving West European Countries. International Migration 49(1): 31–57.

Riccio, Bruno. 2002. Toubab and Vu Cumprà. Italian Perceptions of Senegalese Transmigrants and the Senegalese Afro-Muslim Critique of Italian Society. In The Politics of Recognizing Difference: Multiculturalism Italian-Style, ed., Ralph Grillo and Jeff Pratt. Aldershot, U.K.: Ashgate.

Riccio, Bruno, and Monica Russo. 2011. Everyday Practised Citizenship and the Challenges of Representation: Second-Generation Associations in Bologna. Journal of Modern Italian Studies 16(3): 360–372.

Rodriguez, Robyn Magalit. 2010. Migrants for Export: How the Philippine State Brokers Labor to the World. Minneapolis: University of Minnesota Press.

Rumiz, Paolo. 2010. L'ultima Beffa Agli Immigrati Spunta La Sanatoria Trappola. La Repubblica, March 4. http://www.repubblica.it/cronaca/2010/03/04/news/l_ultima_beffa_agli_immigrati_spunta_la_sanatoria_trappola-2499728/, accessed April 26, 2017.

Sabetti, Filippo. 2000. The Search for Good Government: Understanding the Paradox of Italian Democracy. Montreal: McGill-Queen's University Press.

Salt, J., and J. Stein. 1997. Migration as a Business: The Case of Trafficking. International Migration (Geneva, Switzerland) 35(4): 467–494.

Sarat, Austin. 1990. "The Law Is All Over": Power, Resistance and the Legal Consciousness of the Welfare Poor. Yale Journal of Law & the Humanities 2(2). http://digitalcommons.law.yale.edu/yjlh/vol2/iss2/6.

Sassen, Saskia. 1982. Recomposition and Peripheralization at the Core. Contemporary Marxism(5): 88–100.

———. 1996. Losing Control? Sovereignty in an Age of Globalization. The 1995 Columbia University Leonard Hastings Schoff Memorial Lectures.

———. 2012. Cities in a World Economy. 4th ed. Sociology for a New Century. Thousand Oaks, CA: SAGE/Pine Forge.

Schneider, Jane. 1998. Italy's "Southern Question": Orientalism in One Country. Oxford, U.K.: Berg.

Schuster, Liza. 2005. The Continuing Mobility of Migrants in Italy: Shifting between Places and Statuses. Journal of Ethnic and Migration Studies 31(4): 757–774.

Sciortino, Giuseppe. 2000. Toward a Political Sociology of Entry Policies: Conceptual Problems and Theoretical Proposals. Journal of Ethnic and Migration Studies 26(2): 213–228.

———. 2004. Immigration in a Mediterranean Welfare State: The Italian Experience in Comparative Perspective. Journal of Comparative Policy Analysis: Research and Practice 6(2): 111–129.

Scott, James C. 1998. Seeing Like a State: How Certain Schemes to Improve the Human Condition Have Failed. Yale Agrarian Studies. New Haven, CT: Yale University Press.

Shore, Cris. 1989. Patronage and Bureaucracy in Complex Societies: Social Rules and Social Relations in an Italian University. Journal of Anthropology Society of Oxford 20(1): 56–73.

Sigona, Nando. 2012. "I Have Too Much Baggage": The Impacts of Legal Status on the Social Worlds of Irregular Migrants. Social Anthropology 20(1): 50–65.

Silverman, Sydel F. 1965. Patronage and Community-Nation Relationships in Central Italy. Ethnology 4(2): 172–189.

Silvestri, Elisabetta. 2009. Italy. Annals of the American Academy of Political and Social Science 622(1): 138–148.

Spener, David. 2009. Clandestine Crossings: Migrants and Coyotes on the Texas-Mexico Border. Ithaca, NY: Cornell University Press.

Stanley, Flavia. 2008. On Belonging in/to Italy and Europe: Citizenship, Race and the Immigration "Problem." In Citizenship, Political Engagement, and Belonging: Immigrants in Europe and the United States, pp. 43–60. New Brunswick, NJ: Rutgers University Press.

Stolcke, Verena. 1995. Talking Culture: New Boundaries, New Rhetorics of Exclusion in Europe. Current Anthropology 36(1): 1–24.

Triandafyllidou, Anna. 2003. Immigration Policy Implementation in Italy: Organisational Culture, Identity Processes and Labour Market Control. Journal of Ethnic and Migration Studies 29(2): 257–297.

Tuckett, Anna. 2015. Strategies of Navigation: Migrants' Everyday Encounters with Italian Immigration Bureaucracy. Cambridge Anthropology 33(1): 113–128.

Vertovec, Steven. 2004. Trends and Impacts of Migrant Transnationalism. Centre on Migration, Policy and Society Working Paper no. 3. Oxford, U.K.: University of Oxford.

———. 2007. Circular Migration: The Way Forward in Global Policy? IMI Working Paper Series 4. https://www.imi.ox.ac.uk/publications/wp-04–07, accessed February 9, 2017.

Vigh, Henrik. 2006. Navigating Terrains of War: Youth and Soldiering in Guinea-Bissau. New York: Berghahn Books.

———. 2009. Wayward Migration: On Imagined Futures and Technological Voids. Ethnos 74(1): 91–109.

Willen, Sarah S. 2007. Toward a Critical Phenomenology of "Illegality": State Power, Criminalization, and Abjectivity among Undocumented Migrant Workers in Tel Aviv, Israel. International Migration 45(3): 8–38.

Wolf, Eric R. 1956. Aspects of Group Relations in a Complex Society: Mexico. American Anthropologist 58(6): 1065–1078.

Xiang, Biao. 2012. Predatory Princes and Princely Peddlers: The State and International Labour Migration Intermediaries in China. Pacific Affairs 85(1): 47–68.

Xiang, Biao, and Johan Lindquist. 2014. Migration Infrastructure. International Migration Review 48: S122–S148.

Yuval-Davis, Nira. 1991. The Citizenship Debate: Women, Ethnic Processes and the State. Feminist Review(39): 58–68.

Zaslove, Andrej. 2004. Closing the Door? The Ideology and Impact of Radical Right Populism on Immigration Policy in Austria and Italy. Journal of Political Ideologies 9(1): 99–118.

Zincone, Giovanna. 1998. Illegality, Enlightenment and Ambiguity: A Hot Italian Recipe. South European Society and Politics 3(3): 45–82.

———. 2006a. Italian Immigrants and Immigration Policy-Making: Structures, Actors and Practices. The Making of Migratory Policies in Europe. IMISCOE Working Papers, 12.

———. 2006b. The Making of Policies: Immigration and Immigrants in Italy. Journal of Ethnic and Migration Studies 32(3): 347–375.

———. 2011. The Case of Italy. In Migration Policymaking in Europe: The Dynamics of Actors and Contexts in Past and Present, ed. Giovanna Zincone, Rinux Penninx, and Maren Borkert. Amsterdam: Amsterdam University Press.

Zincone, Giovanna, and Tiziana Caponio. 2006. Immigrant and Immigration Policy-Making: The Case of Italy. IMISCOE Working Papers, 9.

Zinn, Dorothy L. 2001. La Raccomandazione: Clientelismo Vecchio E Nuovo. Donzelli Editore.

———. 2011. "Loud and Clear": The G2 Second Generations Network in Italy. Journal of Modern Italian Studies 16(3): 373–385.

Index

The authorized representative in the EU for product safety and compliance is:
Mare Nostrum Group
B.V Doelen 72
4831 GR Breda
The Netherlands

www.ingramcontent.com/pod-product-compliance
Lightning Source LLC
Chambersburg PA
CBHW030844270326
41928CB00007B/1213

* 9 7 8 1 5 0 3 6 0 6 4 9 4 *